THE SAGA OF THE EARLS

THE SAGA OF THE EARLS

Earl of Zetland I 1877 - 1950
Earl of Zetland II 1939 -

by

ADAM ROBSON

By the same author:
The Saga of a Ship – The Earl of Zetland; 1982.
Edinburgh Borderers R.F.C. – The Saga of a Club; 1996.

THE SHETLAND TIMES LTD.
LERWICK, SHETLAND
2002

First published by The Shetland Times Ltd., 2002

ISBN 1 898852 82 0

A CIP catalogue record for this book is available from the British Library.

Printed and published by
The Shetland Times Ltd., Gremista,
Lerwick, Shetland ZE1 0PX, Scotland.

DEDICATION

Dedicated to Gordon Donaldson, CBE, friend and mentor, a man of intellect, imagination, sensitivity and generosity.

Gordon Donaldson (1913-1993) was a brilliant scholar, but by nature unassuming. He carried many honours without any pretentiousness: Hon DLitt, Aberdeen, 1976; FBA, 1976; FRSE, 1978; Historiographer Royal in Scotland to the Queen, 1979; D Univ, Stirling, 1988; and CBE, 1988. He was also awarded the Norwegian St Olav's Medal for his work in promoting links with Norway, the importance of which he emphasised in his book, "A Northern Commonwealth : Scotland and Norway".

Professor of Scottish History of the University of Edinburgh from 1963 until 1979, he was a profound academic, and beyond his commitment to his students he published over 30 books. He had an avid interest in the history of Shetland and was very proud of his ancestral links with the North Isles. The zest for Ultima Thule found expression in his "Shetland Life under Earl Patrick" (1958) and he edited two Court Books of Shetland which survive from the early 17th century.

On a more personal basis he wrote "Northwards by Sea" published in 1978 and for the first time put into focus those vessels which were for decades the communication between mainland Scotland and the Orkney and Shetland Islands. A second, updated, version appeared in 1978.

Pride in origins, sentiment and emotion played their part in a book of yet another dimension in his writing when he produced his "Isles of Home — Sixty Years of Shetland", in 1983, and in it his sheer love of Shetland shines like the brightest of lights. Yet there was more to come and even in his ultimate 80th year he was penning his "Isles of Home — Seventy Years of Shetland" which, thankfully was almost completed before he passed on in March 1993. His Executors ensured publication in 1994.

In a radio interview during his latter years it was suggested that he, "combined the enthusiasm of youth with the wisdom of age"; it was, in fact, exactly his demeanour and is a fitting epitaph.

Chrissie Mann

John Manson

Photographs

The photographs which appear on the cover are also featured throughout the book. However, there are captions covering all the pictures up to page 1.

Front cover: (top to bottom, left to right) – Captain William (Willie) Spence, of Cullivoe, was her longest serving skipper from around 1920 until 1937; he was a colourful and kenspeckle figure in the North Isles. – The *Earl of Zetland* as she was on arrival in Shetland in April 1877. – Mate Tom Gifford and Ertie Moar prepare for yet another anchorage at Out Skerries during a bright morning in the 1930s. – Mate William (Willie) Sinclair checks as the new *Earl* comes alongside at Victoria Pier in 1947, following an inter-county sporting encounter in Orkney. – The old *Earl* at anchor in the voe at Mid Yell with the Linkshouse flit-boat in attendance, a photograph from the late 1930s. – The motor flit-boat eases away from the second *Earl* at Uyeasound in June 1972. – A view of the foredeck while the then new *Earl* is lying at Cullivoe in 1946; the west coast of Unst, beyond Bluemull Sound, gives a focus to the background. – The ship surges along somewhere amid the North Isles on her long-standing routine.

Inside front cover: (top) The old *Earl* arriving in Lerwick during the 1930s with a good crowd on board. (bottom) The new *Earl* during her trials off Aberdeen in 1939.

Short title page: (top) A particularly attractive photograph of the old *Earl* as she heads north during a routine Yell Sound run in the 1930s. (bottom) The second *Earl* on the day she left Shetland in March 1975.

Dedication page: (left) Captain Willie Spence has lifted a small child onto the top of the conveniently-placed binnacle during a North Isles trip in summer. Behind the captain's right shoulder is a passenger with trilby hat associated with the 1930s; his presence on the bridge confirms the friendly informality which was so characteristic of the first *Earl of Zetland*. It became a near tradition that those who travelled were made to feel very welcome, even on the bridge. (right) Captain Tom Gifford had the unique distinction of skippering each vessel with the proud title *Earl of Zetland*. He was mate to Willie Spence then assumed command in 1937 when his predecessor retired. Thereafter he piloted the second ship from her advent in 1939, throughout the war years then on until 1950 when he took over the *St Clair*. He was awarded the MBE in 1946 in recognition of wartime services then became commodore of the North of Scotland Company fleet in 1959. He is seen here at the engine-room telegraph on the first *Earl*.

Contents page: (left) A fashion-conscious lady passenger is flanked by a male companion, also well dressed, while to her left is the homely and portly figure of Jimmy Garriock, for long chief steward on the old *Earl*. He was a familiar and kenspeckle personality. The lady wears an attractive hat to complement the elaborate fastening, known as frogging, on her jacket. Typical of the early 1900s each man sports a pocket watch with chain and a formal wing collar with tie. The scene is set on the after deck, by the wheel. (right) A moment for a yarn on the pier at Baltasound in the 1950s. Pipe-smoking "Gibsie" Thomson on the left was Customs Officer at the Unst port and would cycle down to the second *Earl* for a chat as much as anything else. He is seen here in conversation with apron-clad Jimmy McLeod of the ship's catering crew, both obviously relishing a fine warm day. Of course the background is the *Earl*'s well-deck and catwalk with a window of the deck shelter below the bridge to the right.

Map page: (top) "Whalsay Willie" strikes a pose with the fiddle on the foredeck during an outing. (bottom left) A wave of farewell from a group of ladies on the foredeck of the first *Earl*. (bottom right) A day of agreeable weather always saw a gathering of passengers on the foredeck.

Inside back cover: A pencil sketch by the author circa 1959, the *Earl* northbound and taking the Robson family towards Cullivoe and a three-week stay with cousins.

Back cover: An early morning in Lerwick harbour as the steamer goes astern from Victoria Pier to start another run up to the North Isles.

CONTENTS

Shetland Museum

Douglas Sinclair

ACKNOWLEDGEMENTS

My indebtedness is to people from near and far; from Shetland and elsewhere in the UK to such as America, Israel and Norway (originally). There have been those who offered detailed information in depth, others who have come forward with anecdotal material, while encouragement has emerged from many quarters, often in practical terms.

Of course this is the second book on the theme of the famous name *Earl of Zetland* and many persons and organisations had contributed to the first publication of 1982; not a few have done so for both productions. I am deeply grateful.

This time the main emphasis is on a pictorial record of the two vessels named *Earl of Zetland* and their people – text apart, a saga in itself – thus I give particular thanks to all those who have provided photographs in such rich diversity. I just hope the selection does justice to a couple of splendid ships, all the folk associated with them, and those who have contributed towards the book.

An alphabetical list may appear to be impersonal yet each name (and, often, close relatives), or title, is of particular significance to the author. Thank you.

Captain Andrew Anderson of Cullivoe, Yell; Marie Anderson of Gutcher, Yell; Raymond Anderson of Aberdeen Journals, Aberdeen; Rob Anderson of Lerwick; John Bevan of London; Charlotte Black of Dunrossness; Nadav Bloch of Ein Hod, Haifa, Israel; the Boat Haven, Haroldswick, Unst; Jennifer Campbell of Dollar; Central Peripherals of Dollar, especially Katy and Marion; Michael Clauston of Orkney; Paul Cook of Dollar; Dennis and John Coutts of Lerwick; John Coutts of Fetlar; Judith Cripps, Archivist, City Council, Aberdeen; Captain Ian Denholm of Dollar; Margaret Donaldson of Dollar; Captain Tom Gifford of Strathdon, Aberdeenshire (originally Bressay); Iain Gray, Archivist, City Council, Aberdeen; Captain Michael Gray of Lerwick; Elma Groat of Lerwick; Benjamin Hardaker, Earl of Zetland, North Shields; Cecil Hughson of Lerwick; Angus Johnson, Shetland Archive, Lerwick; Brian Johnston and Staff, Shetland Litho, Lerwick; Eddie Knight of Lerwick; Robert Leslie, Librarian, Orkney Library, Kirkwall; Nechama Levendel of Ein Hod, Haifa, Israel; Derek Lunn of Hawick; Jane Mack, the Interpretive Centre, Fetlar Museum Trust, Houbie; Chrissie Mann of Lerwick; Isobel Manson of Bressay; John Manson of Cruden Bay (formerly Lerwick); Peter Marfitt-Smith of Newcastle and Earl of Zetland; Maureen McRobb of Glasgow; Mary-Ellen Odie of Burravoe, Yell (The Old Haa Trust); the National Maritime Museum, Greenwich; Nita Odie of Burravoe, Yell (The Old Haa Trust); The Editor, The Orcadian, Kirkwall; Brian Patton of Duns; Joyce Pelella of New Windsor, New York State, USA; Captain David and Elma Polson of Lerwick; Andrew Reid of Lyness, Orkney; Lynsey Rendall, Museum Assistant, Shetland Museum; Jessie Rennie of Moffat; Laurence Robertson of Baltasound, Unst; Sandra Sales of Burravoe, Yell; Magnus Shearer, JP, of Lerwick; Anne Sinclair of Fair Isle; Douglas Sinclair of Lerwick; Brian Smith, Shetland Archivist, Lerwick; Leslie Smith of Baltasound, Unst; Leonard Spence of Quarff; Colva Tait of Lerwick; Ian Tait, Assistant Curator, Shetland Museum, Lerwick; Dannie and Beatrice Tulloch of Aywick, East Yell; Eric Turner, OBE, Aberdeen; A & P Tyne Limited of Wallsend; Catherine Walker, Assistant Keeper (Maritime History), The Maritime Museum, Aberdeen; Tommy Watt, Curator, Shetland Museum; Jimmy Winchester of Lerwick; Robert and June Wishart of Lerwick; the late John Yates of Bressay; Eileen Young, Aberdeen City Council, Central Library, Aberdeen.

FOREWORD

One of the factors – even problems – writing and painting have in common is no matter the nature of the approach, there is invariably an alternative. This is a difficulty I have never satisfactorily resolved although I have managed to avoid making it an excuse for not doing anything! "To travel hopefully is a better thing than to arrive, and the true success is to labour." – so said Robert Louis Stevenson around 1880 about the time the first *Earl of Zetland* was finding her way in Shetland waters.

If the writer thus had his say so did artist Sir Joshua Reynolds about a century earlier: "If you have great talents, industry will improve them: if you have but moderate abilities, industry will supply their deficiency." This is reassuring when there are all the doubts about my proficiency in doing justice to creativity. But assuredly I will pass on in wonderment and wondering …

Research is a wondrous and many splendoured thing; that thrill of discovery; of the totally unexpected; of surprise and delight; of contacts through modern communication – the telephone, the fax machine and the computer – or by that disappearing art of the hand written letter. Ultimately it is all about people and there is the infinite privilege and pleasure of the personal contact in renewing friendships and making acquaintances, very often in yarning at length – even into the night – about matters of common interest regarding Shetland and the highway of the sea and its people; and every conceivable related aspect.

But whatever the joys of "the night afore the morn" there is the cold light of day with the realisation that what has been avidly discussed in all its verve, imagination and colour – its spontaneity – has to be prepared (in solitary confinement) for the finality of the printed page. And therein lies the familiar uncertainty … no matter what approach is taken …

Therefore I offer what ensues with a degree of trepidation and no little humility because the history – the saga – of two ships so incredibly part of an island community for those 98 years cannot be taken lightly. Yet that is not to imply that the tale of the *Earls* is an entirely serious affair of fact, because, given that human element, as hopefully will become colourfully clear in the following pages, the folk bring the ships alive. The late Basil Wishart of *The Shetland Times* commenting on my book *The Saga of a Ship – the Earl of Zetland*, published twenty years ago, wrote: "… the story of the vessel that

became the lifeline of the islesfolk of Shetland. But the *Saga of a Ship* is also the story of the people who voyaged in the *Earl of Zetland* and of the men who manned her. It is a saga of the North Isles of Shetland."

If that writing about the old *Earl*, also published by *The Shetland Times*, was admittedly on the long side it has to be said it was not only a story but a fully detailed historical account. On this occasion the publication emphasises a pictorial record with well over 300 photographs; and yet what was written in a preface for 1982 is common to both books. I conclude this foreword with a modified version of what was presented before.

While there was the literal evidence gleaned from a very wide variety of sources, it seemed appropriate to develop free paraphrases to lend individuality and colour to situations. Therefore certain liberties have been taken in the description.

Then, inevitably, in the complexity of research there has been very considerable detail, especially in identifying folk, and while much care has been taken in checking, and on occasion double-checking, there is the very real risk of error or omission. I have to say "the buck stops here" and for any fault I apologise. Also in such involved human experience there must still remain untapped sources of information and doubtless there will be those who browse through this book who know yet another tale or anecdote about the *Earls*; even as immigrant vessel or floating restaurant!

It is hoped, however, as their careers unfold in the sequence, what emerges will sufficiently illustrate the multifarious facets of life centred around two little ships with a big reputation.

The late Rev. Andrew Hughes, minister of the former St Columba Church in Dollar, would say to his Kirk Session following invaluable service in enabling him to take and dispense Communion to the congregation (before the welcome days of lady elders): "Gentlemen, thank you for all you have done; without you I can do nothing as I aught …" Although acknowledgement is made I emphasise again my indebtedness to very many people. Like Andrew Hughes, I could have done nothing …

Adam Robson
Dollar and Cullivoe
2001

THE SHETLAND OF THE EARLS

Muckle Flugga

UNST

Haroldswick

Baltasound●

Bluemull Sound

Balta

Huney

The Vere

Lunda Wick
Bluemull
Snarravoe●

Gloup●

Cullivoe●

Uyeasound●
●Belmont Muness

Skuda Sound

Gutcher●

Uyea

Haaf Gruney

●Sellafirth

Nev of Stuis

Basta Voe

Daaey

Basta Ness

●Brough Lodge

Whale Firth

YELL

FETLAR

Hascosay

●Houbie

Mid Yell●

Wick of Tresta

Vatsetter●

Lamb Hoga   The Snap

North Roe●

Holm of   ●West Sandwick

Rams Ness

West Sandwick

Aywick●

Ness of Queyon

Gossabrough●

Colgrave Sound

Horse of Burravoe

Lochend●

Colla Firth●

Yell Sound

●Burravoe

Ronas Voe

Ollaberry●

●Ulsta
Bigga

Ness of Copister

North-east Mouth

Northmavine

Orfasay

Samphrey

Lunna Holm

Bruray

Housay●

●Hillswick

●Mossbank

Stour Hevda

Grunay

Sullom Voe

Garths
Voe

Firth●
●Swinister

Linga Sound

OUT SKERRIES

Sullom●

Dales
Voe

Wether
Holm

St Magnus Bay

●Brae

Vidlin●

WHALSAY

●Ve Skerries

Olna Firth

●Symbister
Symbister Ness

PAPA STOUR

●Voe

Swarbacks Minn

Stave Ness

MAINLAND

●Neap

●Muckla Fladdicap

Nesting

●Muckla Billan
●Litla Billan

●Aith

Moul of
Eswick

●The Sneckan

●Hoo Stack

Brethren
●Green Holm

North Mouth

Whiteness   Rova Head
Point of Scaatland

Gremista

BRESSAY

Lerwick●
The Knab

NOSS

Scalloway●
Gulberwick●

Kirkabister Ness

South Mouth

Burra Isle

●Cunningsburgh

Sandsayre
Sandwick●

●Boddam

MOUSA

Fitful Head

●Grutness

Sumburgh Head

The island of Foula is
27 miles west of
Scalloway
&
The island of Fair Isle
is 24 miles south-west
of Sumburgh

Sumburgh Roost

Isobel Manson

THE SAGA OF THE EARLS

The roll-on roll-off revolution of the early 1970s in Shetland effected the demise of the beloved era of the two *Earls* whose domain had been the highway of the sea and whose exploits were in the nature of legend.

They were commanded by men of rare character, with crews who were the very essence of folk-lore and who brought to each ship, integrity and fine professional conduct at sea.

The first *Earl of Zetland* of 1877, a product of the John Fullerton yard at Paisley on the River Cart, a tributary of the great River Clyde, had established herself as a focal point amid the scattered island communities, while her successor of the same title continued what had become a strong tradition of sea communication, particularly in the North Isles of Shetland.

The second *Earl* first took the water at the Aberdeen yard of Hall, Russell and Company Limited in 1939. At 548 tons she was approximately twice the tonnage of her forerunner (252 tons after her lengthening in 1884), while her powerful diesel engines generating some 850 horse-power contrasted her apparently seriously under-powered predecessor. However, in April 1877 those engines had brought the first *Earl* and her complement of crew and passengers in some style to northern climes and she was met by an astonishingly big crowd of islanders as she sailed proudly into Lerwick harbour.

Above: There are not many photographs of the *Earl* before she was altered in 1884 and this picture of her lying at anchor gives a good idea of how she looked before the lengthening. It had quickly been discovered that her after well-deck served no real purpose, thus at the same time as the re-shaping between the funnel and the foremast, its removal gave scope for valuable cabin accommodation. The deck for'ard of the funnel was extended allowing a deck-house to be built, then the actual foredeck was also lengthened behind the foremast.

The reasons for the alteration to her length by 23 feet were known to all connected with the islands and welcomed, although it had not been realised that the boiler had been surveyed and was in need of extensive repairs. In some ways this was an incentive to the Directors – all the one doing. However, there was some deliberation between the Lerwick and Aberdeen representatives of the Shetland Islands Steam Navigation Company Limited before Duthie of Aberdeen's offer of £1980 to do all the work was accepted. The firm undertook to have the *Earl of Zetland* ready for sea by the beginning of March 1884.

Below: The remarkable and historic scene at Victoria Pier and Albert Wharf, on Saturday, 19th August, 1939. Hundreds of Shetlanders have appeared to witness a special moment and are milling around to be part of it, as the new *Earl* looks splendid dressed overall, yet her 62-year-old neighbour looks trim and in fine shape. On the far side of Victoria Pier lies the *St Magnus*. The third ship welcoming the *Earl of Zetland* is out of sight astern of her. Appropriately Lerwick rejoices in sunlight.

Shetland Museum

A WARM RECEPTION

That day, her entire crew felt a consuming pride and confidence which was fully exemplified by the warmth of the welcome provided. It was the evening of 14th April, 1877. As the *Earl's* anchor sought the sea-bed for the first of innumerable occasions, an assorted flotilla of small boats clustered round the ship, something of a token of events to come over the years. An enthusiastic reception was echoed in the local press.

The Shetland Times reported: "On Tuesday morning the *Earl* was visited by crowds of people all day. We have already given a description of the vessel (when recording the launch) and it is only to be added that she is fitted up to a very substantial and handsome manner which reflects great credit upon the Directors and upon Captain Nicolson, who has superintended the arrangements and taken every care to ensure the comfort and convenience of his passengers."

By contrast there had been no specific supervision of the fitting-out of the incoming second *Earl* by any crew member, although it was Captain Thomas Gifford, destined to play a highly significant role in Shetland seafaring events, who brought her into Lerwick harbour on Saturday, 19th August, 1939, some 62 years after the advent of the now veteran steamer. The motor vessel *Earl of Zetland* looked magnificent. Many people felt it was unfair to the so much older counterpart to be critical and make comparisons; the newcomer was just different — a fresh generation of ship. But the distinctive and practical well-deck doors were common to both, the sea alongside still mutually available to the flit-boats of the communities of islands more or less devoid of piers.

The chequered history of the *Earls* would unfold over two or three generations of Shetlanders.

THE INVALUABLE FLIT-BOATS

By and large, the flit-boats were former sixareens widely used for fishing around the islands and were in their heyday towards the end of the nineteenth century though by the early 1900s rapidly being overtaken by the bigger, decked fishing craft. However, they proved to be very practicable for working with each *Earl* in turn, being quite spacious amidships with the tafts removed and the section lined with smooth boarding. Until the advent of the internal combustion engine the old sixareens were admirable work-horses year in year out, albeit taxing on man-power when it came to rowing ashore with an enormous load and precious little freeboard in sometimes choppy waters.

The flit-boat was inevitably a focal point at each port, a symbol of communication at the very least, because when the first *Earl* came on the scene the road system in Shetland was, in real terms, non-existent. Metalled routes were in the distant future — as was the telephone. Therefore a leisurely pace by sea was a fact of life, although in an odd way

it was a competitive world. There would be on occasion a fascinating tactical struggle between the *Earl's* skipper and the flitmen — the former trying to tempt the flit-boat out, the latter trying to tempt the steamer in. The steamer's whistle often echoing over the shores, scattered dwellings and hillsides on a still day, would invariably give fair warning, but the flit-boat would lie at the slip or small pier as long as possible with the thought of a more economical distance to pull on oars, especially on the way back ashore with her load. Considering that every human and animal form, every item of sustenance and existence had to be trans-shipped, there were innumerable occasions when freeboard for a flit-boat would be minimal, although over the decades never was a boat-load jeopardised anywhere in the North Isles — or elsewhere in Shetland. But then the seamanship of the boatmen in going off to, or returning from, the steamer, was born of instinct and long experience and in summer and in winter the heavy former sixareens were immaculately handled.

However there is often the exception to the rule and at sea the unexpected can create problems. So it was with the Whalsay flit-boat on 29th December, 1924. The *Earl* had come up into the bay of Symbister in the winter twilight and by the time the flit-boat was alongside the last vestiges of daylight had faded, with an ever-rising wind from the south-east lifting the waters. Rapidly the situation worsened to the extent that the *Earl* could no longer lie there; neither could the big flit-boat be risked only under oars. She was too unwieldy to lift up onto the heaving well-deck, thus a snap decision was made to cut her loose and with the Whalsay men safely on board the steamer got under way, running before the now severe gale in the black December night. Unfortunately it had been impossible to communicate with the shore — there had apparently been no response to either the *Earl's* whistle or lights. It was only a telegraph signal from Mid Yell to Whalsay the next morning which relieved the Whalsay people of their great concern for their men-folk. The flit-boat was seen no more.

Flit-boat crews at the ports had individual techniques. There was no pattern. At Whalsay two oars were the choice, whereas at Burravoe four were preferred. On the other hand with more than one community round the voe at Mid Yell the flit-boats made use of sail as can be seen in the illustrations on page 36.

At Brough Lodge on Fetlar there was only an exposed slip at which to launch the flit-boat, thus a lighter type of craft which could be reasonably manhandled ashore was regularly in use. Heavier goods for Fetlar were landed fortnightly at Houbie at the often more sheltered south bay there. The only port in the North Isles with a semblance of a pier was Baltasound, thus passengers who had spent most of the day en-route were at least able to step ashore instead of waiting until a flit-boat was first loaded with goods.

Therefore throughout the North Isles the commercial facilities on the highway of the sea were basic in the extreme.

Below: This is an effective illustration of the hand to hand practicality of maneouvering cargo from the well-deck to the flit-boat. A fair amount of upper body strength, a certain dexterity, agility and some timing were certainly attributes. What seems to be a back view of Lowrie Gifford (he had a way of pulling his cap down almost over his ears) shows him pushing a sling full of sacks outwards. The sacks already in the flit-boat appear to have some "special" contents.

The flitman, meanwhile, unties a sling watched by a youngster and a colleague, while the bow of the flit-boat already has a pile of boxes, apparently holding milk "full cream" containers. The smooth boarding common to all regular flit-boats is obvious amidships.

Above: The Skerries flit-boat in the 1950s. Two men, with an empty box, two sacks and one animal going ashore. Judging by the taut rope at the bow the big former sixareen is under tow by a motor boat, while the man at the stern seems to be short of a tiller; little wonder the man in the bow appears to be looking aft rather anxiously.

The flit-boat was named *Moses* while the two men are Andy Johnson (left) and Archie Williamson.

Jimmy Winchester

Elma Groat

A FLEXIBLE APPROACH

The service to all the ports was inevitably done in leisurely style, while the very unpredictability due to the diversity of trade, unexpected passenger movements and the vagaries of the weather led to a timetable which could only be described as flexible. But then, on the basis of what you have never had you never miss, the limitations were universally accepted — if reluctantly on occasion — by the islanders. As was evident in the case of the Whalsay flit-boat even communications by telegraph were limited; certainly not available to the general public. Before the days of telephones, which reached the North Isles only in the later 1930s, an obliging postmistress could be very helpful with her telegraph equipment. "Tinkle, tinkle" on the machine, and there was the information that "she left Uyeasound at 8 o'clock," or "she was in Cullivoe at 10 o'clock," or the depressing message, "she's not come to Cullivoe yet"; or the more satisfactory news, "The *Earl* left Mid Yell a while ago". Of course with the wayward maritime climate of the islands there was no certainty that the *Earl* would even appear, fog and perhaps unexpected heavy weather being the main bugbears. There could be a prolonged and indeterminate wait for the crew of a flit-boat and passengers alike which led to a somewhat philosophical resignation, although a degree of frustration would have been entirely understandable.

There was the situation when Willie Spence — a doyen of skippers — was in command. The old *Earl* was lying in Symbister at Whalsay late on a Friday afternoon and was expected in Lerwick that evening after over an hour's steaming covering the fourteen miles to the south. In the teeth of a south-east breeze that would be the average time for that trip. But there was the unexpected full gale from the south-east, reportedly a particularly vicious version. Three times Willie brought her limited horse-power to bear on the breaking seas outside the shelter of the land-mass and three times he had to take her back to anchor in the bay. Thus there was no option but to lie overnight in the hope that the wind and seas would abate by daylight. Willie Spence, an intrepid master, had a formidable reputation for quality seamanship and was vastly experienced, although his ship had her obvious limitations and as it was she had to be tacked in the face of a gale — that Friday night, however, was too much.

By the Saturday morning the wind had dropped and the sea, ever responsive, had eased. No problem. He ordered "full-ahead" and she made good time to the south, surging through the north entrance to Lerwick harbour and heading towards the familiar berth at Victoria Pier, where the dockers were ready for him.

When "Spencey" — as he was affectionately known — eased his steamer alongside, there came a shout from a stalwart: "Weel Wullie, whit wis wrang dat du didna come wi her dastreen?" The skipper never at a loss for a ready riposte shouted back "I widda come but I coodna get her ta come!"

It seems unlikely that such colourful events and incidents could have been visualised by those enterprising men who had the foresight to anticipate the values of steam propulsion in Shetland waters; they would be too preoccupied by the basics of travel and business enterprise to give any thought to such incidental items. The era of sail was being rapidly overtaken by "da steamers", thus the days of the smacks were numbered.

THE EVOLUTION TOWARDS STEAM

In the mid-nineteenth century the Unst shipping company owned two smacks, the *Imogen* and *Matilda*, which traded between the island and Lerwick, subject, of course, to the vagaries of the northern seas and their fickle tide-runs in narrow sounds between rock-girt shores. The skippers of these vessels gave yeoman service but the limitations were inevitable. Alexander Sandison of Unst was their agent, a man of enterprise and initiative, with the imagination to picture the possibilities of development, which had to come sooner rather than later.

A move was made in 1863. The erstwhile newspaper the *Shetland Advertiser* carried the statement: "We learn with much pleasure that a meeting was held in Unst on the 17th instant (May) to consider the propriety of putting a steamer on the North Isles trade ..." But the imaginative and far-sighted idea never reached fruition because no suitable ship was at that time available.

In mid-1868, however, the Shetland Steam Shipping Company Limited had been founded in Lerwick. On 1st September Alexander Sandison received a letter from their secretary with the suggestion that the two small 10-15 ton vessels, *Imogen* and *Matilda* should be sold and Unst interests should invest in the new firm.

This was then agreed because steam was the obvious way ahead.

Meanwhile the Shetland Steam Shipping Company Limited had been searching for a suitable steamship to serve the islands and they discovered the attractively named *Chieftain's Bride* lying at Glasgow. She was purchased for £2100. Sandison had strong views about a ship which seemed to be unsuitable for Shetland, "having 94 tons burden with 25 horse-power, she is a trash and would be thrown aside where either speed or power is required. Her class for purposes such as ours is fast going out of use ..." His strong criticism was justified when the merchants and travelling public dubbed her "the Crab" since she proved to be adept at moving sideways in the strong tides amid the North Isles. Yet she had the distinction of pioneering steam propulsion in the islands, while no criticism was levelled at her crew who were well supported by the folk and, indeed, one correspondent gave wholesome praise in the local press. The writer considered that, "... I am quite sure ... any success is due to the incredible amount of exertion and labour of her captain and crew. Leaving the regular days of work out of the question, the amount of night work is excessive ... and all this for a pittance in wages. The captain and crew, I may mention in passing, are well known to be as civil and good a set of men as ever sailed on a ship." The writer referred, of course, to William Nicolson and his men.

He continued: "I, for one, would cheerfully enter into the speculation of a new boat to do the whole trade ... twice a week, of sufficient power and capacity for the daily growing trade, and I am certain that influential men ... would come forward ... The result would be a new and commodious vessel commanded by the present captain, if he has not by that time left in despair, giving the shareholders a reasonable dividend ... while at the same time we have laid off the yoke on the truly hard-wrought slaves on board the *Chieftain's Bride.*"

There is no record of Captain William Nicolson's reaction to the remarks but he would be acutely aware of the problems posed by his vessel. He had been brought up in a hard school. He was born at North Ustaness in the district of Whiteness in 1838 and in keeping with the strong island tradition he went to sea, firstly as a cabin boy on a Leith ship working the Faroe and Iceland cod fishing. Life was tough for the young teenager and his wage was a barely adequate six shillings and eight pence per week, yet he persevered with the fishing for 11 years and thrice survived from sailing vessels which were a total loss. His determination benefited him because in 1864, aged 26, he became chief officer of the sailing packet *Queen of the Isles,* trading goods, passengers and occasional mails between Leith and the west side of Shetland, then by 1872 he was

Douglas Sinclair

Left: Captain William Nicolson and his wife Barbara, née McPherson. He was the first to command the steamer, the forerunner of a long line of fine seafarers spanning near-enough a century on both vessels. The couple are seen in the Whiteness area. At this time William Nicolson would probably be skippering the ship.

Left: The Merksworth ship-building facility of John Fullerton and Company on the River Cart at Paisley, a tributary of the Clyde, was noted for quality. This is the yard where the *Earl* was built and, although there is no photographic evidence of her construction or launch, this illustration shows the situation.

A wide cross-section of the population is gathered to watch a small dredger-type vessel taking the water on 20th September, 1917, with the far bank lined by spectators. A much larger ship is on the stocks to the right. The Fullerton yard was operational from 1867 to 1928; the yard built 279 ships. The founder died in 1905 and his younger son, James, continued the business until his death in 1925.

Paisley Museum

rewarded with the captaincy of the erstwhile *Chieftain's Bride,* then, briefly, the temporarily chartered *Lady Ambrosine.*

Five years later the same William Nicolson became master of the brand-new *Earl of Zetland* and, of course, he was the man who, so understandably proud, brought the keenly awaited ship into Lerwick harbour that spring evening of 1877.

Perhaps it would have been somewhat surprising if there had been a smooth transition from the vagaries of sail to the anticipated consistency of steam, but clearly there was an inevitability of gradual change as initiatives spread northwards. The Leith and Clyde Shipping Company had existed since 1790, when Shetland knew nothing but sail, then in 1810 there was amalgamation with the Aberdeen, Dundee and Leith Shipping Company to form what was popularly known as the Aberdeen, Leith and Clyde. Their first-ever steamer to inaugurate a service between the Scottish mainland and Lerwick was the wooden paddler *Sovereign* in 1836. Then, significantly, in 1873, that firm became the North of Scotland and Orkney and Shetland Steam Navigation Company, which played a significant role in establishing steamship travel in Shetland and, indeed, the coming of the first *Earl of Zetland.*

There had been one main Shetland initiative. The *Chieftain's Bride* had served for seven years and certainly was not without her critics, thus she was dispensed with in May 1876. Many incentives existed to establish reliable sea communications and a group of Shetlanders, all deeply involved in the community, met on 25th February, 1876, in the Lerwick office of the North of Scotland and Orkney and Shetland Steam Navigation Company — presently known simply as "the North Company". That day, history was made. By the end of the meeting the Shetland Steam Shipping Company Limited had been absorbed into a new firm named the Shetland Islands Steam Navigation Company with a 50% share held by the North Company, with a group of appropriate co-directors in Aberdeen.

By early June 1876 the company had been registered and certificated, the fee for this having been drawn from the account opened with the Union Bank of Scotland in Lerwick. On 3rd June the board meeting approved plans and specifications for a projected steamer, forwarded by the Aberdeen directors of the North Company who, of course, had an executive role in the Shetland Islands Steam Navigation Company Limited. But a new vessel could not be ready before the spring of the next year; a stop-gap materialised in the shape of another steamer named *Lady Ambrosine,* comparable to the *Chieftain's Bride,* but more functional for the purpose. She was chartered from Glasgow for £80 per month from August 1876; her earnings for October and November amounted to £452.6.3d, with expenses of £382.12 shillings. The surplus of over £69 was thought reasonable, since a loss had been anticipated. She then ran on

rocks at Burravoe, Yell, on 4th January, 1877, and carried away her forefoot, thus had to leave for repairs.

There was the resultant void in the steamer service with an inevitable anomaly when the sailing smacks *Absara, Spell* and *Spy* filled the gap, although sailings were advertised under the name of the steamer's company. So the wind of change was blowing fitfully, albeit the "Almighty's ain wind"!

However, work was proceeding apace down at Paisley where skipper William Nicolson had the fascinating and absorbing task of supervising the fitting-out of the as yet nameless new steamer. At the time, when boilers and steam engines were developing rapidly, it was customary to place an order with the main engineer, in this case James Howden and Company of Glasgow, a highly reputable firm, who then sub-contracted to John Fullerton and Company operating at the River Cart, by Paisley, with building and launching facilities as seen in the illustration above. Howden's price of £6650 had proved to be acceptable after delicate negotiations ended in August 1876 and Fullerton could then begin the hull. Meanwhile, there was lively discussion and subsequent decision-making about a name for the new steamer and, in due course it was hardly without controversy! On 24th January, 1877, prompted by a telegram from the North Company directors in Aberdeen, the Lerwick directors got round the table to look at the issue. They finally settled on a short leet of three names, *Countess of Zetland, Princess of Thule* or *St Olaf.* The last-named seemed to have decided possibilities because it was so much in keeping with vessels in the North Company fleet like the *St Nicholas* and *St Magnus.*

Concurrently, the *Paisley Daily Express* of 1st January, 1877, reported progress at Fullerton's yard: " ... well employed, the vessels launched being: SS *Devon,* 205 tons, SS *Sousa Franco,* 81 tons, SS *Larne,* 252 tons and *Surf Boat No 31,* 30 tons. The vessels now building are a screw steamer for the Shetland Isles(sic) Steam Navigation Company Limited and a screw steamer for the coasting trade in Australia".

Then the Aberdeen directors, Messrs Jamieson (Lord Provost), Mylne, Shepherd and Webster were offered the choice in decision-making about a name for the anonymous hull rising from the stocks at Fullerton's Merksworth workplace. For possible political or, at least, diplomatic reasons the recommendation came back to Lerwick for *Earl of Zetland* or *Countess of Zetland.* There is no record of what the Lerwick directors may have thought, but in any event a letter was despatched to Lord Zetland down in England putting forward the proposals and leaving it to him to decide whether the steamer would be *Earl* or *Countess.* His Lordship was prompt. He replied by letter on 2nd February, 1877, intimating his willingness for either name to be used.

By 16th February the directors in Lerwick and Aberdeen had decided

on a title which was to endure from 1877 until 1975, near enough a hundred years, with only two vessels, then in an extraordinary manner to be revived and to survive into this 21st century — the *Earl of Zetland*.

But over 125 years ago there were repercussions. Many islanders were not happy with the name and were not slow to comment. Letters appeared in the Shetland newspapers and correspondents were certainly forthright. Sarcasm was a factor, not to put too fine a point on it: "As most of the shareholders … must now be aware that their new steamer has been 'gracefully' named *Earl of Zetland* it is to be hoped that they will embrace the first opportunity of awarding a vote of thanks to the directors for the great amount of taste and discernment they have shown in choosing a name that must sound like music in the ears of every native of the islands … it is to be hoped that his Lordship will feel a due sense of honour …

"Shetland, although a poor place in some respects, is certainly not so in either historical or traditional names … is it better to toady to a live Lord than to pay compliment to a Norse hero? … Has he (the Earl of Zetland) done anything with his enormous wealth to further steam navigation to, or amongst, our islands? Has he shared in any of the losses that we have had to bear in opening up the trade with the old *Crab?* Or has he even visited the islands? … it is to be hoped that in return for the honour conferred on him, his Lordship may purchase any shares that remain unsold and do so in a true spirit of charity …" The letter was signed, "A Shareholder".

Another irate shareholder took up the cudgels: " … I was glad to see in your issue *(The Shetland Times)* of 24th (March) that your correspondent had the courage of his opinions and gave expression to the feeling of dissatisfaction with which Shetlanders regard the name … (they) ought to know that they are indebted to the Scottish (Aberdeen) section for the high-sounding name … Well, that she may be successful under whatever name she sails is the prayer of your petitioner …"

Perhaps any name would not have had universal acceptance in the islands. *Princess of Thule? St Olaf?* Regardless of the multiplicity of public opinion, in the fullness of time there appeared to be no dissent when the second *Earl of Zetland* was named at the Hall, Russell yard at Aberdeen as she was launched in March 1939, thus the name had apparently achieved acceptance in the populace and, undeniably, when disagreement had run its course, the name, regardless of human title connotations, came to have a dignity which found expression in the vessels themselves. If a conglomeration of metal and wood can convey a proud demeanour, then each *Earl* in turn earned success in the eyes of the folk; and thus the name has proved to be entirely appropriate over the decades. Indeed, over the long years, keeping in mind "the prayer of the petitioner", perhaps there were the occasions when they plied their trade, the old *Earl* in two world wars and the new *Earl* in the second conflict, when the good Lord intervened for their salvation.

Above: The *Earl* as she was built, depicted by G. Thomson, a Leith artist who painted the North Boats, and whose work is today well valued. This water-colour was produced in 1892. The ship appears to be steaming in Bressay Sound.

The Author

Above: Another version by the same artist, also dated 1892, illustrating the steamer after she was lengthened. Here the ship is seen in a rather stylised sea with shipping on the horizon.

Laurence Robertson

Above: On an unknown mission to Broonies Taing at Sandwick in the South Mainland. The date is probably about 1902. The ship still has her original on-deck anchors, operated by windlass and the manual davits, a lot of work with a vessel lowering and raising her hook many times each week. In Yell Sound alone it would be as often as 12 occasions as she took in Burravoe, Mossbank, Ollaberry, Lochend, North Roe, Westsandwick, Ulsta and again Burravoe; also Swinister, Sullom and Brae were regular ports at various times, and calls could be made at Bardister.

Just what the dark cylindrical or box-shaped object is at the bow remains unclear because the *Earl*'s foresail is stowed in front of it and the two cannot be confused. What appears to be steam obscures people in the background. Two men are in conversation while two others, moustached, the one on the left wearing plus-fours and the other with trousers clipped around the ankles for cycling, are camera-conscious. The solidly-built pier stands today, now a century old and a tribute to those who built it, actually begun at the end of the nineteenth century.

Shetland Museum

Above: Framed between masts, the *Earl* works cargo with a flit-boat alongside at Whalsay, possibly in the late 1920s. In a way this composition symbolises the transition from sail to steam in that LK1075 *Gracie Brown* was the last Shetland sail herring boat, as the era of the steam drifter evolved.

Shetland Museum

Shetland Museum

Above: Despite the initiative and enterprise of those distinguished men who formed the Shetland Islands Steam Navigation Company Limited in 1876, the brand-new steamer *Earl of Zetland* was outdated even by the time she was launched. Certainly she had been optimistically described by the *Paisley Daily Express* of Friday, 2nd March, 1877: "... no doubt ... this commodious vessel will be a great boon to the inhabitants of those distant islands, as well as a source of enjoyment to the tourists who frequent the country ..." then *The Shetland Times* joined in enthusiastically: "... on Tuesday (17th April, 1877) the *Earl* was visited by crowds of people all day ... she is fitted up in a very handsome and substantial manner ..."

The North Isles people liked what they saw – perhaps anything would have been an improvement? – yet there were those who were reticent, even slightly sceptical; they had their thoughts about recent ships like the *Chieftain's Bride* and the *Lady Ambrosine*, and their shortcomings, especially those of the *Crab*. It would need a winter to prove the mettle of the new steamer. Would she be big enough for her task despite what had been officially stated and publicised in the press?

There would be justification for the doubts because trade in Shetland expanded, exacerbated by the unprecedented boom in the herring fishing in the 1880s, and the *Earl*'s capacity was in question only two or three years into her career; although few folk could have anticipated her eventual amazing contribution in Shetland and beyond. Special trips to Fraserburgh, Peterhead and Aberdeen from the herring trade alone added to the busy inter-island schedule; indeed, fish apart, the *Earl* could have well over 100 gutters on board. Big cargoes multiplied and inevitably a vessel of her dimensions – 120 feet – was badly compromised. As it was, Shetland people were not happy with the two South sailings a week in winter and, following a meeting in Lerwick Town Hall in October 1887, the North Company was requested to adopt the third sailing – meanwhile summer only – all year, with the steamer leaving Lerwick each Saturday night. The company declined, which put pressure on shipping space and unavoidably this highlighted the position with the *Earl*.

All the uncertainties led to an exchange of ideas about having the ship lengthened and this photograph perhaps illustrates the problem. Here is the *Earl of Zetland* as in 1878 and clearly she is of restricted capacity, neat though she is, lying offshore at Lerwick in the company of the first *St Magnus*. Coincidentally she was one of the South boats in question regarding the adequacy of the service which, in her case, was almost entirely confined to Leith-Aberdeen-Kirkwall-Lerwick, although she appeared occasionally on the direct Mainland-Shetland run. The *St Magnus* was the last paddler owned by the North Company, their only two-funnelled ship. She was sold to interests in Gibralter in 1904.

THE WAY AHEAD

There was no doubting the fascination with which the first *Earl of Zetland* was greeted. The response of the islanders gave the directors great encouragement and the steamer remained a central focus of attention right through the islands from Sumburgh to Unst, for weeks.

The *Paisley Daily Express* of Friday, 2nd March, 1877, had described in detail the launch into the River Cart; not only that but the paper offered an optimistic opinion on Shetland tourism and weather; " ... but the influx of tourists has been so great and the intercourse between the islands is increasing so rapidly that the want of proper conveyance by water has been very much felt. The pleasant climate enjoyed by the islands in June and July especially, and the many opportunities for shooting and fishing have led to so many tourists selecting to spend a few weeks among the islands which Sir Walter Scott has so vividly described in the 'Pirate'. It may be mentioned that there are Inns on the principal islands."

The article continued: "... the launch ... took place in the presence of a large company ... As the ship left the ways, Mrs John Henderson, sister of Charles Merrylees (secretary to the company at Lerwick), gracefully named it *Earl of Zetland*. Immediately afterwards, it reached the water and floated successfully".

A description of the *Earl* had been eminently positive: " ... built under Lloyd's survey and is classed in their books 90A1 ... engines of 50 horse power inverted and direct acting on the compound principle ... specially adapted for a large passenger trade as well as for carrying goods, the internal fitting up has received careful attention. The engines, engine room and hatches are all placed in the centre so as to allow ample room fore and aft and also increase the steadiness of the boat. There is a large saloon and ladies' cabin in the poop, furnished in a handsome style with sofas, tables, etc. Above the saloon is the poop deck, which will form an excellent promenade for passengers in fine weather.

" ... Forward there is a steerage saloon on the main deck for female passengers and on the deck below a large apartment for male passengers ... there is no doubt that this commodious vessel will be a great boon to the inhabitants of those distant islands as well as a source of enjoyment to the tourists who frequent the country."

The newspaper report confirmed that William Nicolson had superintended the internal fittings then it rounded off: "After the launch Mr Fullerton entertained a select company in Merksworth House, to cake and wine, when prosperity was drunk to the *Earl of Zetland* and the builder."

Any toast will be given in a spirit of forward-looking goodwill, but that offered to the already proud hull was, in effect, a toast to a legend within a lifetime. Yet no one there on 2nd March, 1877, could have the crystal ball of clairvoyance to visualise the saga of the *Earls* today indelibly woven into the fabric of the communities in Shetland, especially those of the North Isles; nor could they anticipate that a controversial name could develop an aura of timelessness which will forever be part of Shetland's maritime history. And not a few toasts have been offered in the context of the *Earls* as will become apparent!

Having returned to Shetland, secretary Charles Merrylees could scarcely contain his elation when he reported to the Lerwick directors that their ship would be ready for trial in April, with delivery to the islands later that month. So it was good.

The Shetland Times of 7th April remarked: "Bailie Robertson and Mr Arthur Laurenson went south by last boat as members of the pier committee, along with Mr Charles Merrylees, for the trial of the *Earl of Zetland* on the Clyde. We trust that everything will prove satisfactory and we will soon have her here. However much our correspondents may quarrel about her name (ships' names do confuse the grammar sometimes) I think we may venture to say she will be welcomed by everybody. Owing to the unsettled state of the weather the isles' carrying trade is in a most unsatisfactory state." Of course this was a reference to the void caused by

the demise of the *Lady Ambrosine* and weather problems for the sailing smacks.

Thus on Saturday, 7th April, the *Earl of Zetland* sailed stylishly into the measured mile off Skelmorlie in the Firth of Clyde, a ship alive. Howden's thoughts concerned his engines; Fullerton appraised the hull shape; Nicolson savoured the moment in its fullness; Merrylees, Robertson and Laurenson considered many things, including the consumption of fuel! Below, a fireman shovelled coal, an engineer eyed his gauges and the *Earl* responded with 10½ knots. They were all delighted.

On Thursday, 12th April, they left for Shetland. There was time in hand and with reduced and worsening visibility and nightfall off the island of Jura, it was thought prudent to anchor in Crinan Bay; then away at the crack of dawn. By midnight on the Friday the *Earl* had the Butt of Lewis off her port quarter and the open sea expanded before her, wind out of the south testing the counter stern in following seas. The west side of Orkney unfolded, then the croft-houses at the south end of Fair Isle with Sumburgh Head looming up before the ship.

From the height of the Knab at the south end of Lerwick the *Earl of Zetland* so far off looked diminutive, yet purposeful with smoke about her funnel and a "bone in her teeth". Steadily she came up and then passed a big crowd of well-wishers who hurried back over to the waterfront to see her actual arrival. It was 8pm on 14th April.

There followed the announcement: "The *Earl of Zetland* will leave on Tuesday morning first for the north of Shetland and will sail regularly thereafter on the mornings of Tuesday and Thursday until further notice. Next week, however, owing to the Sacramental fast day she will make only one trip, taking goods for both voyages on Tuesday first …"

Right: A letter of Authorisation of Registration signed by the Lerwick Directors: Arthur Laurenson was a partner in the hosiery firm of Laurenson and Company and a distinguished Shetlander; John Robertson – nicknamed "Robertson of the trance" – wielded considerable influence in the community; William Irvine, a director of Hay and Company, the major Shetland trading firm; Alexander Mitchell, a solicitor; and Charles Robertson, partner in the grocery firm of R. & C. Robertson, also serving on Lerwick Town Council as a bailie.

SHETLAND ISLANDS STEAM NAVIGATION COMPANY (LIMITED),

Lerwick 5th May 1877

To the Secretary
Shetland Island Steam
Navigation Co Limited
Lerwick

Sir,
We the undersigned Directors of this Company authorize you to Register the SS Earl of Zetland" in the Books of the Mercantile Marine Office here as the property of the Company. —

A Laurenson
Wm Robertson
William Irvine
Alex Mitchell
Charles Robertson

Below: A well known photograph of the fast paddle steamer *St Magnus*. She certainly has boilers fired here! In the distance, and significantly, the then new *Earl of Zetland* is at anchor amid a variety of sailing vessels. The time will be around 1880, before a pier became established at the capital of the islands. The nature of the Lerwick foreshore can be seen, with its indiscriminate range of beach, slip and small jetty. What a labour it would be to row ashore by flit-boat the immense variety of cargo coming from the south! But a pleasingly built small boat is drawn up in the foreground.

Shetland Museum

A STEAMER AT WORK

In the little ports to the north of the mainland and the isles, there was keen anticipation and excitement. The significance of the *Earl's* coming was highlighted when she called at Haroldswick in Unst and the school children were out en masse to greet her. Most folk liked what they saw but there were those who were reticent, even sceptical; the experience with other steamers had not been good. It was easy enough to maintain timetables in the soft days of summer, although they were prepared to make allowance for delays when the islands merged into a shroud of fog, the biggest hazard of all. Still, this ship had something about her it was said. She looked the part. It was also said that she had cost over £7000, which was correct — £7000.13s.11½d, to be exact!

At the end of July 1877, the directors presented a first report in which it was minuted that, "The *Earl* has been well appreciated by the travelling and trading community ... and has secured a very fair return." And within weeks the steamer dealt with her first salvage case when she towed the derelict schooner *Milberg und Engstrom,* of Drammen, from south-east of Bressay up to Lerwick.

Surprisingly, an overture by Merrylees through Mylne in Aberdeen to the Post Office for a mail contract was met with bureaucratic delay. From time immemorial mail had been subjected to the uncertain and vulnerable method of post-runner and boat, under oar or sail. In fact, to this day, just across from Cullivoe in Yell, there is the "Post Geo" on Unst, which is a suitable inlet with a beach where a boat could be drawn-up.

Eventually, at the end of February 1878 the Shetland Islands Steam Navigation Company was offered four shillings per week by the Lerwick postmaster to take the mail from Lerwick to Whalsay on regular voyages. Yet this route was but a fragment of the company's proposals and by the end of May 1878 the directors had given up hope on achieving anything further with a strangely reluctant Post Office.

But business expanded in parallel with innovative and immensely popular leisure trips. It was written of Foula: "Quite a sensation was caused by the first visit of the *Earl* ... having on board some south-country and Lerwick gentry on a pleasure trip ... being the first steamer that has ever anchored here ... it is hoped that he (Captain Nicolson) will make many more trips with her yet, to this romantic and isolated island ..." Another correspondent wrote: "Having found the former trips enjoyable ... I resolved that I would improve my geography by having a look around the coast of Northmavine ... how little people know of the lie of the land, distances and general information of their own local districts. At the examination of one of our schools a class was asked about the geography of Palestine, but one cannot help feeling that a little more attention might be given to the geography round our own doors ..."

Unwittingly the writer had touched on the unexpected in his or her comment about the Holy Land; certainly no one in their wildest dreams could have visualised that one day the *Earl of Zetland* would be sailing to Palestine in 1947 with a precious cargo of humanity destined to help form the infant state of Israel.

Such completely original initiatives by the Shetland Islands Steam Navigation Company had a powerful appeal. The directors had the imagination to use opportunities to the full and on the August trip to Out Skerries "Jeems" Williamson's fiddle had the folk dancing on the *Earl's* deck, albeit caught unawares on occasions as the steamer rose and fell in a slight swell. For the usually somewhat isolated Skerries folk the visitors' coming was a moment to savour and the hundred or so trippers were welcomed with open arms. Some friendships were renewed, others formed; it was not easy to bid au revoir to the warm island hospitality. The *Earl* then put into Symbister Bay at Whalsay and as she lay at anchor all on board enjoyed the catering of R. & C. Robertson, who had been appointed as suppliers.

Meanwhile, Charles Merrylees, the secretary, had been promoted to manager of the North Company from January 1878. His ability and faithful diligence in business for over 20 years were highlighted and it was said he would be well appreciated south, in Aberdeen. His successor was William Shand at the remuneration of £50 per year.

The ship was paying her way, with an expansion in revenue from approximately £2144 in June 1877 to £2643 in 1878. Briefly there was talk amid the Lerwick directors for a corresponding ship for the west side of Shetland but there was no practical support from the directors of the North of Scotland and Orkney and Shetland Steam Navigation Company in Aberdeen; "... it is a matter for the local directors of the Shetland Company to promote. If they see their way to give the thing a trial ..."

Although nothing came of the suggestion, five years later, in 1883, the *Lady Ambrosine* — long recovered from her mishap at Burravoe — arrived in Shetland waters to ease the pressure on the *Earl* in the summer herring season when the special runs were made to the north-east of Scotland ports. Large numbers of herring gutters and cargoes were carried. Thus the *Lady Ambrosine* was re-introduced in the April at £105 per month, skippered by John Scott, mate of the *Earl*. She was collected at Fraserburgh and given a "floating brief" to be run during the herring season in conjunction with the inter-island and the south steamers.

Such pressures led to the lengthening of the *Earl of Zetland* as described in the captions accompanying the photographs on pages 6 and 9, although the question could be asked today as to why the co-directors in Lerwick and Aberdeen could not have anticipated the inadequacy of the ship's capacity only seven years after her appearance in Shetland. In any event the peerie steamer was making an impact in a variety of forms. There had been a small financial return from the salvage of the *Milberg und Engstrom,* then she picked up the disabled brig *Superior,* of Aberdeen, on 13th November, 1881, and £50 went to the *Earl's* owners. Captain Nicolson received £20, while £30 was distributed amongst the crew.

Right: If there was a pier at a port – and there were several – it was not always of the strongest construction and any bigger vessel had to approach with caution. The original Cullivoe pier was subject to quivering and shaking if there chanced to be an inadvertent bump in going alongside.

From the evidence here, North Roe pier of the 1920s and earlier came into the flimsy category, and judging by its rather sparse inner supports it was very vulnerable; "exercise with caution" would be the appropriate catch-phrase. Yet at least it could be used by the steamer, the important factor being enough depth of water. It was not always possible on the ebb.

However, here is the *Earl* depicted on a postcard, across the end of the pier at North Roe, her for'ard derrick angled out. Going by the open bridge, the photograph must have been taken early in the century, although the date stamp on the card is "North Roe, Lerwick, 22nd Aug '36". But postcards could lie in a shop year by year for a long time. This one carried the message: "Dear H and L. Having a very enjoyable time up here. The weather is lovely and everyone is mostly very busy. Looking forward to a 'fly cup' when I come down. Hope you are all well. Love from Helen." The card is addressed to Lerwick and was marketed by "E. Nicolson, North Roe".

Douglas Sinclair

Of course the boom time for picture postcards was in the Edwardian era, essentially the first decade of the twentieth century. George V came to the throne in 1910 and public enthusiasm continued until 1914, when the First World War intervened. The "golden age" had come and gone, yet over the decades the postcard has remained a hugely popular means of communication to this day with an enormous world-wide market.

National Maritime Museum, Greenwich

Above: At anchor in Burravoe in the early 1890s. A solitary figure stands on the new "bridge" and some passengers linger around the decks. The *Earl* flies the "Red Duster" at her stern. The extension to the hull has a good look about it. A subtle sheer has appeared, while her decks are much more spacious. The lifeboats have been moved 10 feet forward and the deckhouse has been provided with a ladder up to a railed top from which to con the ship. The longer foredeck has given cover for the derrick winch and the crew who work it – rather better placed than those who navigate and steer!

Duthie's had produced an excellent standard of workmanship, much to the satisfaction of master and crew, while the Shetland public reacted enthusiastically. The carrying capacity was doubled, speed fully maintained and working expenses were not expected to be greater. She was described as "a much more serviceable steamer, in all respects as good as new."

Her timetable was unremitting, between the Yell Sound and Unst passages, week by week, year in year out, goods, passengers and animals featuring in great volume. The schedule for April 1884 immediately after her lengthening is featured on page 10.

Passengers seemed to be well disposed to the *Earl*, as was Harry Pearson Taylor, a Yorkshireman who had studied medicine in Aberdeen and had graduated in 1890, had accepted a call to relieve a practice in Shetland and decided he liked the islands and wished to stay. He did so, and for 45 years was a G.P. on Yell from June 1890 until November 1935, captivated by the place, people and way of life, to the extent that he created a book entitled *A Shetland Parish Doctor*. He wrote colourfully and explicitly about steamer and flit-boats: "… a flit-boat and other smaller craft came alongside, the owners of the small boats taking off their relations, friends and goods for themselves, while other passengers, mail, animals and general cargo for the local shops were deposited in the flit-boat … those of us who had further north to go amused and interested ourselves in watching the proceedings of the steamer and the skipper of the flit-boat. The badinage which took place between those worthies, although at times unprintable … would certainly have made a Thames bargee envious and astonished a Billingsgate porter. The skippers of the flit-boats were usually the victors in the wordy, but always friendly and humorous conflicts. This could be accounted for because the officer — generally the mate — superintending the transfer of goods was required to exercise restraint while the skipper of a flit-boat could let rip!"

The career of the old *Earl* was punctuated by incidents, frequently to other shipping and occasionally involving herself. Already, there had been the two salvage affairs. A third episode brought loss of life, yet a

miraculous save. She had been on annual survey in Aberdeen and returned to Lerwick on Saturday, 30th January, 1886, to the news that James Jamieson, the skipper of the local smack *Columbine* had been knocked overboard by the boom and drowned, that his two crew of unrelated Smiths had gone in the *Columbine's* dinghy in a fruitless effort to save him and that by a quirk of fate the smack, having been hove-to, had got under way again. That was bad enough in itself as she headed offshore in a stiff and strengthening breeze and increasing seas. But aboard was a solitary passenger, Betty Mouat, who was travelling from Grutness to Lerwick with knitwear to sell from the women folk.

The two Smiths, Jeremiah the mate, and Oliver, deckhand, struggled ashore in the dinghy to break the news to observers who already knew there was something far wrong as they watched the smack's erratic movements. John Bruce of Sumburgh, owner of the *Columbine,* found the only available suitable vessel was a small steamer, the *Gipsy,* lying at Mid Yell and she was immediately chartered to search. She did so for 25 hours, covering 200 miles, while the *Earl* left at 4am on the Monday to join in. William Nicolson took her 30 miles east-north-east in near gale force snow-laden winds which had gone westerly earlier. They sailed east for ten miles and south-east for ten miles. Nothing. All ten crew on the steamer doubted if the *Columbine* could have survived; later they joined the throng in Lerwick, disconsolate at the thought of another drowning.

Yet survival there was. Miraculously, Betty Mouat did not succumb as the smack ran ashore on the island of Lepsoe near Ålesund in Norway, providentially at a beach where she could be saved. She was feted in Norway and the rescue hit the headlines in the national press; back in Lerwick, Elizabeth Mouat was driven round the town in an open carriage

with Bailie Robertson, a director of the Shetland Islands Steam Navigation Company, before a big gathering of well-wishers. A subscription list was opened. Queen Victoria donated £20, as did John Bruce, owner of the *Columbine*. A collection on board the *Earl* brought in £11.7.6d, then the overall total was £400.

Throughout it all Betty Mouat maintained a modest dignity; she was happy to return to her quiet, retiring way of life and did so for another 32 years, being just into her nineties when she died.

Lerwick harbour works had been gradually improving, with the herring industry a particular incentive for improvements. In May 1876 a conference in Lerwick had agreed on the necessity for a berthing pier; in 1877 Lerwick Harbour Trust was formed. By 1883 Sheriff Principal Thoms had laid the foundation stone for a pier to be named after Queen Victoria, while to the *Earl of Zetland* would fall the privilege of being the first vessel to berth there. Thus it came about on Wednesday, 23rd June, 1886, that a big crowd of townsfolk, supported by the town band, watched the peerie steamer go alongside the Victoria Pier into what would be her regular berth at the north side for six decades to come.

Some weeks later the *Earl* visited Fair Isle for the first time and for the inauguration of the Wesleyan Church there. The Reverend William Moister preached on the theme: "The glory of this latter house shall be greater than that of the former". His message might well have related to the ever-developing progress of steam propulsion as against the uncertainties of wind power! This was illustrated when the schooner *Pet*, of Wick, drove ashore at Cunningsburgh in December 1885 and was towed to Lerwick, followed by the loss of the smack *Lady Nightingale*, which missed stays in the swift tide of Yell Sound, came down on a lee shore, struck a rock off West Sandwick and was lost. The *Earl* brought her crew of three down to Lerwick. Another salvage task materialised when a steamer, the *Merjulio*, of Leith, collided with the rock known as the Skate, off Maryfield on

Bressay. The inter-island steamer's men earned a couple of hundred pounds in fees, towing the *Merjulio*.

The mid-1880s brought changes in the officers. William Nicolson was promoted to the *St Clair* and he was replaced by John Scott, born in South Shields with Shetland parents. His father had died and his mother returned to Shetland where young Scott grew up in Twatt, Aithsting. He went to sea in 1865, had experience in local and Faroe cod fishing, then went "deep sea" for eight years before joining the steamer on 13th September, 1877, at the invitation of his friend William Nicolson. After Scott's promotion, Tom Moffat was appointed mate and he was with the *Earl* for 35 years, a fine record.

Within a short time they salved material from the remains of the steamer *Borgfelde* which had wrecked at Hillswick, then the *Earl* towed the barque, *May*, of Mandel, to Lerwick. Further incidents followed in quick succession, all indicative of the hazards of sail. In December 1888 the Norwegian brig *Normand* had had all hands to the pumps keeping the sea from encroaching on her cargo of coal, from Burntisland to Christiania (former name of Oslo). They made it to Lerwick but dragged anchor and went ashore between Lochaber Baa and the Holm of Cruister. She was towed off and taken to the other side of the harbour where the coal was discharged, rather far from its destination.

The astonishing sequence of recorded sea accidents continued. In January 1889 the schooner *Snaefell*, like the *Normand*, dragged and ran aground in the vicinity of Gardie House. She had had a bad time north-east of Shetland but made port. This time she could not be budged but she came off the ground on a very high tide of her own accord. Also in January, the steamer hauled the barque *John*, of Stockholm, from the North Isles. She had been denuded of her main and mizzen masts in fearsome seas off Unst but made it to Baltasound, where the *Earl* came to her assistance.

Left: Captain John Scott MBE returns to his ship on 19th August, 1939, to help commemorate a famous occasion. Half a century has elapsed since his captaincy of the *Earl*.

Shetland Archives

Below: Vast crowds of Shetlanders come to support the formal opening of the Victoria Pier as a proud *Earl of Zetland* inaugurates berthing. A steam crane on a barge and another on the quayside contrast the delicacy of the bunting of the steamer and on the shore. The year is 1886.

Shetland Museum

A MOVE TO NEW MANAGEMENT

At the time of the lengthening alteration in 1884 the Shetland directors had to look at the question of a temporary replacement vessel. William Shand contacted Charles Merrylees in Aberdeen and it was agreed that the North Company steamer *Queen* should take in the Unst passage fortnightly (rather than charter a ship), while the local smack *Cynthia* would be chartered for Yell Sound ports. At the time, the 448 ton *Queen* had a form of roving commission taking in diverse calls ranging from Leith, to Inverness, to Caithness, to the west side of Shetland to the North Isles, indeed in 1872-73 she had even voyaged to Iceland, mainly for ponies!

Divergence of opinion between the Shetland and Aberdeen directors had emerged in February 1884. It had appeared that the North Company recommended the purchase of a derelict lying at Stornoway for £250 to be moored at Baltasound as a floating pier for convenience in the herring season when the *Queen* would be on the fish trade. The local directors begged to differ in that they reckoned the Aberdeen outfit had more to gain than they. A compromise was reached when the smack *Petrel* was hired by both companies as a floating store "on most favourable terms".

Financial factors were always a concern. The enlargement of their steamer plus boiler repairs produced an account of over £3500, which forced the Lerwick directors to negotiate a loan of £1500 from the North of Scotland Bank. Suddenly there were doubts about the viability of the Shetland Islands Steam Navigation Company, accentuated by the North Company placing the *Queen* on the Leith, Fraserburgh, Lerwick and North Isles traffic — this because of pressure due to the fish trade and to prevent outside parties encroaching. The situation was becoming a dilemma for the Lerwick directors.

By May 1884 they had decided to recommend amalgamation with the

Right: According to the clock in the engine room the time is 10.05am on board the *Earl*, as morning sun slants in, probably through the skylight. The control wheel for the main valve shines through fastidious care and constant use. This was probably photographed in the 1930s.

Below: Port identification in photographs is not always easy and this is no exception … but somewhere in the North Isles? Low-lying land? It is open to speculation. Exhaust steam from the cargo winch flurries round the bows as a smart fourareen is rowed ashore and the big flit-boat prepares to go alongside the steamer. Meanwhile, long-skirted ladies and companions grace the after-deck; the skipper, possibly Peter Johnson, stands on the exposed bridge. It is the first decade of the 20th century.

Above: The *Earl*'s stem touches on the pier structure as she angles in from the harbour for the very historic opening occasion. It would appear that there is decorative "gingerbreading" at her bow and, presumably at her stern. It seems likely that this was short-lived because later photographs show no evidence, although at least one contemporary painting of 1892 by G. Thomson, the Leith artist, shows such decoration.

The long, flowing skirts worn by the ladies of the late 19th century are in evidence.

North Company to the shareholders, although time drifted by without concrete action and finances continued to fluctuate, although the travelling public were using the *Earl*. The employment of the *Queen* still rankled. In 1887 a letter was sent to the North Company complaining about her involvement and its adverse effect on the finances. Then, ironically, the *Earl of Zetland* had serious boiler problems and had to be towed from Garth's Voe near Mossbank, right to Aberdeen — by the *Queen!*

This proved to be a catalyst for the amalgamation of the two companies. It was 1890, the 13th year of the Shetland Islands Steam Navigation Company and their ship the *Earl of Zetland,* unlucky in that an identity was about to be lost yet fortunate that ship and service would be put on a sure basis. The shareholders were well enough aware of the fragile financial state of their company, thus it was not surprising that 75% of them gave the Lerwick directors a mandate to link up with the North Company. Bailie Robertson chaired the meeting on 10th June, 1890, in which some views were polarised. A speaker was adamant that the local directors had proved themselves utterly incapable. This was countered with the opinion that they deserved a vote of thanks and that all blame should be put on the Aberdeen men!

The Old Haa Trust, Burravoe

Above: Characters abound in Shetland folklore and Peter Clark of Unst would qualify in his day. He was a frequent and familiar traveller on the *Earl*, for he sold tea on Unst and Yell and was often seen in typical stance on the foredeck as here portrayed, carrying his work-worn basket. If the arms of his jacket seem a modicum on the long side, they served to keep his hands warm on a cold day!

There is the tale of Peter's dog which was known to accompany him from a port like Uyeasound to Cullivoe. About the turn of the century, early nineteen hundreds, the ship was still rather primitive in fittings and the anchor chains emerged from the spurling pipes in the foredeck and hung free without any guard in the gloom of the fo'c'sle before entering the chain locker below. Peter, who had come aboard with his dog, happened to be in the fo'c'sle as the ship got under way for the short run between ports, had looked for a convenient projection on which to tie up the animal, and had hitched it to a link in the chain.

Peter Johnson, then skipper, ordered an anchor down to await the next flit-boat, sadly the anchor chain to which the dog was attached. Instantaneously the unfortunate creature shot skywards to an untimely end. But the passing of Peter's dog was the reason for the chains being boxed in – it's an ill wind that blows nobody good!

The view of the Shetland press was that the time for fighting was now past. There had been a chance when amalgamation was first mooted in 1884 for the Shetland shareholders to act but they had not done so ... The primary object was the extension of trade in the islands ... this had been a success ... trade was now greatly developed.

A second extraordinary general meeting in the November confirmed the resolutions passed in June ... the company, now in liquidation, showed a net profit of £374 ...

Symbolically a letter was sent to the Register of Shipping, Port of Lerwick:

"Lerwick, 1st December, 1890

Sir,

I request, as authorised by the Shetland Islands Steam Navigation Company Limited, Lerwick, that the registry of the steamer *Earl of Zetland* of Lerwick, 68187, be transferred to the port of Aberdeen.

Yours Faithfully

W. M. Shand, Secretary"

The peerie steamer, indifferent to human foibles, responded to the needs of the North of Scotland and Orkney and Shetland Steam Navigation Company. In 1890 she was ready for special trips on Mondays "when sufficient inducement offers". She loaded 15 tons of fish at Lerwick and 35 tons round at Scalloway on a January Saturday night, sailing from the west side at 10am on the Sunday and was 30 hours on passage to Aberdeen. Again, in May 1891, the *Earl's* long-suffering and patient crew took her away to relieve the *St Olaf,* on overhaul (predecessor of the first *St Ola* circa 1892) in Orkney on the Pentland Firth mail run.

Even by 1891 the Shetland mail service was not satisfactory ... the Company were offering to run five per week ... the Post Office was at odds. Then the *Earl's* timetable meant that mail from the North Isles of both Thursday and Saturday was subject to fragmented schedules. The timing situation was compounded because the North Company sailing bill announced, "North Isles Passage. From Lerwick every Saturday night or following morning for Uyeasound and Baltasound ..." The studied avoidance of the word "Sunday" was no doubt intended to allay offence but, in fact, it was generally just into the Sabbath when the steamer left Lerwick.

Angered by this desecration of the Lord's Day, numerous Shetland ministers were intensely critical, the more so since it was alleged drinking took place at some of the ports. In April 1893 the Synod met and unanimously agreed that a letter should be sent condemning the Sunday sailings. William Shand replied fairly. Every Friday after 5pm a steamer left Aberdeen with mail and arrived in Lerwick through Saturday. Outgoing mail was shipped south on the Monday evening. He pointed out that the *Earl* would be impossibly restricted if part of the Sunday was not used, having six ports at which to call on the week-end run to the North Isles, before connecting with Monday's south-bound boat. He also mentioned that this was solely for the benefit of the people of the North Isles. The outcome was that although the Synod still had serious reservations, it was agreed the practicalities were vital; and thus the issue was left. Yet it had to be admitted that any limitations were relative. A "post-runner" service had been set up by private enterprise in 1820 and a "runner" meant exactly that. The "postman" would take two days from Lerwick to Unst including rowing or sailing over Yell and Bluemull Sounds. This put the contemporary criticisms into a perspective in what was practical and sensible.

With the apparent success of the special outings to Foula and Out Skerries, the North Company set out to encourage excursionists to join the more routine type of voyage as far as Unst. One happy participant described, "... shaking the dust of the city off the feet and go to Unst, leaving Lerwick on the Sunday and returning on the Monday." He described the *Earl's* new silent departure from Victoria Pier: "... it was Sunday (evening) and the still of the sabbatic rest seemed to prevail everywhere; scarcely a breath of wind ruffled the surface of the water", while "the sound of the church bells inviting worshippers to the evening service came stealing over the sunlit and sparkling waters in tones sweet and mellow". Captain Scott came down from the open bridge and mingled with the passengers, as was his custom. At Whalsay all the big herring boats were at anchor, while their men, "lounged about the doors of the houses, smoking their pipes and enjoying their well-earned Sunday rest ..."

The ship then called at Mid Yell and Uyeasound, dealing with mail and,

therefore, seemingly the pleas had not fallen on deaf ears: "… although it was midnight before we reached the shores of Baltasound there were a few people astir and lights gleamed from several windows, while gathered on the pier were islanders as were expecting to meet their friends."

The North Company, having already embarked upon ambitious summer cruises to Norway with their *St Rognvald* in 1886 — the Hardanger, Sogne and Ronsdal Fjords for £10 — became the first British shipping line to try that market. The experiment was so valuable that they ordered the first *St Sunniva* as a purely cruising/passenger vessel; such ambitious plans worked in parallel with broadening the appeal of the *Earl's* normal sailing programme within Shetland itself. The plans expanded. In 1898 an elaborate series of round trips was publicised, making use of all the company's routes to and from Shetland and between Lerwick and the North Isles in various combinations. For example one could switch from the *Earl* at Ollaberry to the west-side steamer at Hillswick, or one could spend four successive days (Sunday to Wednesday) on the *Earl* doing first the North Isles route and then the sequence of Yell Sound ports. This was progressive thinking; the Company, of course, had to be seen to be involved in developmental and positive marketing because there was always the threat of competition, apart from keeping up profit margins.

Indeed, by the turn of the century, rivalry materialised in the shape of the Shetland Islands Steam Trading Company Limited, with registered capital of £12,000 made up of £1 shares. By May 1903 the steamer *Mona* had been chartered. Posted to leave Leith on 22nd June, she was due to call at Aberdeen, Dunrossness and Sandwick before visiting Lerwick and going on to the North Isles ports. Opinion at Lerwick was that she looked a smart vessel, perhaps better fitted to cargo work, although passengers who had come north with her seemed well enough pleased. At the same time the *Earl* was away, taking care of the near-new *St Ola's* route in Orkney when she was on overhaul.

In the autumn of 1903 the directors of the Steam Trading Company chartered the SS *Trojan* to replace the *Mona* during the winter months. The *Trojan* was a steamer of 260 tons, a trifle bigger than the lengthened *Earl*, and within a fortnight she was the subject of controversy in that she usurped what was already, almost traditionally, "the *Earl's* berth" on the north side of Victoria Pier. A misunderstanding … Captain Allison, the harbour master, was at lunch; the *Trojan* having arrived earlier than expected. The matter was complicated when the *Earl* herself appeared and was forced to go alongside at the south-boat's place on the other side of the pier, under the command of a new skipper in Peter Johnson who hailed from Skeld in Sandsting on the West Mainland, John Scott having taken over the *St Sunniva* in May 1902.

The wrangle developed in an exchange of correspondence between the Steam Trading Company and Lerwick Harbour Trust. Mr John W. Robertson, the company secretary wrote that the harbour master had come to the pier and "expressed regret" that the *Trojan* was lying there, then half an hour later had re-appeared "… just when we had got under way with the discharging and ordered us to shift the vessel". Arguably, the "expressed regret" was enough of an implication but the *Trojan's* master and crew did not see it that way and the steamer remained where she was.

Although the incident was a one-off affair Captain Allison was accused of partiality, "… if they could believe the stories told …" but ultimately he was instructed "to endeavour to make such arrangements with steamers

Below: Just how many funnels the *Earl* had has never been ascertained but it can be safely assumed not a few! Also they seemed to vary not only in width but in height. This version is perhaps once removed from the "Woodbine" variety! The binnacle stands in "splendid isolation" on a completely exposed bridge, while the canvas dodger in front of the wheel hardly looks designed to withstand a gale! Yet the canvas served for decade after decade.

A young captain Peter Johnson faces the camera wearing his tie and smart wing collar, but who is steering the *Earl* is debatable. The rather elegantly-clad young lady's hat and dress suggest the early twentieth century – 1905 in fact – but she seems unaware of the wheel. Her companion gazes downwards and, surprisingly, there is a crouching figure on Peter Johnson's right. The helmsman perhaps?

Shetland Museum

Above: The seat by the dining saloon skylight, with its metal protective bars, makes an admirable stance for a tiny girl of the Edwardian era, with her elaborate bonnet and long white pinafore. A steadying hand is available nearby … just in case!

using the pier as would prevent any inconvenience or loss of time in future."

In contrast to the North Company and their steamer *Earl of Zetland* now of some 25 years standing, the Steam Trading Company acquired their third ship when the *Minihinde,* of Belfast, appeared. She was renamed *Norseman* and came into operation in March 1904 with a very competitive fare structure. The reductions were warmly welcomed by Shetland business interests and travellers and suddenly the North Company announced, "… at present the modification of their services to Shetland, consequent to the falling off in goods and livestock through opposition". Of course the 409 ton *Norseman* was actually doing a Leith to North Isles of Shetland trip … she even transgressed on the *Earl's* leisure runs, being billed to make an excursion to Whalsay, Yell and Unst, followed by another to Baltasound on Victoria Day of 1904. Simultaneously, the North Company advertised a trip to Collafirth and Ronas Voe, weather permitting. Thus, the two steamers were in direct opposition the same day but if anything, the *Earl* had a tactical advantage with the prospect of passengers visiting whaling stations, then in full production. The response from the public was encouraging when 150 joined her at the Victoria Pier — north side!

Meanwhile the *Norseman,* billed for Unst, did not have much luck; she had had the misfortune to run aground briefly at Fraserburgh on her way north and arrived in Lerwick late, with the result she left for Baltasound with only about a dozen trippers — the *Earl* had scored over her rival! The *Norseman's* failure was symbolic; for the four-year-old Steam Trading Company had run up debts of £6000 and it was no surprise when in May 1908 assets were sold off in a sad end to a worthy motive.

Above: A lighter moment on the *Earl of Zetland* about 1905. Peter Johnson had taken over from John Scott as skipper in May 1902 and remained in command until 1912 – a ten-year tenure. Here in a corner of the wheel-deck he indulges in a frolic with two unknown companions. This photograph was taken not long after the rails had been sealed off by good-looking teak panels, although the rails themselves remained exposed on the outside! Obviously the wood provided a modicum of a wind-break – if not actual comfort – in an ongoing sequence of "improvements" over the years.

Wooden benches were distributed around the *Earl's* decks as can be seen in the wide variety of photographs but creature comforts were in short supply, facilities remaining distinctly spartan on deck to the end of her days. Yet by way of mitigation her dining saloon was a haven of warmth and wholesome food on a cold day …

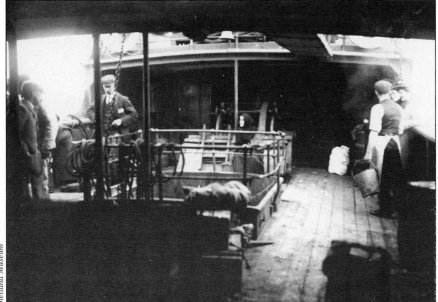

Left: The domestic touch. Jim Petrie, the cook of the era in the early 1900s, has probably emptied such as tattie peelings over the side and now has a word with two attractive young ladies. A gentleman on the left is maybe contemplating the only relative nature of the *Earl's* timetable, while a traditionally-clad woman sits by the open hatch.

THE TWENTIETH CENTURY UNFOLDS

Each phase of the career of the old *Earl* was punctuated by incidents of assistance to other vessels and their crews. The late 1870s and into the eighties, nineties and, presently, the new century, saw accidents, albeit in diminishing numbers as steam ousted the uncertainties of sail. It was near enough the turn of the century when the Mid Yell owned *Jessie* came to grief off Uyeasound, losing not only sail but anchor. That the aid given was appreciated was evidenced by Charles Mann and crew of the *Jessie* in a letter to the Shetland press: " … we were in great extremity when the vessel (the *Earl*) came to us and we think we would be neglecting our duty if we did not in this manner tender our best thanks to all who assisted us …"

On 17th February, 1900, the Norwegian barque *Hedevig,* homeward bound to Frederickstad, met a hellish storm off the south end of Unst, became unmanageable and was thrust towards the north coast of Fetlar. She crashed into the tiny island of Daaey a mile offshore and ground in her death throes, while her crew fought ashore in the maelstrom of white surf. Two men were lost. It was a shepherd in the employ of Sir Arthur Nicolson who spotted the men on Daaey and, as seas abated, the islanders launched a boat. The survivors were given hospitality by Sir Arthur, while the *Hedevig's* mate and crewman who had died were buried in the Fetlar graveyard at Tresta before the rest of the crew sailed for Lerwick on the *Earl*. The storm had made a lasting impression on North Isles folk and over the years, if memories were rekindled, it was referred to as "the Hedevig Gale".

There followed the fishing disaster of December 1900 when the district of North Delting was devastated by the loss of four boats and 22 menfolk, today commemorated by a particularly lovely memorial at Northlee, Firth's Voe, by Mossbank. Circumstantially, the *Earl* was not involved in that; while she had been due in Fetlar about the time of the appalling family deprivation she, in fact, had been confined to Lerwick by the same gale until 9am on the Saturday, some 24 hours behind her scheduled departure. A telegram from Mossbank had somehow not succeeded in communicating the extent of the problem but the owners were criticised for seeming failure to do anything at all in such a dire situation.

The *Earl* had remained essentially trouble-free over her quarter of a century of work in northern waters until Saturday, 7th June, 1902, when she was attempting to enter Baltasound. Herring fishing activities were in full swing. The steamer had gone to Wick to bring up fishworkers and they came in their hordes, the fisher lasses full of optimism and high spirits, the men, coopers, a hard industrious breed, all bound for Scalloway, Burra Isle, Ronas Voe, Cullivoe and Baltasound. By the time the ship came to the Unst port the number of passengers was down to sixteen but Captain Johnson was faced by a forest of masts and spars of a mass of herring boats occupying the bulk of harbour space. Peter Johnson took the only available stretch of water along the north side of the voe, moving cautiously not far from the shore. Abruptly, there was a grating noise as the *Earl* ground to a halt on what was assumed to be a discarded ballast heap of stones: there was little concern. Engines full ahead and astern had no effect; surely she would ease off in the rising tide. But that was not to be because suddenly there was water in the engine room, which encroached steadily until it filled the hold and washed all through the accommodation, part-submerging the well-deck, galley, animal stalls and right aft through the ladies' cabin, then covering the carefully polished stove and plush seats in the dining saloon. The sea reached up almost to the portholes; to all intents and purposes the *Earl* had sunk!

Five days later, when the tug *Empress of India* arrived from Aberdeen, the steamer presented an odd sight lying on an even keel but submerged almost to deck level at high water. Steam pumps from the tug dealt with the offending water after a large gash under the engine room was found to

Below: Another angle on the Victoria Pier, shared by the *Earl* and the second *St Giles*, which had a ten-year period with the North Company. Having appeared in 1903 she would be relatively new here – in fact she looks spic-and-span. Both ships are working cargo judging by the exhaust steam about the *Earl*'s starboard side and the presence of the crane boy on the *St Giles*. Many a young Shetlander went to sea initially as a crane boy on a North Boat.

Shetland Museum

Shetland Museum

be the culprit. A temporary repair enabled the *Earl* to limp to Lerwick, hence to Aberdeen for full reconditioning.

Shetland newspapers expressed Peter Johnson's appreciation: "... anxious to return his sincere thanks publicly to all the people of Baltasound for having shown such kindness to the crew of the *Earl* while she was submerged there. Especially he would like to thank Messrs Anderson, Edmonston and Sandison for giving accommodation to the crew." Public comment was made about lack of markers for the ballast heaps and much sympathy was shown to Captain Johnson for his misfortune.

That the steamer had fully recovered from her mishap was revealed by her work rate three weeks later. She took fish workers south to the Scottish mainland on a Sunday from the North Isles, returned to Lerwick on the Tuesday, sailed up to West Sandwick on the Wednesday and on to Baltasound during the Thursday.

Next, almost inevitably it seemed, in April 1903, the 684 ton barque *Nina*, of Porsgrund, was swept into Yell Sound with only a stump of a mast remaining, being driven before a northerly storm. She had been abandoned but when the waterlogged hulk came abreast of Ulsta, local men boarded it, possibly with salvage in mind; but there could be no control and they were all hazarded. Fortuitously, the *Earl* appeared and although a tow was rigged, she could not cope with the burden and the *Nina's* timber cargo spilled along the Firth Ness shoreline and she disintegrated on the rocks, the would-be salvors fortunate to get away with their small boat. And the timber washed up quickly disappeared!

Although the bulk of accidents came about through wind and heavy seas, fog was always a potential menace. It was an irritating inconvenience at the very least and could be frightening in its very emptiness, sea and land merged into a grey nothingness. Men could be so affected as to misjudge situations — even allowing for perceived local knowledge.

North Company vessels had been hazarded: the first *St Rognvald* was lost in a pea-souper at Burgh Head, Stronsay in Orkney in April 1900, followed by the first *St Giles* at Rattray Head on the Scottish mainland in September 1902. It was a curious twist of fate when her successor of the same name ran ashore at the north-east end of Mousa in October 1904.

Above: A splendid shot of three ships owned by the old North of Scotland, Orkney and Shetland Steam Navigation Company, illustrating the community involvement as a dense crowd is gathered on the pier and on the foredeck of the ill-fated first *St Sunniva* which is departing for Aberdeen. The two dockers at the extreme right of the pier have just cast off her headrope. Behind the *Earl* is the *St Rognvald* (1901).

The time is confirmed as the first decade of the 20th century by the *Earl's* open bridge, and the recess in the pier, bottom left, which was filled in between 1913 and 1915, as shown when this photo was taken. Steam drifters and trawlers lie in Bressay Sound.

Providentially little sea was running and Captain John Scott ordered a boat away to Sandwick to telegraph for aid.

Unlike the *Earl* at Baltasound on the ballast heap, the *St Giles* slid off the offending rock on full astern, and then at full speed, but taking in water, she covered the short distance to the shingle beach at Sandsayre where she was put ashore, resting upright and with her pumps coping against the invading sea. The *Earl* had not left on her North Isles run from Lerwick and, with steam already up, she came alongside the stricken steamer to take off passengers, livestock, mails, cargo and luggage for the 11-mile return trip to the island capital in improving visibility. A week later the *Earl* sailed back to tow the *St Giles,* now temporarily repaired, once more into deep water.

In April 1905, the drifter *Emily Reaich* was stranded on a baa off the tiny island of Orfasay, near the Ness of Copister at the south tip of Yell. Peter Johnson brought his ship to the rescue of the seriously damaged and rudderless fishing boat, attached tow-ropes and after an hour's hard work the *Emily Reaich* broke free, although taking some water. She was lashed alongside the *Earl,* and in progress reminiscent of the *Chieftain's Bride,* alias "Crab", the two ships reached Burravoe for beaching of the drifter. Peter Johnson was not to know then that his *Earl of Zetland* would be similarly badly compromised within a few years. As it was, she suffered a broken intermediate shaft in May 1906, south of Whalsay, and drifted helplessly. A boat was launched to row the 12 miles to Lerwick, a hard 3-4 hour pull, and her men were thankful enough to have the relaxation as the *St Giles* took them and their boat back to the waters around the Muckle

Fladdicap near Whalsay where the *Earl* awaited the tow — now the turn of the *St Giles*!

Over six years from 1906 till 1912, there were four major incidents. The first was at the end of December 1906 when the barque *Nordwind,* of Hamburg, on a voyage from Gothenburg to Melbourne, Australia, fell on her beam ends off Out Skerries. The skipper and two crew were, sadly, drowned but 17 survivors were grateful when Captain Johnson offered the hospitality of his ship for the voyage to Lerwick.

Seventeen months later the *Earl* had 12 men on board, survivors of the Norwegian whaler *John,* of Sandefjord. An exploding oil lamp in her accommodation had triggered off a blaze which could not be contained and the crew took to the boats, forced to watch as their vessel burned out and was swallowed up, 75 miles south-east of Unst. Another Norwegian ship, the fishing steamer *Ludolfreade,* had taken the men to Baltasound.

The third affair featured an abandoned barque, *Pioneer,* yet another Norwegian. She had left Liverpool for Skien near Porsgrund on 21st November, 1910, caught sight of the coast of Norway then was disabled by a fearsome easterly gale. Her skipper lost his life in efforts to cut away wreckage and the mate and crew fought a losing battle as the vessel, deprived of sail and steering, was inexorably driven towards Shetland in hitherto unknown awesome weather. The doomed barque, her cargo of coal still intact, was left to her fate as the crew escaped to eventually win ashore at Eswick in Nesting.

Whalsay had also suffered from this gale of gales. The fishing community was stormbound and often enough the men were at the croft-house gables looking for a break in the leaden sky. As the wind eased and the sea responded they were amazed to see a ship, seemingly out of control, and with no sign of human life, wallowing in the tideway at the south end of the island.

Three boats went out of Symbister and the men contrived to not only board the 900 ton *Pioneer* but manoeuvre her into Linga Sound where she was anchored, a sorry looking sight yet with cargo unspoiled. It was then, subsequently, that the *Earl* had a participating role, for she carried the salvage money for the Whalsay fishermen, who were glad enough to have £24.10/- each, for it was well nigh Christmas 1910!

The south-east has, from time immemorial, been a source of worry about bad weather in Shetland. Such a storm played havoc with shipping in January 1912. *The Shetland Times* carried the headline: "Great Storm in Shetland. Mail Service Unhinged." The *Earl* had to lie over a weekend at Mid Yell, something she had managed to avoid for 20 years. A third barque, the *Advena* from Sweden, was within sight of the Norwegian land when she was assailed by frightening seas — the folk in Shetland were talking about the spray being carried over the lighthouse on the heights of Sumburgh Head. The *Advena* was driven relentlessly towards the islands and she came to land at Out Skerries, where people watched as the ship slewed round in the confined south entrance and in a smother of whiteness crashed on wave-battered rocks. One moment there were seven dark figures on board the rapidly disintegrating *Advena,* then only two who

Shetland Museum

Above: A departure moment at Lerwick with a massive crowd of folk to see off "da steamer". The end of the pier is jam-packed, while the now-moving spectators spill along the big cargo shed where the *Earl* is lying, sharing berths with two sailing craft, apparently a fishing boat and a big smack. In front of them are two small rowing boats, and somehow it is all symbolic of the transition from sail to steam after the protracted era of proceeding by "the Almighty's ain win' an' no' wi' the Deevils fire an' brimstane".

The scene is set in the late 1880s, only a few years after the alteration to the *Earl* in 1884. As it is, her so-called bridge is no bigger than the roof of the tiny cabin below, although some concession has been made to "comfort" in that a white material now covers the rails!

The departing "sooth boat" is the first *St Rognvald* built in 1883, thus she would be almost brand-new here. She pioneered cruising to Norway and was an immediate success, which led to developments in her layout, like a smoking room and a "music saloon".

Unfortunately on 24th April, 1900, sailing from Lerwick to Kirkwall, she was wrecked in fog at Burgh Head on the Orkney island of Stronsay. However, here she is in days of yore surging away, a froth of water at her stern and a plume of smoke about her funnel, with the backdrop of the Lerwick lodberries and the Ward of Bressay.

proved to be Ragmar Larsson and Karl Yonsson, saved by the Skerries men. Both survivors sailed to Lerwick on the *Earl*.

From time immemorial loyalty and integrity have been associated with men in all the great seafaring nations of the world and clearly the crews of the now indispensable North Isles steamer had become personalities of note. Her first skippers had shown seamanship and friendship and were backed up by worthy shipmates. William Nicolson, the first captain had, of course, gone to the *St Clair,* followed by John Scott to the *St Sunniva.* Now Peter Johnson was deeply involved with the *Earl* and he had an able deputy

Above: Another stalwart in "Lang Jeemie" Jamieson, glimpsed doing his stint at the wheel, wearing muffler and, apparently, Fair Isle style knitted gloves. This would be in the 1920s.

Shetland Museum

Gordon Donaldson

Above: Colin Henry at the wheel during the mid-1930s

in Tom Moffat, who, at the time of the *Advena* incident had been mate for over twenty years. He had to be quick off the mark from his home in Market Street, Lerwick, on a winter's morning to begin working cargo at 6am, prepared to play his part in loading. There were no dockers in the North Isles then, no lines of demarcation, no industrial action. A man did his day's duty and more if need be.

The mate had a work-intensive task; directly answerable to the captain in crew supervision; controlling the warps, lowering and raising the anchor at each port; storage and distribution of cargo and livestock; an affable attitude to passengers. Also, and importantly, he had to bear the idiosyncrasies of the flitmen through the North Mainland and North Isles, and many a scathing remark in the traditional banter had to be countered in a manner inoffensive to the company and the passengers, as implied by the doctor, Harry Taylor.

It is not always fair to single out individuals, yet sometimes attitude and length of service highlight people. Colin Henry would be one of the longest serving seamen. He came from the little community of Gutcher in Yell and had worked on the *Earl* for a decade before he decided to move wife and family to Lerwick, from which base he served for another 25 years to emulate Tom Moffat's spell of thirty-five. Colin had a kindly nature, friendly and helpful to many a passenger in the throes of seasickness, while he was a familiar figure at the wheel, hands protected from the bitter cold by knitted mittens, often renewed by fisher lasses who appreciated his agreeable disposition.

Then there was John Fraser from Cullivoe in Yell, a survivor of the 1881 fishing disaster when 10 boats and 58 men perished. He lived in Lerwick and such was his commitment to his beloved ship that he was one of those who would venture down to the Victoria Pier to check her moorings on a wild night of winter weather. This was a seaman devoted to the *Earl of Zetland.*

Shetland Museum

Above: Tom Moffat who was mate for 35 years, from the mid-1880s. On the *Earl* the mate had to be a combination of everything from stevedore to acting skipper, and to Moffat was attributed the remark: "I cannot work and navigate at the same time!" No doubt it was made in a moment of pressure because he had a loyalty and commitment which served the steamer, and all associated with her, particularly well. Of course he was mate at the time of the Lunna Holm incident and had acted responsibly throughout when the ship was at great risk.

MILESTONES AND
THROUGH WORLD WAR ONE

The remarkable range of work for the ship never lessened. Passengers in abundance, livestock and goods cargoes, pleasure trips, postal services, the Up-Helly-A' annual festival; even political activities. It was back in 1906 that Mr Cathcart Wason, Liberal candidate, chartered the steamer to take Skerries voters to Whalsay and those from Fetlar to Mid Yell, although Mr Dunlop, the Unionist candidate, did not wish to be involved in the expense. The Liberal majority was 2816 — perhaps poetic justice had been done!

Relatively poor postal arrangements persisted. Even although the *Earl* dealt with much of the mail, in the mid-1900s horse and gig plus open boats were still used. Letters from the previous week-end sometimes did not reach Unst until the Friday, while Skerries was poorly served. The drawbacks were an ongoing limitation and, despite some progress, the problems remained.

Early in September 1909 the steamer carried 1097 lambs in one of the special autumn livestock voyages. In loading at More's station at Leiraness, the concentration of hundreds of disturbed sheep, barking dogs and shouting men produced a babble of noise carrying over the water to Lerwick, as the lambs were funnelled into every available area on board; deck, 'tween decks and cargo space were all utilised. The din of bleating animals crammed into the hold and acrid odours were in sharp contrast to the fiddle airs, shouts of revellers and smells of roasting Shetland lamb wafting from the galley on pleasure trips.

Up-Helly-A' had become a focus for the *Earl's* movements. The 1910 celebration was no exception and, "... notwithstanding the cloud laden and grey sky a large number of young people undertook the journey to the capital ... The SS *Earl of Zetland* brought down visitors from the North Isles on Monday afternoon and later in the evening these were added to by the steamer's arrival from Sandwick." Obviously, although Sandwick is only some 12 miles from Lerwick, the roads and transport were far from being practicable and the sea remained the essential highway.

For many years it was the custom that the firing of the signal gun, the lighting of a flaming torch on the *Earl* heralded the start of the festivities, and from 1889 the feature of a locally constructed Viking galley which was the focal point of a procession through the streets made an exciting impact. Then the climax of hundreds of procession flaming torches tossed into the galley at the burning point charged the January night with a spectacular column of fire. The participation by the old steamer was further evidence of community involvement. The tradition of the Viking fire festival continues into the 21st century under the leadership of the Guizer Jarl.

The year 1912 dawned like any other with New Year celebrations, then keen anticipation of Up-Helly-A' that last Tuesday in January. In May, amongst other outings the steamer carried 200 passengers on a trip down to Grutness, home port of the *Columbine* of Betty Mouat fame. Some visitors landed at Sandwick and others later found their way up onto the heights of Sumburgh Head. It proved to be yet another outstanding day for the *Earl of Zetland*.

There were the standard visits to ports throughout June and into July. Indeed the morning of Friday, 26th July, 1912, was little different from any other except as the cargo and passengers were put ashore on the Whalsay flit-boat the first tendrils of encroaching fog surrounded the ship. Within minutes it was a blank mass of greyness. As they got under way Johnson rang down to engineer Tom Sutherland for appropriate speed reduction, making allowance for the ebb-tide, in the five-mile stretch up towards Lunna Holm. Tom Moffat and crewman John Fraser were wraith-like figures as seen from the bridge, peering into the seemingly impenetrable fog from the bow. They had seldom seen worse in what was a near-flat calm, only the tidal currents disturbing the sea's surface.

Magnus John Scollay, AB, at the wheel, responded to the skipper's careful course changes — he had steered similarly in countless situations. He understood how to adapt and adopt, while passengers like Gracie Robertson of Burravoe knew her folk would take her when she appeared. The *Earl* was never that punctual. In any case they were not all that late; only four miles or so to Burravoe, past Lunna Holm and across the mouth of Yell Sound.

Moffat and Fraser saw the vague shape simultaneously: "Holm ahead!" Peter Johnson grabbed the engine-room telegraph, and below Tom Sutherland reacted to "Full speed astern." But it was too late. The grating

Shetland Museum

Above: The caption printed on the photograph offers the basic information ... but no comment on the weather, although no doubt it fails to dampen the spirit of the occasion. Once again the *Earl* offers a presence at a notable happening. Behind the fourareens laid at the Albert Wharf is the Shetland schooner *Ariel*, a fine craft in her time.

The Old Haa Trust, Burravoe

Above: Although far from a clear image, this photograph illustrates the parlous state of the ship following her close call in Yell Sound. The water is not much below deck level at the stern, with a slight list to port and the state of her dining saloon aft can be imagined with the flooding in of the sea!

This view is from Overby at Burravoe.

of iron on rock sent a chill through 85 stomachs as the steamer grounded on an underwater shelf; and the tide had another two hours to fall. The time was 12.15pm. Just over an hour later a Burravoe boat under oars emerged from the murk, the anxious occupants having heard the siren booming its deep throated alarm three miles distant. They almost immediately returned to arrange the telegraph alarm to Lerwick.

Passengers had been put ashore on the grass-covered holm a mere boat-length away, tarpaulins had been rigged to give some respite from the persistent drizzle of wetness through the fog, and women and children, including a three-week old baby, huddled together in their discomfort. A dozen or so male passengers had elected to remain on board but could only witness the desperate efforts of the crew to free the *Earl*.

By four o'clock the tide had turned but water was seeping into the hull; the shaft tunnel flooded; the sea was finding its insidious way into the engine room; the donkey pump spewed water overboard. At 5.30pm the ship moved on the tide on an even keel and gently lifted off the offending rock shelf, then was pulsating with engine vibration as Tom Sutherland responded to the telegraph. He also had every available pump in action. Despite all their efforts, the ship was gradually settling and he knew if the fires were extinguished that would be the end — the sea-bed in Yell Sound.

As the steamer, significantly down by the stern, was swallowed up in

the miserable fog and drizzle, the passengers left temporarily on Lunna Holm speculated on the fate of the *Earl*. None could be optimistic. An hour passed; two hours; nearly three, when the Burravoe flit-boat, with two other craft, ghosted out of the gloom and flat calm to ease alongside the rocks of the holm to rescue the passengers. Desperate shouted questions brought the answer: "… She's beached at Burravoe . . !"

The news of the stricken vessel had brought the folk out of their houses and the little pier at the voe entrance had been crowded as the labouring *Earl* limped past. There was dismay when they saw how low in the water she was, then incredulity that she had survived at all. To Peter Johnson's vast relief the ship was gently grounded on shingle at the far side of the voe opposite Overby. The illustrations on pages 19 and 20 graphically convey the situation.

By mid-evening, still with summer daylight, the sixty or so passengers from the holm had been absorbed into the ready hospitality of the homes in Burravoe all guided by the minister Rev John Watson, who himself took a group to the manse. Many hands cleared mails and luggage from the now desolate *Earl of Zetland,* preparatory to the arrival of the *St Sunniva* in response to the Lerwick telegraph signal. She reached the Yell port at 2am on the Saturday, loaded passengers, mails and luggage and then visited the ports of call, all agog with news of the mishap.

It had been a nerve-wracking situation for Captain Peter Johnson, although he could console himself there had been no panic, no loss of life and his ship was going to survive. There was sympathy for his predicament and plenty of goodwill. There had been situations with North boats before; the *St Giles* had gone on Mousa eight years previously (1904) and Peter

Johnson had taken the *Earl* to Sandsayre in succour; indeed he had saved the fishing boat *Emily Reaich* in 1905, beaching her in the selfsame Burravoe.

Although the outcome of the stranding was the voluntary resignation of Peter Johnson from the North Company, such was the appreciation for his work that he was presented with a purse of gold sovereigns by Mr J. C. Grierson, county convener: "… all who travelled knew him to be an excellent seaman and thoroughly capable in every way."

In the inevitable change of skipper Captain Mackenzie of the *St Nicholas* took over the captaincy in August 1912, although he was then succeeded in the early spring of 1913 by David Burgess who had sailed as mate of the *St Rognvald*.

By 1913 domestic matters were being overshadowed by events in Europe. As far back as 1904 some units of the German fleet anchored in Bressay Sound, causing some misgivings in official circles. Increasingly, in the following years British Naval presence showed around Shetland. In June 1913, warships of the Third Destroyer Flotilla were deployed in exercises around Shetland and crew and passengers on the *Earl* saw the spectacle of high-speed warships in Yell Sound and in east-side waters. Then massive boom defences were rigged across the south and north entrances to Lerwick harbour and it became routine for the *Earl* to negotiate through the boom near Rova Head.

During the war years the North Company maintained a steady timetable. In 1915 the steamer left Lerwick early on the Monday for Uyeasound, then called at Cullivoe, Brough Lodge, Mid Yell and Whalsay on her return the same day. She did the Yell Sound ports on the Tuesday,

The Old Haa Trust, Burravoe

Above: The date of the photograph is 28th July, 1912. The old *Earl* is a forlorn sight, beached – but only just before she foundered – at Greenhead in Burravoe. Another short distance in deep water and she would have gone, probably forever. The time to cover the three miles from Lunna Holm, where she grounded on 26th July, must have seemed like an eternity for skipper and crew.

Temporarily abandoned, the punctured hull rests on a shingle bottom as she now awaits a salvage team – had she gone, what a remarkable history would have been prematurely ended; and yet she was nearly 35 years old already. Her starboard lifeboat – and port unseen – had been used to ferry passengers initially to Lunna Holm.

The green turf of the holm had been little more than a boat-length away. In fact Gordon Donaldson observed how a male passenger had remarked to Tom Moffat, the mate, "Boy is du tinkin ta gie her a corn o' green girse ida moarnin?" Moffat's response was never recorded!

In an apparently successful attempt to prevent the hull keeling over, her derricks have been swung out with long hawsers attached. There is evidence of two men in conversation in front of the *Earl*'s funnel and there may be a small boat moored at her port side.

returning on the Wednesday from Ollaberry at 7am. At the week-end she sailed up to Baltasound and other ports on the Friday and was back in Lerwick on the Saturday. There were few delays to her timetable due to the war, yet the crew were uncomfortably aware of its proximity.

Initially the wartime scene was set in distant waters as German warships sought out and destroyed merchant shipping, but British naval might and tactics gradually eroded the enemy power. This forced a circumstance which was difficult to counter and arrest — the submarine. The German response had been premeditated and carefully planned. Through the unseen underwater threat they desired to cripple Britain's sea communications and leave her in a state of seige, born of starvation of supplies. It was designed to shatter the economy from Shetland's Muckle Flugga to Cornwall's Land's End.

The submarines sank ship after ship, confidently appearing within sight of land to strike terror into the heart of a community. Shetlanders realised with dread that the war had been brought right to their doorsteps by the U-boat when during a bright June morning in 1915, within a few miles of the *Earl's* frequent route by Out Skerries, the herring fleet was faced by the daylight surfacing of a raider which systematically sank by gunfire 15 fishing boats. It might well have been a slaughter of the innocent, but a U-boat commander, with a degree of chivalry, spared two boats and allowed all the crews to take their frightening tale to Lerwick.

Stealth and cunning under the covering sea allowed submarines to come close inshore and shelter in a place like Whalfirth, the long narrow inlet on the west side of Yell. After the war it was a German businessman who described to a Shetlander, the Nev of Stuis and the geo at the foot of the Lumbister Burn at the entrance to Whalfirth, the rugged slopes above the inlet tenanted only by sheep and with the nearest habitation at the Herra, well down the inlet. It was, therefore, easy enough to row ashore and kill off a sheep to make a marvellous delicacy in an otherwise rigid and featureless diet. This seemed the epitome of carrying the war to the enemy camp!

It was not surprising that those who crewed the *Earl* and those who travelled on her felt vulnerable during the almost daily voyaging up the east side of the islands — local talk was often about the sightings of U-boats. She remained unmolested, however, with more delay caused by winter weather than enemy action; also she was the steamer with the doubtful distinction of using Lerwick harbour boom defences more than any other! In one January gale in 1916 the *Earl* was forced to abandon her Friday morning North Isles passage until the Monday when she headed north at 5am. Deep snow brought all land-bound transport to a halt and the winds persisted throughout most of the month, so strong that in Weisdale a sixareen was lifted off the beach, killing two sheep when it fell! Although there were other deep snowfalls it would be thirty years, in 1947, before similar blizzards ravaged Shetland and threw into disorder road communication to the extent that the second *Earl of Zetland* provided the lifeline amid the islands for weeks on end.

Often enough the North Isles vessel carried conversation about shattering events. In February 1916 northern Unst folk were badly shaken by reports of the battle within sight of Muckle Flugga when the 16,000 ton *Alcantara,* an armed liner, took on the strength of the German cruiser *Greif* at the expense of both ships. It was one of a diminishing list of individual battles because the British began to appreciate that there was strength in numbers and this brought the initiative of the convoy system which was to prove valuable, although not invulnerable, in two World Wars.

The North Company suffered the sinking of the *St Magnus,* torpedoed near Peterhead with the loss of three lives, yet there were 412 voyages to Lerwick in safety before peace came in 1918. A second ship, the *St Margaret* was on charter to G. & I. Burns of Glasgow when she was struck by another U-boat thirty miles east of the Faroe Islands. Four crew were lost but 18 survived.

When it came, the end of the Great War was met with vast relief and joyous celebration, tempered by the thought that a host of young Shetlanders had paid the ultimate price. Church and Town Hall bells at Lerwick echoed round the harbour on 11th November, 1918, while, in company with other shipping, the *Earl of Zetland* at Victoria Pier was decked overall, her crew watching the Lerwick Brass Band playing before a great gathering of townsfolk. And, as if to sympathise with the human situation, the heavens opened up a fantastic display of the aurora borealis from a deep base in the north-east, superb streamers of coloured light shimmering above. The "war to end all wars" had come and gone.

Shetland Museum

Above: A unique wartime view taken on 13th June, 1915, as His Majesty's Transport *Vienna*, with her two funnels and long spar at the foremast, calls at Lerwick to convey the troops of the Shetland Company of the Gordon Highlanders to Aberdeen for active service. Behind the *Earl*, on the left, is a destroyer and on the right probably the second *St Magnus* with the characteristic twin ventilators immediately in front of her bridge.

Magnus Shearer

Above: The *Earl* about to leave for the North Isles. Given a reasonable hour of day it was fashionable to see the steamer off and here she is all set to go on a Sunday at 2pm with a goodly number of passengers and even greater crowd on the pier. A big pile of sacks and boxes on the left makes an admirable vantage point for the younger element, including a bare-footed lad.

This group includes, on the left, the wife (light coat) of the North Company agent Alexander Stephen and grandmother of former Lord Lieutenant Magnus Shearer, while the naval uniforms indicate wartime reservists RNR (Shetland Section). The year is 1915.

Shetland Museum

Above: It is near the beginning of the First World War and the *Earl* provides transport for Shetlanders, members of the Shetland Companies of the Gordon Highlanders. They were to serve with distinction in France with the Third, Fifteenth and Fifty-First Highland Divisions – albeit with heavy losses. Therefore the photograph has an added poignancy.

BETWEEN THE WARS

Long serving skippers, characters like Nicolson, Scott and Johnson, had each established his own individuality yet with one common factor of good communications with the crew, company officials, steamers' agents at the ports and all who travelled. They created an informality on board which had become something of a tradition over the 40 years of the steamer's existence. Then William Spence was appointed just after the war. Of course his service in the conflict had ranged from the Dardenelles to the likes of Ardrossan as described in the captions on page 23. Spence and the *Earl* became synonymous. He was part of her although initially his relationship was somewhat fragmented. After a short time on board in 1919 he became mate on the *St Sunniva,* commanded the 350 ton *Fetlar* owned by the North Company for some months, then, when she was sold in 1920, he returned to the *St Sunniva* again, as deputy. The apparent North Company policy of change among their captains returned him to the *Earl* for a number of weeks in 1920/21, then he skippered the *St Clair* from June till November 1921 when he was sent back to the North Isles passages.

For 17 years thereafter the *Earl of Zetland* was the main outlet for Willie Spence's outstanding seamanship and he was familiar with success of an adventurous and confident bearing. Thus when he was let down by his ship on a Saturday in January 1922 it must have been an anticlimax for his expectations. Yet she had done what she could with her somewhat limited power.

A Norwegian full-rigged ship, the *Maella,* had anchored off Maryfield on Bressay, riding light and having come in with a convenient south-easterly wind. After a short visit to Lerwick her skipper awaited a change of wind direction to negotiate the relatively narrow channel at the south mouth but this was not forthcoming and he decided to approach the North

Above: Perhaps all inter-island vessels in the global sense have engendered a wonderfully congenial and intimate atmosphere, but the old *Earl* had her own very special fellowship. The fraternity was a close-knit world of its own and many individuals had a remarkable and intense loyalty to the ship. It was not unknown for John Fraser, a Cullivoe man who lived in Lerwick, to go down and check the moorings of his beloved steamer in her berth at the Victoria Pier during a menacing night of wind. Fraser was a survivor of the Gloup fishing disaster of 1881.

Then there were the links intensified through the flit-boats of the communities. The steamer was a prime focus and to all intents and purposes a microcosm of the island population, especially in the earlier decades when there were a dozen and a half calls outside Lerwick. Such a background, plus the layout of the ship, led to an unusual companionship between crew and regular passengers. This was highlighted in that navigation was not something remote. When Willie Spence became skipper in 1919 the bridge rails were cased in canvas but otherwise the layout was identical to what it had been for years. He, like captains before him, such as Nicolson, Scott, Johnson, Gifford and Burgess, stood amidst the travellers when issuing orders. This produced a feeling of "all being in it together" and removed all mystery from navigation.

This quizzical-looking group on the *Earl*'s after deck is typical. Taken probably about the time of the appointment of Spence, this photograph seems to symbolise the "togetherness". Rather surprisingly Captain Spence sports only one ring on his sleeve, but then so did a predecessor, Peter Johnson. On the extreme right is Sammy Harrison who became engineer immediately after the First World War. The other men appear to be dressed in their "Sunday best", especially the gentleman with the bowler hat, velvet collar on his coat and one gloved hand! Then there is the fashionable watch chain on the waistcoat of the man to Spence's right. Perhaps they are all en route to such as the Fetlar Show? What descendants might these passengers have today?

Chrissie Mann

Above: The cargo chain of the derrick cuts through this well-deck scene in which Willie Spence flaunts what has the look of a filleted haddock. To his left are Sammy Harrison, engineer; Jeemie Jamieson, crewman and an unknown steward. To the left of the haddock is part of the cargo winch under the break of the fo'c'sle.

It was said that the catering on board the *Earl* left little to be desired, fresh fish and eggs, lashings of tea and bread and butter – all in abundance. And of course on a day of biting wind the dining saloon could be a most congenial haven with the bogey stove going full blast and further enhanced by the deep scarlet cushioned seats, polished brass surrounds on the portholes and with sepia-coloured photographs of Shetland scenery interspersed.

When the old *Earl* was somewhat prematurely "retired" in 1939 the Unst folk met on 4th August to pay homage to their favourite steamer. It was in the Baltasound Hall that Rev James Binnie, parish minister, reminisced about the ship and paid tribute to the hospitality and catering. He said: "… and the attention and courtesy of the officers and crew … is proverbial … passing from the sublime to the commonplace, but necessary, creature comforts, one remembers the really good cup of tea on the *Earl* and the crisp yellow fried haddocks, tails in mouths, served between Whalsay, Skerries and Mid Yell …"

Company for a tow. The North Isles ship was an evident choice being so readily available, thus a hawser was passed at the *Maella's* anchorage and the two ships moved slowly into Bressay Sound with the wind from the south airt. They were off Bressay Lighthouse when the hawser snapped and there followed prolonged manoeuvring to prevent the big ship drifting ashore. Willie Spence ordered full power but then a second problem developed when the strength of the wind and tide combined was too much for the *Earl's* engines and there was the ignominy of the *Maella* towing the *Earl*!

Left with no choice Spence signalled that they would put back into Lerwick. When they reappeared at late evening, there was amused comment from the populace, although the doughty skipper would have his response ready!

Coincidentally the next day the wind went westerly and the Norwegian made a fine sight as she set sail for Tonsberg in Norway. Meanwhile the *Earl* pursued her usual routine, the subject of some good humoured banter!

Eighteen months later, in 1924, she was associated with a different kind of incident when she brought from Yell to Lerwick 14 crew members of the steamer *Jane,* of Gothenberg, which had foundered after running on the rocks of Linga at Gutcher. The ship of 500 tons had come to Lerwick from Boston with a load of coal, discharged, voyaged north to Baltasound for a cargo of 475 barrels of herring, then sailed for Lerwick at 11pm on a clear smooth night. Unaccountably, caught by the strong tide off Linga she had rammed the island and had sunk in deep water. There was no loss of life. And there were those on the *Earl* who thought back to 1912 and her own stranding at Lunna Holm!

By the beginning of the third decade of the 20th century the Great War's terrible destruction was still vivid in mind yet everyday life was a necessity, thus normality gradually evolved again. Domestic issues steadily came to the fore. There had been regular maintenance on the *Earl* and in 1922 there was a significant change. The Shetland press described how "that old friend of the travelling public, the *Earl,* has just been fitted with electric light throughout. The contract for the work was in the hands of James Thomson electrical engineers of Aberdeen. The current is generated by a GEC dynamo driven by a Ruby engine … There are about 60 lights throughout the vessel, including navigation lights and passengers'

Chrissie Mann

Willie Spence; a proud and warm-hearted skipper and his ship – for'ard, 'midships … aft, on board the *Earl*, snapshots taken in the thirties. He was born in Cullivoe, North Yell, in 1870 and destined for the sea from the outset in a community very well noted for its seafarers. Like too many Shetlanders of a bygone era, economic hardship near the poverty line curtailed early ambitions, then the unexpected arrival of a school of whales and his part in driving them ashore – when whales were killed commercially – provided enough cash for the fare "sooth" and he joined the brig *Ocean Belle* of Blyth.

Sailing vessels on which he served included the *Jane Porter* of Belfast, *King James*, as described on page 42, *Wasdale* of Liverpool and *Carrick* of Glasgow; then the steamers *Lord Elise, General Gordon, Raphael, St Hillier* and *Saxon*. As if determined to prove that "variety is the spice of life" he returned to Shetland attracted by the herring bonanza and made his first acquaintance with the *Earl of Zetland* in 1900 when he crewed in her for a fortnight. Since he had married it suited him to work locally, thus for some years before the First World War he served on North boats *Queen, St Giles* and the first *St Sunniva*. The membership of the Royal Naval Reserve, and the War, took him variously to China, the Red Sea and the Dardanelles … colourful indeed … and rounding off as a coaling officer in Ardrossan then, secondly, as a pilot under the convoy scheme, working out of Lerwick for three months and Methil, in Fife, for nine.

Thus Willie Spence came to the *Earl* immediately after the war, in 1919, a seaman of vast experience and great distinction and about to make a unique contribution to the well-being of the islands and a way of life. The bluff figure of Spence was the subject of many a photograph.

For'ard: The skipper leans casually on the teak boarding of the wheel-deck, perhaps anticipating an anchorage. 'Midships: A more formal and proud captain of his ship, standing abaft the tiny cabin below the bridge. At the top of the ladder the bridge itself seems to have been taken over by passengers and a curious face peers down, to the left of the binnacle! 'Midships: By the funnel. A neatly dressed lady passenger smiles for the camera and the skipper offers a friendly hand. A lad looks to be seated on the "box" at the base of the funnel, well remembered by the author as a comfortable warm place on a chilly passage. And aft: … always amenable, Willie Spence cuts a sartorial dash for an unknown photographer, standing beside the seat by the engine room skylight, the never-used life-rafts to the right.

Chrissie Mann

Chrissie Mann

Jemima Hughson

Above: Fetlar stalwarts Lawrie Brown, on the left, and Tommy Thomason pull hard towards the waiting *Earl*. Seated in the bow of the flit-boat between them is Willie Shewan, while a fourth, unknown figure seems to be on a taft amid some cargo!

The load-line of the steamer is obvious and the tall slender funnel plus white canvas covering on the bridge rail suggest the late 1920s.

Shetland Museum

Above: An enterprising unknown photographer has caught an unusual angle on one of the smaller flit-boats alongside. In the dramatic foreshortened perspective the view at first seems further forward than in actuality, and the shot is probably abeam the after hatch. An interested male passenger leans on the rails between the life-rafts and the starboard lifeboat, while the silhouetted figure on the bridge is probably Captain Spence.

Meanwhile, the peerie boat is well laden. How many more to board her? Is it a suitcase on the stern? Unusually, in this print the flit-boat seems to be at the starboard doors of the well-deck, not often used due to the catwalk above.

accommodation and crew's quarters. There is also a deck cluster for loading and unloading cargo, giving much superior facilities, especially at the country ports. There can be no doubt as to the improvement in the lighting and this last advance in equipment puts all the company's vessels on a level, the SS *St Ola* having been fitted by the same firm last week."

Electricity came as a revelation. The mundane, routine tasks of filling, lighting and maintaining old oil lamps were reduced to a flick of a switch, the new-found brilliance lighting up hitherto shadowy corners on board. Considering how for 44 years, and for six months of each year many of the steamer's tasks were accomplished in semi-darkness, or darkness, those who spent a lot of their working lives on board appreciated beyond measure what had been done. Many said it was not before time.

In 1920 a traditional feature which reappeared in Lerwick was Up-Helly-A', while excursions had lost none of their popularity of pre-war years. Only the weather did not relent. January 1922 was bad. On the 22nd, a Saturday, the *Earl* made it to Symbister and unloaded mail and cargo. Beyond Whalsay she faced ferocious waves which forced the crew to sling oil bags over the side as they aimed for Mid Yell and sanctuary.

On the Sunday morning she won through to Uyeasound where there was danger in unloading as the flit-boat plunged madly alongside, even in relative shelter. Beyond Skuda Sound the waters were in a boil of whiteness in surf and spindrift. A decision was made to run back to the haven of the splendidly sheltered Mid Yell voe. On the Monday they tried for Baltasound again: this time the *Earl* battered her way through the north-easter and came safely into the narrows of Balta Isle and the wind-torn waters of the voe, but at least to a sheltering pier.

A temporary respite in the wind power permitted a return to Lerwick on the Tuesday, yet back came the gale ensuring that the warps stayed on at Victoria Pier until the next Saturday due to the storm, which had persisted for a full week. Considering the frequency of such exposure to gale-force winds it was surprising that major mishaps to the *Earl* occurred in near windless circumstances; the ill-fated situation with a Baltasound ballast-heap in 1902; the stranding on Lunna Holm in 1912. Twice the *Earl of Zetland* had had a problem. And there came a third hazard.

Captain Spence was temporarily on the south run and Donald McMillan, who hailed from Tiree in the Western Isles, was skippering the steamer as she approached Lerwick at the north entrance late on the evening of Thursday, 28th August, 1924. It had been a good day. The *Earl* had transported a considerable number of people north to Fetlar for the popular agricultural show held annually there and a happy band of trippers reflected on the success of the visit to a cordial community. A smooth sea enhanced the congenial atmosphere on the deck of the steamer, thus near-disaster could not have been further from the minds of the crew or passengers. Indeed the unruffled surface of the water served to hide a baa of notoriety which proved to be the peril for the *Earl of Zetland*.

The treacherous underwater rock had been known as Skibba Baa until 1874 when the whaler *Nova Zembla* was coming into the north entrance. Robbie Ramsay, a Yell man, and reportedly a harpooner, was at the wheel when the skipper, according to popular belief, remarked: "Isn't there a rock somewhere about here Ramsay?" He had just uttered the words when the *Nova Zembla* ground her underside on the rock. "Dey ir dat and you're upon im!" The whaler was not seriously damaged but from that day onwards it was known as Robbie Ramsay's Baa.

Thus from an apparent very normal situation the *Earl* was badly compromised. She had greater way on her compared to the Lunna Holm accident; there was a horrific grinding of metal on solid rock; she was completely stranded with a distinct list to port. Sammy Harrison reported water in the engine room, so Donald McMillan had signal rockets fired in the darkness to alert the authority in Lerwick.

A fishing boat, the *Mizpah*, appeared in response to the distress rockets and the 60 or so passengers were transferred in a sea which allowed the vessel to nose close alongside the *Earl* in deep enough water. By 1.30am they had been taken safely to Lerwick leaving the steamer to a rather uncertain immediate future.

Full daylight revealed that about half the starboard side rested on the baa with bows and stern overhanging. She still listed to port to the extent that as the tide rose the sea filled the main hold, engine room and crept through the accommodation. The ship herself never budged, aided by the weather which was a model of consistency; for a third time lady luck was favouring the *Earl of Zetland*.

By 1pm on the Saturday a salvage vessel, the *Henry Lancaster,* appeared from the south and following a temporary repair by divers, the

steamer was pumped out. She then was taken to Victoria Pier to be met by a curious and speculative crowd; they had a vested interest as she was already not far short of half a century old and warmly known as "da auld *Earl*" — very much "wir steamer".

On Tuesday, 2nd September, she left for a month's stay in Aberdeen for renewal of plates and a new and larger rudder.

Variously, the *St Sunniva, St Magnus* and *St Fergus* were seen on the North Isles and Yell Sound passages until the *Earl* came back and Donald McMillan re-assumed command on Sunday, 27th September, 1924.

Taking into account the constant movement of the *Earl* in the year-round commitment amid such a mass of unmarked outcrops of rock, which could only be known through intimate knowledge of local geography, it is not beyond expectancy that local problems arose. The men who commanded the "sooth boats" had no easy task in the rigours of winter, yet if it blew up they had areas of sea in which to heave-to or run; no North Company ship ever sank in that great mass of water between Sumburgh Head and Kinnaird Head on the Scottish mainland, by Peterhead. Thus in some respects their voyaging held fewer risks than did those of the inter-island steamer. North boat losses were due to collisions with the land, apart from wartime sinkings.

The inter-island vessels, however, had land, visible or invisible, as a constant companion, with seas smooth or rough, a gentle swell or high breakers; yet it was the proximity of the unyielding gneiss or blue-grey limestone of baa, or skerry, or indented coastline which posed the risk factor. And so it was that Lunna Holm in 1912, and in turn Robbie Ramsay's Baa, had almost brought about the downfall of the *Earl* in August 1924. Then four months later a ship deprived of her steering, being driven onto a lee shore in storm and darkness illustrated the variety of events which could so easily go wrong.

The loss of the Whalsay flit-boat on 29th December, 1924, has already been mentioned to highlight the uncertainties of inter-island voyaging over the decades, but that situation had been compounded further. To cut adrift the flit-boat had been an invidious decision off Symbister and yet towing was out of the question with the risk of a fouled propeller in following seas. That judgement was difficult enough in itself but Donald McMillan

again skippering when Willie Spence was briefly on the *St Sunniva,* was faced by an added major problem on the self-same occasion.

Since the *Earl's* anchor had begun to drag and she had not the power to face the gale, running was the only option and, the flit-boat abandoned, this went reasonably as the counter stern rose well to big following seas. The skipper ordered a course north-north-east knowing that he had open water for 15 miles or so west of Skerries and up to the Fetlar coast, with the formidable Lamb Hoga and Rams Ness ahead in the black night, then Colgrave Sound and the shelter of Mid Yell in prospect.

The old manual wheel with its chain and rod system needed two men, with the rudder subjected to severe buffeting again and again and they had to work hard at keeping control, with the steamer yawing in the steep seas. For an hour they staggered to the north until tension on the wheel abruptly ceased and the *Earl* lost direction, deprived of her steering.

John Henderson, the mate, who had taken over from Tom Moffat, hurriedly checked amid the stinging spray on the after deck and found that the quadrant at the rudder head had snapped. Even the reserve wheel at the stern was useless. An alarming situation had developed, for the hour's steaming had taken them well up towards the Fetlar banks somewhere ahead in the impenetrable blackness. Engineer Sammy Harrison supplied a large, fully extended spanner which was keyed onto the rudder-head stock and the steering was then controlled through the after winch drums, the operation done in extreme weather circumstances. Even Jimmy Willie Spence, the chief steward and the "ship-wrecked" flit-boatmen were involved. Below, the two firemen, Jack Anderson and Hugh Hughson ensured well-tended fires while, in contrast, a handful of passengers suffered sickness. Midnight had come and gone before the *Earl* was under control.

Below: The compact lighthouse on Symbister Ness and a solitary sheep provide a setting for the *Earl* as she steams towards her anchorage at Whalsay on a peaceful day. Beyond the light is the entrance to Dury Voe with the Mainland to the south of Stava Ness featured on the left.

Shetland Museum

Come grey daylight Mid Yell folk were astonished to see the very familiar steamer which was the subject of much speculation; also at a later date when Hay and Company sued the North Company for £150, being the value of their lost flit-boat. In the light of evidence Sheriff Grant found in favour of the defendants, thus Captain McMillan was exonerated. The hugely problematical predicament had another twist to it in that the insurance underwriters, impressed by the resource and seamanship displayed after the rudder quadrant came adrift, decided to award Donald McMillan and his crew with £50.

There was a final minor, though amusing aspect. The Up-Helly-A' celebrations had always given scope to creative writing in the islands and it was — and is — customary to feature current or recent events in the "bill". Inevitably the Whalsay flit-boat incident was a talking point throughout Shetland and at the January 1925 festival jocular reference was made:

"Oh for the days when Scotts[1] was rife,
A body could travel without fear of life,
Where loaf and saucermeat and aa sic so,
Came oot o'da steamer wi freshness aglow.
These were the days when aa da flit-craft,
Wisna left ta be washed up less oars and taft,
Or towed wi da tide,
And cast off wi a grin,
And a wave o' da hand,
And GUT-CHEER[2] ye win[3]."

1. Captain Scott
2. Gutcher, in Yell
3. Go.

The Author

Shetland Museum

Left and above: There were days when anywhere on the exposed deck areas of the old *Earl* were inhospitable, to say the least, when wind, rain – sleet, or snow – spray or even solid water, drove passengers below. The bridge and wheel-deck were totally vulnerable when the weather blew up, with oilskins scant protection on a wild day. Willie Spence was known to come off the bridge with his lips cracked and bleeding through exposure. Since the *Earl*'s steering gear was entirely manual the wheel could have a kick like a mule and was known to have dislocated a shoulder. Frequently in winter it demanded two crew to cope.

The illustrations emphasise the vulnerable foredeck. In the photograph the ship is butting into what may well be a south-easter between such as Skerries and Whalsay, making the deck untenable. No doubt the cover on the hatchway will be firmly in place! The author uses the photograph to dramatise the effect of the sea breaking over the bows, also bringing in the foremast to enhance the contrast between the formal shapes of the ship and the flying spray. The medium is scraper-board.

Captain Donald McMillan had a long career with the North Company for his work continued into the years of the Second World War and he was in command of the second *St Rognvald* built in 1901, when there was the extraordinary experience of being attacked by a captured British bomber with a German crew, on 27th December, 1940. There were no casualties and the ship was undamaged. Then on 20th October, 1942, he was skippering the third *St Magnus* of 1924 when she was bombed and machine gunned near Fair Isle. A solitary bomb missed by about 50 yards and there was minor damage from bullets, though no casualties. Such hazards were to be the lot of both *Earls of Zetland* in due course. In a range of honours and awards to North Company personnel after the war Donald McMillan received the MBE.

By the mid-1920s Willie Spence seemed to be firmly established in his remarkable connection with the steamer the *Earl of Zetland*. The routine work he took comfortably in his stride, but more than any man he had confidence to move his ship in weather which might well have confined her to shelter. Somehow there seemed to be more occasions when the black bows showed starkly against the light welter of sea, her whistle steam

momentarily white on her dark funnel as Spencey announced her arrival on a bad day. Now the *Earl* could roll in a beam sea but the heavily built Captain Spence was always loath to accept adverse remarks about the sea-keeping quality of his ship, always maintaining that any rolling she did was due to his pacing from side to side on the bridge!

Like others before him Willie Spence gleaned the personal and particular lore of coastal navigation by gradual experience and local word of mouth, working the ship in the infinite variety of flat calm to howling gale, brilliant sunlight to blank fog; and into seasonal black night. It needed great sensitivity and awareness. The *Earl's* scrap-log would record proceedings; indeed a pencil note in Willie Spence's handwriting from the early 1930s noted the conditions in dense fog at sea level — yet sometimes with a glimmer of light above.

" … 4.30pm Hove up and proceeded
4.35pm Full away. Dense fog.
Board of Trade Regulations in operation.
5.43pm Eased down.
6.00pm Stopped and sounded (whistle)
6.25pm Sounded.
6.30pm Sounded.
6.45pm Sounded
Moderate south-westerly. Ebb tide."

Spence may have been a man of independent spirit, bold and adventurous but never foolhardy. If anchoring was an obvious need then he would anchor. It was like that when the steamer lay motionless in the stillness of another pea-souper, only the plop of water around bows, belting and stern, intermittent conversation on deck, the chink of crockery below, the subdued hum of a dynamo and occasional roar of blown-off steam interrupting the blanket of silence. The captain waited on the bridge, forearms on the canvas dodger, his patience contrasting some increasingly restless passengers only a few feet below him. "Captain," said a female passenger, "when can we go on?" He indicated the fog. "But there's blue sky above." Willie Spence glanced yet again at the opaque and oppressive wall, like cotton wool, looked back at the woman and intoned: "Aye, lady, but yon's not the way we're heading!"

Leisure trips remained a feature. On 18th July, 1925, a hundred people went north for the day, well entertained by George Stark, the blind fiddler and his band. They went ashore at Mid Yell to play for an enthusiastic audience. Fiddle music was generally a feature of the *Earl's* holiday jaunts. There was one in August 1927 and *The Shetland Times* commented: "… annual regatta and aquatic sports … For the afternoon, when the sports were completed, the North Company had arranged an excursion trip round Bressay. As one participant remarked: 'The *Earl* left Lerwick at 3 o'clock on 3rd August on a three hours trip at a fare of three shillings.' And the combination of threes apparently proved a good omen, the trip having been most successful and enjoyed by all who went. Captain Spence and his crew did all they could to make the voyage pleasant, while Mr George Stark, the blind fiddler, and his companion Mr Jordan, entertained the outing with cheery music." In fact, the old steamer had become something of a focus for Shetland fiddle-playing. Characteristically, Willie Spence utilised this in his own inimitable manner. Steward Robbie Gray was one of those musicians and Willie would say, "Man Robbie awa doon below tae da galley and we'll have one or two slow airs." And Robbie would play and Spencey would say to strangers to the islands on board indicating the seals on Lunna Holm as the ship sailed past, "Listen now, listen. You'll hear da seals; see them dere. Now you'll hear them." Whether or not the tourists gave much credence to such suggestions was never recorded, but they were sources of great amusement.

Such casual visitors to Shetland disappeared during the winter months although in January each year Up-Helly-A' attracted some incomers from south. Otherwise the even tenor of island life was uninterrupted, unless some major outside event influenced affairs. Withdrawal of labour by strike action was in principle anathema to the Shetlander and the islands remained little affected by industrial unrest, although there was national post First World War unease about low wages and unemployment. This culminated in the massive General Strike of 1926, which in Shetland was considered to be a "brutal and primitive" method of settling the issues. "History would be searched in vain for a parallel to the events which have transpired in Britain since Saturday, 1st May."

The country ground to a halt and with the cessation of mainland train

services, mails and goods to the islands were instantaneously terminated. The *Earl* lay alongside at Victoria Pier for the unprecedented spell of seven days, still and silent, until the national strike was ended unconditionally by the General Council of the Trade Union Congress and was "received with great satisfaction in Shetland".

Yet the post office organisation was still under public scrutiny and criticism. Amid a welter of complaints, in a letter to the Shetland press in March 1928 a writer rather grudgingly conceded: "We must admit that the mail service to the North Isles has been regular now for some time. Much praise is due to Captain Spence who has brought the *Earl* many times to Baltasound under unfavourable conditions, darkness and so on, and at the same time not disregarding the good service of the other masters." The letter emphasised the irregularities on Unst, in that the *Earl* having come into Baltasound on a Friday, did not discharge the mail for the Haroldswick Post Office until the Saturday morning when the horse and gig came over to Baltasound pier with the outgoing mail. It was pointed out that as a result no letter could be answered by return.

Such anomalies were partly the outcome of slow transport on land — not that ships epitomised the essence of speed — but by 1928 there was the transition already established from "Shanks pony" and pony and trap, or gig to petrol-fuelled internal combustion engined vehicles. In many respects in mid-April 1927, when R. W. Tait and Sons asked Peterson the coachbuilder of Market Street in Lerwick to build a bus on a Chevrolet chassis, it was the beginning of the end for the long-established sea routes. Although time would make its impact, it would be no cataclysmic destruction of the shipping route held dear by so many Shetlanders and in fact, another astonishing 47 years were to elapse before the final demise of the consecutive service of those two fine vessels named *Earl of Zetland*.

Isobel Manson

Above: In December 1911 David (Davie) Gray, who had worked in the office of the shipping company, took over as Purser on the old *Earl* and was destined to be a man closely associated with the ship right through until just before her departure from Shetland. In fact he served selflessly until December 1945 after a 40 year association with the North Company.

Davie Gray had the strongest of commitments to his beloved steamer. Enhancing his slightly-built physique he had an outgoing and warm personality, his overall-clad nimble figure a familiar sight to passengers and flit-boat men alike, as he cheerfully dispensed tickets at his office below the bridge or climbed down into the semi-darkness of the hold armed with his wad of invoices and orders to sort out cargo at each port.

There had been the abortive attempts to usurp the *Earl's* monopoly on the sea routes to the north mainland and the isles, all unsuccessful, but another more insidious infiltration of her domain appeared in the early thirties. The newspaper notice said it all: "Overland Route to North Isles. Ganson's Passenger Service to and from the North Isles every Wednesday will continue to operate as follows: Leave Lerwick 6.45am. Leave Mossbank 10.15am on arrival of motor boat from Yell. Travel by Ganson's – The Pioneer Overland Service".

In the long term there could be only one winner as the roads in Shetland rapidly improved, however it was the same David Gray – sadly, fighting a rearguard action – who reputedly came up with the idea which was implemented by the North Company, that the *Earl* should have a Tuesday/Wednesday sailing to connect with the direct "sooth boat" from Lerwick. It was said that the shrewd Davie was told he could take the steamer to Uyeasound or anywhere else he wanted on a Tuesday afternoon!

The photograph suggests a gentle and unassuming character, here flanked – but only just – by Willie Spence and Tom Gifford, and yet he was a personality of concentration and a model of consistency whose heart was in the right place.

A SHIP AND HER PEOPLE – A PICTORIAL ESSAY

Shetland Museum

Above: At rest from a busy schedule. There is no sign of life on board as the ship lies alongside, well up the Victoria Pier and basking in the afternoon sunlight. The stem of an unknown North Boat is close up by the *Earl*'s counter stern. The corrugated construction of the former freight shed shows up well in this kind of light, while buildings behind are subtley defined. Prominent on the left is the Queens Hotel with its weather-worn sign. On the right the back of the Post Office, and above it the St Magnus Scottish Episcopal Church with its tower, and surmounting that a glimpse of the Bruce Hostel for girls from rural areas, many of whom were in secondary education in the late twenties when the photograph was taken. The skyline is greatly different today, with new buildings.

Judging by the lack of movement on the pier and in the street behind this could be a Sunday, and yet there appear to be people working with animals, possibly Shetland ponies, on the pier behind the *Earl*'s bow. Meanwhile a solitary spectator looks at the *Earl* from the corner of the shed. Notably just below him on the *Earl*'s bridge deck is the steering binnacle not normally noticeable in photographs of the ship.

Right: The finely-shaped counter stern is shown to advantage, enhanced by the thresh of wake as she gets under way. This photograph is unusual and almost certainly taken from the Brough Lodge flit-boat. The land off the *Earl*'s port side is likely to be the top end of Hascosay, with the peat hills of Yell beyond.

Waving vigorously, the lady on the left and her companion are probably departing guests of Sir Arthur and Lady Nicolson. Judging by their dress styling and the canvas covered bridge this will be around 1930. Gone are the days of the steamer's thin and somehow inappropriate funnels.

Fetlar Museum Trust

Two panoramas of contrasting eras; perhaps a quarter of a century between them. **Above:** Lerwick harbour early in the first decade of the 20th century and the *Earl* lies across from the first *St Rognvald* of 1883, a pioneer of cruising in the Norwegian fjords by 1886. Sailing craft abound elsewhere towards Bressay. **Below:** The unusually tall funnel of the first *St Ninian* towers above the North Isles steamer, as two steam drifters head south through Bressay Sound. Others cluster around the pier on what is a fine day in high summer in the 1930s.

As seeming evidence of the herring fishery, barrels are stacked on the far away quay at the small boat harbour, while the Lerwick lifeboat *Lady Jane and Martha Ryland* lies at her mooring in a near flat calm. The yacht *Soldian* owned by Theo Kay of Lerwick is just behind her with the triangular steadying sail.

Unknown

Above: An exceptional aspect of a typical flit-boat situation. This would be in the thirties – probably 1932/33 – and the port is Cullivoe in Yell, the sheltered voe lying behind the spit of land above the *Earl*'s after rail. The rat-lines in her main-mast rigging look a trifle flimsy! She has upped anchor and the first revolutions of her screw are churning up the sea, leaving the flit-boat in a backwater with her crew sorting out the oars. The cargo seems to range from sacks and tea chests to baulks of timber, contrasting the simple but stylish shape of the old sixareen. Sea-bird droppings on the gunwale imply that she will be permanently at a mooring in the voe apart from going off to the steamer. Ordinarily her crew would be four but eight men are on board. Those whose identity is known are, second from the left Willie-Andrew Anderson of Midfield; Magnie Sinclair of Muckle Haa, steamer's agent; standing with his back to the camera, Albert Nisbet, and to his right Jeemie Jamieson. Seated behind the youthful standing figure of Willie Anderson of Meadowbank is Jimmy Willie Spence of Houses. Sadly Willie Anderson was to lose his life at sea in the late 1930s.

To this date the *True Love*, the peerie flit-boat of this era, serves as a shed roof, carefully maintained by Jamie Nicholson, son-in-law of Jimmy Willie Spence.

Below: Probably taken from the well-deck of the old *Earl*, this angle shows the lines of a former fishing sixareen to advantage. The standard practice with modified craft like this of lining the cargo area with boarding is obvious enough, although this one is extensively patched; which was not uncommon!

This is a flit-boat probably at Mid Yell and the photograph featured in a calendar for 1986. The men at the oars are Jamie Sinclair, Simon (Simie) Sinclair and Peter Petrie, accompanying the Board of Agriculture stallion. The sling used for lifting it from the *Earl* is under the animal's rear legs.

The Old Haa Trust, Burravoe

Right: An unusual and particularly eye-catching grouping of passengers observed from the bridge on a rather damp, drizzly day, judging by reflectings of fittings on the deck … and no mistaking the name of the ship! Below it in the gloom of the space around the cargo derrick winch stands a solitary bucket, while the bell is prominent from this angle. It would be rung in Lerwick prior to departure, a sound which could echo up the Lerwick lanes on a still morning and was very evocative for local folk and visitors alike.

Judging by the wash set up by the bow this is the *Earl* at sea, although to whom the fisher lasses are waving so enthusiastically could only be speculated upon. A passing vessel? A herring boat? Are they 'sooth' girls possibly on their way to such as Baltasound for the gutting? Their dress is of the early teens of years of the twentieth century, notable through the long skirts, tight waist bands and knitted shawls. Their baggage on top of the life-jackets indicates wicker baskets. The two men at the bow seem indifferent to their female companions! But at the end of the nineteenth century the ship could have as many as 150 gutting lasses on board.

Douglas Sinclair

Douglas Sinclair

Left: The foredeck was very often a popular subject with the box and other cameras of early days and frequently offered lively subject matter because travellers were wont to gather there on a day of agreeable weather. Not surprisingly, too, the *Earl* appeared regularly on a range of postcards over the years and this one was sent to London with a halfpenny George V stamp on it. Judging by a rather obscure date-stamp the year may have been 1913. The message on the card was: "Dear Sis, Just a PC, thank you for the one you sent me. I hope you will like this one. You seem to have fairly enjoyed your holiday. We have been having lovely weather up till now. It is awful cold and windy. With love from us all. Mary. Write soon." The card is personalised in an interesting historical sense in that Mary's sister Annie, to whom the card is addressed, was also the sister of the colourful character, docker "Jeemie Sheeksie".

The photograph illustrates yet again the age of the hat in all its diversity in Shetland. Even a straw boater, worn by the gentleman on the left, complements the homburg-hatted man on the right whose interest has been caught by something at water level. A babe wrapped in swaddling clothes nestles in mother's arms, while another lady seems to find the pile of ropes a not uncomfortable seat. Meanwhile the *Earl* ploughs on her way.

Right: Willie Leask, the Lerwick docker, well-known as "Whalsay Willie" strikes a pose with a fiddle on the foredeck during an outing. By his right elbow is Wilfie Goudie, while third from his left hand is Nana Moffat. A breezy day judging by the flag at the bow, while bright sunshine adds to the event.

Isobel Manson

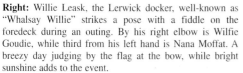

Shetland Museum

Left and below: Not every photographic image is crystal-clear but an atmosphere or situation can be conveyed adequately enough. The two prints do just that, both photographs taken at Ulsta, Yell, in the 1930s.

In the upper version there is what appears to be a solitary sheep considering a leap into the sea towards the *Earl*, with an alert dog keeping an eye on things.

Below, a dog – the same animal perhaps – stands on the pier, eyeing the two boats while folk tend the sheep hemmed in by herring barrels in the foreground. Another dog lies by the little railway line used for running bulky items by trolley down the pier.

Shetland Museum

Chrissie Mann

Left: On the back of the original snapshot owned by Mrs Derek Mann of Lerwick, grand-daughter of Captain William Spence, were the words: "SS *Earl of Zetland* arriving Lerwick, Monday, 20th August, 1934. With the compliments of the photographer". Therefore this would appear to be an offering from another well-disposed traveller, the photograph probably taken from the stern of one of the south boats lying at Victoria Pier.

The ship glides gently in, with figures grouped on the bridge, emphasising the informality of the *Earl of Zetland* and the relaxed, invariably friendly, atmosphere which characterised the ship for all of her 69 years serving Shetland and the people. Willie Spence's broad shoulders can be seen just to the right of the signalling light on the bridge, while Mate Tom Gifford prepares to supervise the bow lines. At her permanent mooring in Bressay Sound is one of the coal hulks serving the islands at the time.

Right: Low early morning sunlight offers a dramatic effect at the north-east entrance to the sheltered harbour of Out Skerries. Mate Tom Gifford at the rails awaits the order from Willie Spence to drop anchor, while Ertie Moar, cap well down over his eyes, contemplates a fine day for the job as he stands here, about to operate the much-used windlass. Attached to the port rail is the boathook very often utilised to clear seaweed from the raised anchor or to assist in mooring a boat alongside.

If the Out Skerries group of islands, lying as they do about 10 miles east of Lunna Ness on the mainland, had been served only erratically in the days of the smacks at least the coming of the *Earl* in 1877 gave a much needed consistency to the service. Of course Skerries as a port was off the beaten track and initially there was only a fortnightly call when the steamer covered Yell Sound destinations, thus the little island remained relatively isolated.

Isobel Manson

Below: Framed! There is no apparent record of a lifebelt ever being used by necessity in the history of either *Earl* but here is a near use for one. While the lifebelt is hardly in pristine white state, nevertheless the decorative North Company flags show up quite well between the lettering. Sammy Harrison, engineer, is the subject, resting on the pile of ropes by the steering wheel aft. He was a young townsman of Lerwick who joined the ship at the end of the war in 1918. He was there on Thursday, 28th August, 1924, when the *Earl* collided with Robbie Ramsay's Baa and Harrison had to report water in the engine-room, then he evacuated the vessel with others.

It was Sammy Harrison who came to the rescue in December 1924 when, after the Whalsay flit-boat was lost, the ship's rudder quadrant-head at the stern had snapped in the fury of a south-east full gale. Harrison organised a temporary repair in darkness and flung stinging spray. What credit he received is not known, except that the insurance under-writers impressed by the resource and seamanship shown in difficult conditions by Captain Donald McMillan and his crew, gave an award of £50 to them.

Below: By 1930 the old *Earl* was more than 50 years of age and perhaps beginning to show her vintage in styling if not in appearance, but no expense had been spared in annual overhaul and maintenance. Indeed when she was subsequently advertised on the market after World War Two in 1946, the sale offer stated "has always been employed in an easy general cargo grade and has been kept up regardless of cost. She will be found to be in excellent condition for a vessel of her age".

The care is confirmed in this aspect of the fore-deck and its shipshape appearance, with crewmen grouped in the right corner, two of whom are hauling on a rope with the legs of another man seen high up in the rigging, probably dealing with ongoing maintenance.

Barrels galore on the pier are probably tar or fuel, while buildings at the rear have been either demolished or sold. Aitken and Wright's General Store was eventually removed to make way for a modern TSB building while the old Harbour Trust office, white-painted and featuring a clock, was developed as Harbour House, Shetland Voluntary Services Centre.

Shetland Museum

Shetland Museum

Above: The teak boarding of bridge and wheel-deck stands out behind the dockers in a standard loading scene of the 1930s. In the foreground there is a merchant's barrow of the type used by a firm like a grocer R. & C. Robertson of Commercial Street. Behind it the wooden chute used for sliding items down into the well-deck can be seen. The lad with the white coat has probably brought the barrow down to the steamer. As indicated by the waft of smoke about her funnel, the *Earl* is preparing to sail.

Above: With fencing stakes over at the starboard side of the well-deck, purser Davie Gray's theme song might be, "… don't fence me in!" The docker or crewman on the left is probably handling a type of wooden box used for conveying Shetland Library books to the outer isles.

Above: Looking aft on the port side from the bridge, with the *Earl* in her customary berth at Victoria Pier in Lerwick. The day looks a trifle short on good visibility but the ship seems set to leave judging by the hint of passenger presence to the right of the funnel, with steward McLeod lugging a suitcase aboard. Other baggage lies on the whinstone sets of the pier. The view highlights the *Earl*'s life-saving equipment, with the radial davit for the port boat seen in detail. Behind the ropes is a sectioned life-raft, neatly placed by the rails.

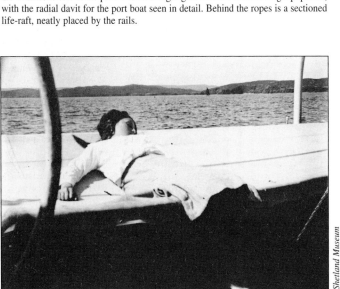

Above: Tom Gifford, seen behind the bridge canvas dodgers, brings in the steamer. Various people anticipate the arrival, including children in the well-deck and a gentleman, standing on the seats provided on the wheel-deck, who wears a hat of the kind favoured by the Boy Scouts in pre-World War Two days. The docker striding forward to take the bow rope is described as John Robertson who is not unlike "Whalsay Willie" seen on the *Earl*'s foredeck in another photograph.

Left: Total relaxation! Warm sunshine and a comfortable spot are just right for this lass, asleep on the cover of a lifeboat on the *Earl*. Is this the port side of the steamer northbound? Inshore, there is evidence of a squaresail.

Magnus Shearer

Isobel Manson

Above: A day of better weather in this grouping as light flows in from the port side of the ship. This angle catches the steering mechanism casing abaft the wheel on which rests the arms of crewman Magnie Fraser, brother-in-law to Tom Gifford. Family connections on board the *Earl of Zetland* are highlighted yet again.

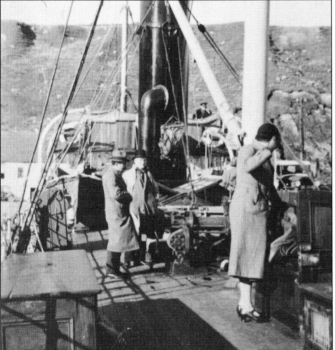

Chrissie Mann

Above: Although the day is bright, the clothing worn by passengers suggests cool conditions. The gentleman in the trilby hat on the left is Sheriff R. J. Wallace. He later was to accept on behalf of the Gilbert Bain Hospital in Lerwick, a gift of £100. This was given by James L. Smith, the manager of the North Company, as a memento of the old *Earl* at the time of her "retiral" when the brand new motor vessel of the same name arrived in Lerwick on 19th August, 1939. Meanwhile the lady by the dining saloon companionway adjusts her hat with a gloved hand. Her shoes are in the style of the mid-thirties. On the bridge Willie Spence seems to be looking pensively aft, over the canvas dodger. If there is a cold wind the engine room staff are doing their best to make the most of it below, because the skylight is wide open.

The ship has her bows on to the small pier at Ollaberry and a motor vehicle is parked on what must be the end of the jetty. Presumably it will be the top of the tide since the steamer seems to be, at least partly, alongside

Left: Another view of the first *St Clement* which was a weel-kent steamer at northern ports when she relieved the old *Earl* each autumn. While on such duty she ran ashore in Saltwick, near Aywick, on Yell, in heavy rain on 18th October, 1928. Despite damage she could steam to Aberdeen. Sadly she was sunk in a German air attack on 5th April, 1941, a fate which might well have befallen the *Earl* the same year, on 4th October.

Chrissie Mann

Above: There are very many views of the ship at Victoria Pier yet there is still variety, each photograph having its own characteristics. This one is no exception. Willie Spence is "standing tall" on the wheel-deck, no doubt aided by some object behind the teak boarding. Beside him is Tom Gifford and the other officer on the right is likely to be purser Davie Gray. There is a dark-haired lass between them. The crew member on the bridge could be Colin Henry. All the canvas dodgers around the bridge area and at the foredeck are furled.

Chrissie Mann

Above: Three *Earl of Zetland* stalwarts linger for a moment on board the ship. On the left, Robbie Gray, joined at the age of 16 as a cabin boy and was chief steward in the Second World War. His daughter Margaret remembered "... my father loved being on the *Earl*, although it was hard with long hours. We lived in Lerwick and my sisters and I made regular trips to Baltasound for our holidays. My father, then cook, was usually busy in the galley making huge roasts. We would go in there because it was lovely and warm ... in bad weather when mothers were too seasick to get out of their bunks to make up their babies' feeds, he would fill the bottles at the galley and take them to the children. Of course the mothers were most grateful and many were the knitted socks and scarves he received each Christmas ..."

Jimmy Willie Spence, from Cullivoe in Yell like skipper Willie of the same name but not directly related, was an earlier chief steward at the time of the loss of the Whalsay flit-boat in 1924, and played his part in fixing a jury steering rig. He was a well-known figure, affable and popular.

On the right is the youthful Freddie Pottinger, originally cabin boy and ultimately catering manager of the North Company in Aberdeen before his retirement to Lerwick. It was he who remarked "the *Earl* is a lifeline". He also was on the old *Earl* when she sailed from Lerwick on 20th December, 1945, bound temporarily for Stromness to assist her old counterpart the *St Ola*, then had the unenviable task – after another brief sojourn for *Earl of Zetland II* in Shetland to relieve pressure on shipping space – of sailing to Aberdeen, finally, on 21st June, 1946, and beginning to strip the old steamer of her domestic fittings. He had the doubtful privilege of being the last Shetlander to stay on board what was by then a lifeless vessel tied up in Aberdeen harbour. He could not then anticipate her amazing, if brief, career as an immigrant ship.

Douglas Sinclair

The Old Haa Trust, Burravoe

Above: Of course Baltasound was the most northerly port of call for both *Earl*s and featured a "full-time" pier which was a major asset for the steamer, since she could go fully alongside whatever state of the tide. Until after the Second World War there was no other pier of any consequence in the North Isles. In a general sense somehow Shetland missed out on piers; even Lerwick did not have one until 1886! Orkney, meanwhile, had fared much better.

The Baltasound pier had owed its origins to the gigantic herring bonanza in the final years of the nineteenth century and into the twentieth when, indeed, in 1902 there was the incredible number of 650 boats based in Baltasound – not that they tried to cluster around what became the Baltasound pier for there were many wooden stages and jetties around the voe.

An old hulk had been sunk initially at the outer end of the main jetty to provide stability, then an open wood and metal structure linked the shore for a pier owned by the Sandison family and used for shipments of talc mined on Unst. Eventually the Sandisons sold out to the Shetland Islands Council and a splendid harbour facility was constructed at the end of the twentieth century. The crews of the old *Earl* would be incredulous!

In this print the *Earl* gleams in afternoon sunshine, looking her best, while fishing craft cluster around, offering a forest of masts in reality, and reflections in windless conditions. Although her decks seem deserted her derrick is in the working position, while, surprisingly, there appears to be a large crowd of people gathered on the pier by the *Earl*'s bow. Perhaps they are fishermen from moored boats, some of which could be Swedish.

Below: An attractive setting at Mid Yell in the late 1930s. In many ways this symbolises the North Isles scene of the period, with a glimpse of a pier of somewhat dubious quality … the *Earl* at anchor; a flit-boat at the well-deck; houses at North-a-Voe; the rocky foreshore and the hill behind. The ship looks smart and in pristine shape, including what looks like a freshly painted lifeboat.

There is leisured activity at the flit-boat with her sail, so characteristic of Mid Yell, while on the after hatch stands a small car giving a strong hint of trends in transport in the North Isles. What port it is destined for can only be speculated upon but of necessity a pier is needed – other than the structure in the foreground! Certainly flit-boats were not intended to carry vehicles.

Above: The grace and style of sail. Mid Yell featured big flit-boats in keeping with what was always the largest of the Yell communities and, of course, the crews were happiest when sail could be raised. This, probably viewed from the *Earl*'s well-deck, or perhaps the pier, shows the shape of the flit-boat's hull to advantage, while the jib is very much economy size. Charles Spence is at the helm and Tom Pole stands at the mast on the short foredeck. It is a "passengers only" situation. The bearded gentleman amidships seems to be addressing the ladies.

Chrissie Mann

Above: The photographers' photographed! Willie Spence and Tom Gifford pose for a group of young ladies standing by the starboard lifeboat. They in turn are snapped by someone on the bridge. In this close-up of the funnel the whistle lanyard is very prominent above. Where the ship might be north of Lerwick is very much open to question. She could be somewhere south of Whalsay en route to Victoria Pier …?

Bruce Spence

Above: A warm occasion on the shore at Brough Lodge. Captain William Spence stands before his ship in the company of Lady Herschell and her son Rognvald, today Lord Herschell. The former Vera Nicolson, only daughter of Sir Arthur Nicolson of Brough Lodge, had married Lord Herschell after the end of the First World War. The Herschell-Nicolson union had been greeted with enthusiasm by the Fetlar folk, although there were two religious factions on the island; diplomacy and tact prevailed, and the wedding ceremony was shared by the Rev J. A. Campbell and Rev R. S. McAffer on 1st November, 1919.

That the marriage was popular elsewhere was evinced in a magazine's society notes: "Court, by the way, pleasantly titillated by the news of the engagement of Lord Herschell to Miss Vera Nicolson. The cheery Lord H. was in waiting for over twelve years, and was vastly popular as a man of rather more erudition than most court servants, added to a well-developed taste for music. Miss Nicolson is also not uninterested in the more cultured side of life, tho' she has made quite a study of modern dancing. And now must fly – Love and kisses from Eve."

Above: There are all the signs of a work-intensive area in the well-deck. Goods and victuals for the people swing through the open hatch; travellers and animals alike, traverse the battered wooden sheeting covering the deck; at each port there is the intensive clatter of the winch with its exhaust steam, under the after part of the foredeck.

Lowrie Gifford (left) and Robbie Gray take a relaxed view of things between ports. The ship's bell dangles invitingly overhead to their left.

Above: The load of sheep will mean a hefty pull for the two oarsmen, seen at Brough Lodge, on the left identified as Lowrie Brown and on the right, Johnny Hughson. Looking thoughtfully at the animals in the bow is George Williamson perhaps contemplating market prices! The *Earl* awaits their arrival in a flat sea, although the men will need to row round to her port side for well-deck access.

THE THIRTIES

The decade opened disastrously for the North of Scotland and Orkney and Shetland Steam Navigation Company Limited. When the news broke in Lerwick with the firing of a maroon at 6am on the morning of 10th April, 1930, that the lovely clipper-bowed *St Sunniva* had run hard aground on Mousa in thick fog and that her survival was unlikely, the information was met with incredulity. Only a year before she had returned to the direct passage between Aberdeen and Lerwick, having been renovated from the lower decks up at considerable expense over a spell of three months. She had been a centre of interest at Victoria Pier and much admired as a modernised steamer after 21 years on the main route. But now her 864-ton hull was apparently in danger of being swamped by the eager sea.

The island of Mousa was the only projecting land between Buchan Ness and Lerwick. A degree or two off course and a ship could be too far inshore for safety. So it was with the *St Sunniva*. The Bard of Mousa near the south-east corner proved to be her downfall; not that she was moving unduly fast because her skipper had cut-back around Sumburgh Head with its lighthouse, unseen in the darkness and drifting fog. But he had sea room then.

It was 3.40am when her plating was ripped by underwater rocks in a gigantic gash which left the future of the *St Sunniva* in dire straits. Temporarily she heeled over to port and more than 40 passengers, including women and children scantily clad, straight from their bunks, came on deck to the roar of escaping steam and the deep mournful wail of the steamer's siren, noises accentuated by the reports and swish of signal rockets. They were directed to the boats swung out in readiness to put them ashore on Mousa.

When information reached Lerwick, the *Earl of Zetland* and the fisheries cruiser *Vaila* immediately sailed for the wreck. Over an hour later both vessels stood by the doomed *St Sunniva,* now well down by the bows, her passengers despairing spectators on the rugged rock pile of the Bard of Mousa. Of course, twenty-six years previously, in 1904, the *St Giles* had also come to grief in fog on Mousa although her skipper, crew, passengers and cargo escaped the potentially serious consequences when the steamer slid off the rocks and was beached. The *Earl* had rendered assistance then too. But the sight which met the *Earl* and the *Vaila* that April day in 1930 was heart-rending.

Both ships lay close by, as what could be salvaged was removed and transferred by ship's boat while the sea remained calm. Passengers had already been taken onto both rescue vessels and watched disconsolately as the *St Sunniva* settled deeper, her stern rising high from the sea.

While the aft accommodation remained accessible, crew removed crockery, cutlery, table-linen, bedding, rugs, cushions — all the items likely to be of practical use — although they could not cope with the well used piano, so much a part of the ship's amenities. For several days the ruptured hull remained in benign conditions until the wind went south-east, strengthened, then as the hull began to disintegrate in the resultant seas,

cargo ranging from sacks of letters and parcels, and foodstuffs to barrels of petrol, was thrust ashore on the rocks. Some letter-mail was salvaged, taken to Lerwick on the *Earl,* dried out then delivered on the Friday and Saturday.

Finally, the lovely *St Sunniva* lay strewn out in pieces on the sea-bed. Her tragic demise was a bitter blow to all who had come to hold her in affection over 13 years. If only a token it can be, nevertheless the ship's bell salvaged from the wreck-site, today on display amid North Boat souvenirs in the Shetland Museum, is a precious reminder of halcyon days. It was in 1972 when Shetland divers probed through the kelp surrounding the wreck and gladly discovered such a fitting symbol of a distinctive steamer.

By June 1931 there was a replacement ship described as: " … a triumph of sentiment and beauty over utility …" The *Earl of Zetland,* bedecked by bunting, was one of several vessels to welcome the *St Sunniva II* into Lerwick harbour. She was a beautiful craft, with her bow-sprit and figurehead, clipper bow, shapely counter stern, pristine white hull and well-proportioned buff funnel. As she had come north, significantly she slowed down and lingered by the wreck-site of her predecessor, then had a warm welcome in Bressay Sound from many spectators, her white hull glinting in the evening light. Yet, tragically, like her forerunner she met an untimely fate. Commandeered for war purposes in August 1939, she survived various assignments including the abortive Norwegian campaign before serving as a rescue vessel in North Atlantic convoys and, ironically, she had no chance when, reportedly, she iced up in the black void of a winter night in January 1943 and went down with all hands. She was there in the pallid twilight off Newfoundland; in the pale dawn she had gone.

The first years of the 1930s unfolded without undue drama — sailing vessel numbers had steadily diminished — although there were incidents. Even before the incipient threat of the road services, efforts were made to usurp the *Earl's* reign. John S. Ratter, the Cullivoe merchant, had acquired a 52-foot motor-boat, *Islander,* designed to offer a faster service from Lerwick to the North Isles. She appeared late in the spring of 1931.

She was scheduled to leave on a Sunday afternoon and was proving relatively popular, when only a few weeks into her career a faulty magneto left her wallowing helplessly, dangerously near the notorious Brethern reef. Fortunately the *Earl* had left Lerwick some time later and happened on the disabled launch. A line was put over not a moment too soon and the *Islander* was towed back to Lerwick. Thirteen passengers transferred to the old steamer.

A year later Ratter's boat had an encounter with Whiting Baa, north of the Ness of Queyon near Aywick, East Yell. The baa remains deceptive into this twenty-first century, being indiscernible in calm conditions. Off Aywick the *Islander* stopped to pick up passengers and their luggage from a small rowing boat; she had just got under way when she struck the reef and was firmly held. Two other fourareens fishing for mackerel, and the

Below: A scraperboard by the author depicting the fate of the *St Sunniva* on Mousa in April 1930.

Aywick boat, were alongside within minutes to take off passengers and luggage leaving the skipper and engineer of the motor boat standing by. Again, coincidentally, the *Earl* appeared on passage between Mid Yell and Burravoe and uplifted the folk from the small boats.

The *Islander,* necessarily abandoned, broke her back across the baa in an exceptionally low tide; it spelled a sad ending to John Ratter's imagination and enterprise.

Another scheme to compete had indifferent success. A vessel named *Innovator* was commanded by John Henderson, a former mate of the *Earl.* That she had problems was illustrated by a newspaper report of January 1933. In a prolonged gale the *Earl,* bound for Lerwick, had to shelter near Mossbank. The same storm affected the *Innovator.* The report highlighted her problem: "The local passenger and cargo boat *Innovator,* skipper John Henderson, left Lerwick on Monday for Whalsay to take a consignment of fish to be sent south by the *St Rognvald.* On the way north it was found necessary to cut adrift the small boat — shades of the Whalsay flit-boat incident — which was being towed by the *Innovator.* About 200 boxes of fish were taken on board at Symbister and the vessel had a rough trip to Lerwick, a good deal of anxiety being felt for her; however she weathered the gale well."

Such depressions in the weather were in keeping with economic trends of the early 1930s. The herring industry had gone into recession because of European market decline, and fishing as a Shetland preoccupation became subordinate to other indigenous industries. A shortage of herring compounded the situation, reducing the number of outlying stations. The old *Earl* no longer carried the great complements of gutters, curers and coopers of another era.

Into the mid-1930s the emphasis in terms of large passenger numbers was on leisure excursions. These were many, varied and immensely popular. In May 1932, for the Victoria Day Celebration the esteemed steamer was advertised to depart at 9am for Whalsay, Burravoe, Mid Yell, Fetlar and Uyeasound with the Lerwick Brass Band engaged to play selections during the trip. Members of the Thule Model Yacht Club were due to sail their craft in a regatta at Burravoe with the enthusiasts there … but the weather militated against the sailing event.

The Fetlar Agricultural Show coincided with the Lerwick Regatta Day in August 1933. Instead of the annual cruise round Bressay the steamer transported judges, officials and spectators north to Fetlar at the crack of dawn, leaving Victoria Pier at 3am!

A couple of years later, in July 1935, Willie Spence took the *Earl* and about 180 trippers round Bressay, with a call at Noss where the raucous calls of the seabirds threatened to outbid the sounds of the combined George Stark's and Radio Jollies bands. So successful was the trip that an identical outing took place a fortnight later, a feature being the large number of visitors to Shetland taking part. The aged steamer could certainly provide the atmosphere, mostly enhanced by the full regalia of her dressed-overall bunting.

Invariably Spencey added his own brand of colour, whether it be the special festive occasion or routine voyage. C. A. Manson of the Lerwick Post Office staff contributed an article to the Post Office magazine in 1936: "I left the Head Office at 10am on Friday and boarded the mail steamer *Earl of Zetland.* Captain Spence's good seamanship and geniality are well known as great assets to his passengers with a knowing twinkle to the

Shetland Museum

Above: Judging by the bunting at the foremast and the obvious informality on the bridge – nothing new – and deck, this is a special outing; a Victoria Day holiday perhaps. A bright light helps to define shapes of ship and passengers. The engine-room skylight is wide open, while the bridle round the funnel securing the mainmast stays is particularly well defined. Dress of people on board indicates the early-1930s. Captain William Spence is just visible above the bridge stairway.

Gordon Donaldson

Above: A fair weather angle from the foredeck as the *Earl* ploughs her way back down Yell Sound in the days of calls at West Sandwick, one of the two ports on the west side of Yell. The other was Ulsta, now the vehicle ferry terminal. The year is 1930.

Colin Henry is steering but no one appears to be on the bridge. The rather makeshift canvas dodgers at bridge and wheel-deck are much in evidence, contoured by the slanting afternoon sun. The light and shade emphasise the shapes of the cluttered fo'c'sle and the hatch-cover tied back against the guard-rails abaft the much-used anchor windlass confirms the fine bright day.

unwary landlubber. 'Sailing in a fog would be dangerous here,' remarks a timid tripper. 'Yes', says the captain reassuringly, 'but we carry large shovels with which to clear a passageway when it becomes too thick.' Then someone spots the log-line. 'Oh that. It's for catching fish'. These and similar asides are punctuated by his business-like 'Nor' west by west half west' to the helmsman …"

Since its opening in June 1886, the Victoria Pier had been a priceless asset in bringing shipping into the heart of the island capital and the *Earl of Zetland* was a feature in her berth, a pulse of island life and trade. Lerwick folk found the pier splendidly central and it was fashionable to observe the steamer movements. However facilities were always under review, thus in 1923 a suggestion had been made about enlargement but lack of finance delayed progress until 1930 when a proposal appeared to widen the pier at its base on the north side tapering to a mere 20 feet at the point.

In the opinion of many, including Willie Spence, this would make berthing vulnerable. He aired his views in the local press: "… a grant had been obtained for the purpose of widening the Victoria Pier … I would respectfully suggest for … consideration that any widening should be done parallel with the existing pier, which is at a well-placed angle and convenient for going alongside in every kind of weather. During the 11 years I have been Master of the *Earl of Zetland* I have never had any difficulty in getting alongside … if the angle of the pier is altered … would be untenable with a north-east gale …"

Undeniably extension was needed. The pier was a crucial gateway to all Shetland but had become congested; the big transit and storage shed in the middle, left little space at each side for the milling throng at arrival and departure of steamers as well as the motley array of stacked goods. Despite

the limitations, Lerwick Harbour Trust apparently did not have suitable finance available, while the Scottish Home Department never seemed more than lukewarm. Yet that the famous pier was important historically and practically showed on 23rd June, 1936, when the 50th anniversary was celebrated. The *Earl of Zetland* and second *St Sunniva* were dressed overall, the *Earl* having had the privilege of being the first vessel to berth at the Victoria Pier half a century before.

At length, by 1937, the Harbour Trust's finances allowed consideration. In fact the project reached the tendering stage and a price of £36,632 was agreed, however the order was not confirmed until 29th September, 1939, by which time there was a war on and, in theory at least, the old *Earl* had gone and a fine newcomer was in the familiar berth. Willie Spence never saw any development, but neither did he have to be concerned about possible problems of berthing in adverse weather at Lerwick.

Timetabling of the domestic routes of the North Isles steamer fluctuated. In December 1930: "The *Earl of Zetland* or other steamer, will sail as under, weather, etc. permitting, liberty being reserved to alter the arrangements as the necessity of the trade or any emergency may require …"

Essentially the old *Earl* made two trips weekly to the North Isles (usually Sunday-Monday and Friday-Saturday) and one to the Yell Sound ports (Tuesday-Wednesday), though the Yell Sound run was reduced to once fortnightly (Wednesday-Thursday) between the World Wars and after the Second War it was abandoned.

A third North Isles voyage had existed on occasion, as in 1908, and was introduced again in 1937, then after the Second War there were three North Isles runs each week, generally outward one day and inward the next, yet there were certain exceptions. From 1892 to 1939, despite the early reservations of the Shetland Presbytery, whereas in summer the steamer left Lerwick on Sunday afternoon and proceeded to Baltasound, returning on Monday, in winter she left Lerwick on Monday at 3am and, going only

Above: A young and cheerful Lowrie Gifford at the anchor windlass. It was nothing new for Shetlanders, brothers, to crew in the same ship and Tom, skipper, and Lowrie, crewman, did just that. They also served loyally on both *Earl*s, transferring naturally from one to the other. In fact, Lowrie Gifford sailed as bo'sun on the first *Earl* on 21st June, 1946, when she voyaged finally to Aberdeen for presentation to interested parties. With luck, she might fetch the £6000 sought in the printed sale notice.

This illustration shows detail of the windlass, the lum from the stove in the crew's quarters, the open foredeck hatch and the bell on the foremast. The bell was placed there latterly but was known to be fitted at the break of the well-deck. The solitary passenger, partially hidden, has the dubious windbreak of the rails being canvas covered – year 1938.

Above: Youth has its fling with Burravoe the likely venue. A delighted lad, wearing his schoolboy cap of the 1930s, "takes a trick" at the wheel on the stern, sitting astride the steering casing amid the pile of mooring ropes. No doubt the wood of the casing is decorated by the words *Earl of Zetland* as carved on the sides and featured in a later photograph after the impounding of the old steamer at Haifa in 1947.

Shetland Museum

to Uyeasound, was posted to leave there at 8am and return to Lerwick the same day. The third North isles run, in 1908, was a one-day affair on a Thursday. The Yell Sound trip, in its later and declining era, was also a single day, on alternate Thursdays.

From 1946, with the new *Earl*, the programme included a one-day round of Whalsay, Mid Yell, Brough Lodge and Uyeasound, on a Wednesday, alongside the more extended two-day runs, on Monday-Tuesday and Friday-Saturday. It is important to record historically the ports visited over the years. Only two featured on both the North Isles and Yell Sound voyages, being Symbister in Whalsay and Burravoe in Yell. The many ports in the North Isles included Gossabrough, Bastavoe, Gutcher, Cullivoe, Baltasound and Haroldswick; indeed on occasion the old *Earl* would continue beyond the north-east tip of Unst and go past Muckle Flugga towards Bluemull Sound or Yell Sound, offering tourists sight-seeing opportunities.

The customary round in Yell Sound featured Burravoe, of course, Mossbank, Ollaberry, Lochend, North Roe, West Sandwick, Ulsta, Burravoe (again) and Vidlin. Then Swinister, Sullom, and Brae, even Bardister, were ports in early days. In the hectic period of the herring fishery, before and after 1900, the steamer sometimes continued from North Roe round to the attractive Roeness Voe and, on occasion, Hillswick. There were some destinations which lay off the main track of the North Isles and which were covered in different ways at various times. Houbie on the south coast of Fetlar, inserted between Whalsay and Burravoe on the Yell Sound programme, and Out Skerries, which at one time was fitted in fortnightly at the Yell Sound visits but later was a weekly call on one of the North Isles runs. Baltasound was used regularly for overnight berthing — or Uyeasound for anchorage if that happened to be the *Earl's* turning point, then on the Yell Sound voyage she lay at North Roe and, in earlier days, at Brae.

The gradual encroachment of "the Overland" on the traditional sea services meant that the number of ports visited by the *Earl* — "or other steamer" — was almost insidiously eroded, for it did not happen overnight. It was thought by the public that with the arrival of the new *Earl* a new and better era in North Isles travel had come, but in effect, she was too late. The

wind of change was beginning well before the mid-20th century, as mainland and Yell Sound and, indeed, North Isles names disappeared from the sailing notices. Purser David Gray of "da auld *Earl*" had anticipated the erosion, as described elsewhere, and suggested the Tuesday-Wednesday sailing to link with the direct boat. It was an example of the march of progress in competition and the losing battle to contain the growing problem for the sea route. Yet in the final analysis the matter at stake was not about the romanticism of the province of two splendid ships but that which was going to best serve the commerce, industry and general trade of the islands and the swift movement of people by road or by air. The outcome was destined to be as inevitable as night following day.

Limitations in postal arrangements lingered on even into the 1930s and proposals for improvement still appeared. While, for example, Whalsay and Fetlar District Councils accepted the existing service, a lengthy letter from Unst made the point "that the present steamer service is no better than it was 40 years ago." A petition from Unst sought to increase the mail deliveries by the overland route while other communities feared this might jeopardise the very existence of the *Earl*. The Unst council stated that mail which left Aberdeen by steamer on Friday reached Lerwick the next day but was not delivered in the most northerly isle until Monday. Also mail leaving Lerwick Post Office on Friday before 9am reached Uyeasound too late for same-day delivery at the north end of Unst.

If the steamer left Victoria Pier at the scheduled time of 9am perhaps same-day delivery would be possible, but invariably the *Earl's* derrick was swinging cargo from pier to hold, taking on goods and mail off the ship from Aberdeen far past the appointed hour. She might cast-off as late as

Below: A particularly interesting close-up of the bridge, clear in its detail. Despite the addition of teak-boarding in the 1930s the original bridge rails always remained, while the concertina-like canvas dodger would be up and down "yo-yo" style, depending on the weather. In real terms it offered scant protection. To the left is the wooden case for the skipper's binoculars. The engine-room telegraph is supplied by a Scotstoun, Glasgow firm; the indicator seems to be at something other than "Stop", probably "Finished with Engines". The binnacle is a beautifully decorative sculptured feature in its own right.

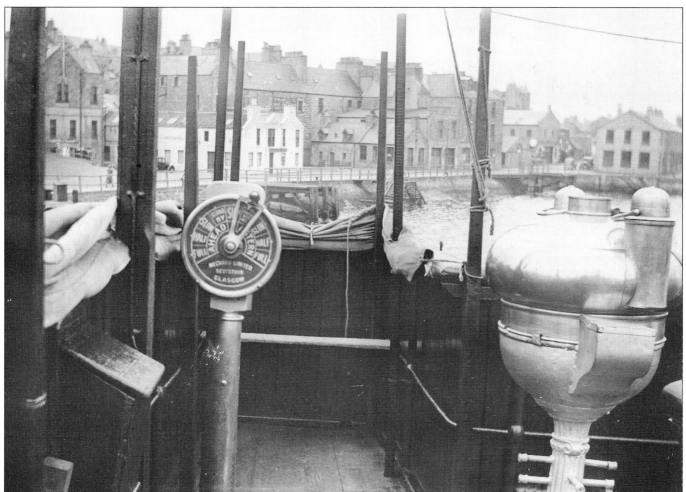

Shetland Museum

10.30am … thus there were anomalies and uncertainties, far short of what was acceptable.

Whatever man-made limitations existed, the maritime climate posed its own restrictions. It is not difficult to imagine the disruptions in the winter of 1936. From 1st December until Boxing Day, 32 occasions of gale force winds were recorded at Lerwick Observatory. That month there were 17 days of storms, followed by 15 in January 1937, the 23rd day of the month seeing the heaviest seas for years. Even in March, severe winds, accompanied by sleet and snow, created havoc not only in Shetland but south in Scotland, England, Wales and Ireland.

It was an incredibly bad winter, and the one preceding the retiral of

Chrissie Mann

Above: In the dialect, "a lad o'pairts" generally denotes a man of versatility and initiative. There is the jocular corollary to this: "… and most of them still working!" Willie Spence had had a varied and most unusual career before his devoted tenure of "da auld *Earl*"; indeed fortunate to survive to have the parts still working.

Perhaps the set of the jaw and demeanour in this portrait by the engine-room telegraph conveys the determination he would have needed in extreme circumstances of shipwreck. He had enlisted as a seaman on board the Glasgow-registered iron barque *King James* and sailed abroad. Eventually she loaded coal at Newcastle, New South Wales, in Australia – a cargo which never reached its destination. Far into the Pacific Ocean spontaneous combustion set the cargo alight; the crew fought the deep-seated fire in daylight and darkness until forced to abandon ship. For two long days the 42 crew agonisingly watched her burn, a slow consuming destruction, until she sank in a boil of water and cloud of smoke and steam, leaving the pair of ship's boats to try for the American coast in worsening weather. They lost contact with each other, and between the two, reportedly, 18 died in diabolical storm conditions, then when in the cold light of day land was sighted by crew in Spence's group the big seas made landing impossible. It became "every man for himself" and ultimately the redoubtable Spence won ashore on Santa Rosa island off Los Angeles. He learned that from his boat only the skipper, sailmaker and an apprentice had emerged, suffering from exposure. There were 24 survivors from the *King James*.

Captain William Spence, who must have thought the weather was making strenuous efforts to have the last word. Little wonder, because on one occasion the valiant Spence had uttered another famous remark in which he described gale-force winds as "a stiff breeze". In the New Year period of 1936-37, wind forces of 95 miles per hour looked like Mother Nature trying to call his bluff!

There were various situations over the long weeks of persistent depressions coming in. The *Earl* left the pier at Lerwick one morning, reached the north harbour, was forced to anchor, then had to return. Even the berths in Lerwick were subjected to a battering. The south boat *St Catherine* had her upper belting on the starboard side damaged in the surge against the wall of Victoria Pier. On the same day, Saturday, 23rd January, 1937, the *Earl* had struggled from Lerwick to the North Isles. On her return she reached Whalsay at 1am on the Sunday, hove-to in the lee of the land, then in the grey daylight of the Monday Willie Spence took her into better shelter at Vidlin. At 10am on the Tuesday another attempt was made only to be thwarted by the shipping of a series of enormous seas. On returning to Vidlin a boat was launched, at risk even in the anchorage, and some passengers, including a stretcher case, were landed to be taken by car on the rough roads to Lerwick. Another abortive attempt to sail was made, denied by mighty waves which threatened to swamp the old ship. Eventually the wind moderated enough to allow her a passage to Lerwick. It had taken from Sunday until Wednesday at noon. A stiff breeze indeed!

If the dauntless Spence had had such problems with which to contend there were times without number when he won through to an isolated community and earned the gratitude and goodwill of the folk. This was abundantly demonstrated during a sequence of events in the months of April and May 1937. North Isles people met together in crowds in Mid Yell Public Hall on 19th May to pay tribute and say farewell to a Shetlander of presence. Each of the North Isles was represented officially by a notable member of the community.

Appropriately it was Dr Harry Taylor, the general practitioner on the island of Yell, who gave the initial speech. He spoke of Willie Spence as the pilot of the dear old *Earl of Zetland* and how those who knew the coast between Lerwick and Baltasound – studded as it was with skerries, baas and sunken rocks, maybe never charted – erratic tides and climatic conditions, dense fogs, cruel winter gales, darkness, sleet and snow; only they could realise the strain on the skippers.

Robert Smith of Mid Yell, a Shetlander, emphasised the point. The *Earl* had come to make a special call at Gossabrough, north of Burravoe on Yell, during her return Yell Sound trip to Lerwick. A south-easter was blowing, but gale or no gale Spence had brought the steamer. The flit-boat men were of two minds about venturing out to the *Earl* with Robert Smith but, maybe influenced by the Spence presence they went, shipping water from time to time. Smith had clambered up from the bucking flit-boat and the *Earl* got under way. He said: "The worst was yet to come! Already under way two hours and twenty minutes, I noticed the Skerries o' Neepoback (off Burravoe) abeam to starboard and we appeared to make no headway. I mentioned it to Captain Spence and asked him if he thought we should ever reach Lerwick. 'Of course we will,' he replied. 'That's nothing. I'll keep her head to wind a bit longer, and in a quarter of an hour there will be the south tide and I'll lay her head to the Out Skerries and get the tide under her bow,' We did arrive at Lerwick 8½ hours after leaving Gossabrough! I mention that as an example of the prowess and skill of Captain Spence. In fact he seemed to be in his glory fighting the elements …"

Peter Sandison, the Cullivoe merchant, augmented this with the tale of Gibbie and Ursula, who had had their supper. There was just a heel of loaf left on the table and there was the din of a fierce gale outside. Gibbie held out the remains of the bread to the dog. "Boy," said Ursula, "dunna gie yon ta da dug, for we hae little ida hoose and du kens da *Earl'll* never come wi dis wadder." "Haud de tongue, du dusna ken Wullie Spence for as shur as daylight, come da morn doo'll hear da whistle o' da *Earl* ida voe." And Gibbie and Ursula were not to be disappointed. The *Earl* came.

The Rev William Carson from Fetlar confessed that his seamanship was confined to a couple of nautical manoeuvres – that of "splicing the mainbrace" and that of yelling louder than usual for a steward for help in saving the saloon carpet from disaster when the *Earl* behaved skittishly, as she often did in spite of advanced years! But he bore witness to Captain Spence's skill in handling his vessel off the open beaches of Fetlar, offering maximum shelter to the flit-boats; and his consistency in bringing the steamer. William Carson had only one regret – the Captain was not a Fetlar man. He said: "There was a Scotsman who attributed every famous person

to Scotland, until an Englishman countered: 'At any rate you cannot claim Shakespeare, the greatest of them all.' 'Maybe,' said the Scot, 'but he was good enough to be Scottish.'" And accordingly the minister thought they could lay claim to William Spence. What he could do, and would do, was confer on him the Freedom of Fetlar, "… so that any time you desire to boast, you can tell the world that you are a Fetlar man."

Dr Gilchrist, formerly the Yell doctor, then with a Whalsay practice, mentioned the notorious stretch of sea between that island and Lerwick and how Mr Carson's remark reminded him of the traveller who was informed by the steward that he could not be sick in the cabin, to which the victim replied, suddenly overcome, "Can't I!" Anecdotes abounded at the presentation and John Stewart from Unst reminded the audience of the consistency of the *Earl's* visits under Captain Spence; they had been rewarded with more sights of the familiar black funnel then ever before. He mentioned that the *Earl* was a very old ship and had seemed to bear a charmed life … "she still survives and as far as we can judge she will still be around when we are all dead! In fact she has gone over the ground so often that one would imagine she could find the way herself!"

Wallets of treasury notes from islanders of Unst, Yell, Fetlar and Whalsay were given: "Presented to Captain William Spence … in appreciation of his faithful and efficient service while Captain of the *Earl of Zetland*, 19th May, 1937."

Willie Spence was taken aback at the depth of feeling displayed by the isles folk: "… I have in my time weathered many a gale and braved many a tempest, but I must confess that speech-making fairly puts the wind up me. Words fail to express my appreciation of your reception tonight and I am deeply grateful to you all … I have always tried to do my best and while, as you all know, the *Earl* is no race horse, I have always managed to get her to crawl along somehow …"

Other presentations made in the April were from shipmates, the Lerwick office staff and the Post Office in Shetland. The *Earl's* crew members were represented by noted purser David Gray: " … I am honoured in making this presentation to Captain Spence … I have known him as long as I've known the company's steamer. As mate he was most energetic, always ready to help … he gave up command of larger ships to take over the North Isles trade which was at that time very irregular. Since then he has made the best use of the material at his disposal … This inscribed ebony stick is a remembrance from the crew. I hope you will be able over a number of years to sport it and never require to lean on it. This is my honest wish and I am sure the wish of us all …"

The Lerwick office staff of the North of Scotland Orkney and Shetland Steam Navigation Company Limited added their warm esteem when Alexander Stephen, the agent, handed over an engraved dressing case, while another gift was proffered by the Postmaster in Lerwick, Mr F. C. Young.

Thus William Spence of Cullivoe departed formally from the shipping scene, to be replaced by his mate, Thomas Gifford, whose captaincy of the revered steamer was to be coincidentally brief, lasting two years, before the coming of a second *Earl of Zetland*.

Only a week after his appointment Captain Tom Gifford took the old *Earl* to the southern approaches of Bressay Sound to help welcome the second *St Clair*, a brand new product of the Hall, Russell yard at Aberdeen. Dressed overall the two steamers approached Lerwick in brilliant sunshine, watched by a great number of the population, the old ship perhaps looking her years when set beside the handsome buff-funnelled *St Clair*. Yet a moment of joy and cause for rejoicing in another improvement in communication for the islands.

Throughout the summer of 1937 Captain Gifford coaxed the ageing *Earl of Zetland* round her oft-traversed route. In the August he supervised the immensely popular round-Bressay trip for a hundred passengers who were rather more relaxed than the survivors of a Norwegian trawler who had come south on the *Earl* from Baltasound the previous week. According to reports the *Aldebran*, a 55-ton fishing vessel, had been swamped by a freak wave north-north-west of Muckle Flugga and her crew, mostly rudely shaken from their bunks, hurriedly launched a lifeboat from a badly angled deck before the vessel foundered. The men, many in night-attire, contrived to keep the lifeboat head into the seas before being rescued by a Swedish ship and put ashore at the Unst port. It had been an agonisingly narrow release from death, an ever-present risk factor for those who challenged the might of the ocean.

Even so, in 60 years of voyaging, year after year, in such close proximity to fickle wave and unyielding rock the old *Earl* had never been

Above: The oft-photographed wheel which had some style with its carved spokes and brass fittings. Here the female touch is much in evidence, while Magnie Fraser, and the skipper seem relaxed enough to let the ladies get on with it. Yet Magnie rests a few fingers on the top of the wheel, just in case …

Above: It's all in the family; skipper Willie Spence and helmsman Ertie Moar were half brothers. Ertie is suitably oilskin-clad for a wet day in summer while Willie strikes a characteristic stance, wearing his sea boots.

Their immediate surroundings by the wheel show the fittings as they were in the 1930s and, indeed, beyond. Could it be that the pleasingly decorated wheel has survived the breakers yard on a Haifa beach in 1950 and is a cherished souvenir of some Jewish enthusiast?

In the photograph the pipe on the deck carries the chain and rod manual steering gear aft to starboard and port and on to the quadrant at the stern. It may have been primitive but it worked, although on a bad day it certainly did ask questions of man-power!

associated with loss of life. It was a proud, though unsung, record. If then, the sea could not claim a victim directly, nor the ship be responsible, none the less there was great sadness when William Carson, a familiar figure as the Fetlar minister, collapsed and died on-board in September 1937. Only four months before that he had been paying warm tribute to Willie Spence.

A public figure, and benevolent by nature, Rev Carson had been at an education committee meeting in Lerwick but looked unwell as he boarded. Moments later he staggered and was helped below where steward Robbie Gray did what he could as the *Earl* steamed towards Symbister. An hour later, Captain Gifford summoned the Whalsay physician, Dr Orr, by megaphone, but by the time he boarded the ship from a small boat the patient had gone to meet his Maker, dead from a cerebral haemorrhage. Despite the lack of precedent the *Earl* went back to Victoria Pier to land the body. The following Sunday William Carson was taken to Fetlar on the old vessel for burial on the island of his ministry, known as "the Garden of Shetland".

Right: A dramatic view from aft, confirming the simplicity of the deck layout. Judging by the canvas-covered bridge rails the time would be in the mid-1920s. The bluff figure of Willie Spence stands by the engine-room telegraph and the old-fashioned binnacle with its decorative base is light against his dark clothing. In this perspective the funnel looks massive, while the "box" at its base is very evident. This was a fine, warm place to sit on a chilly day, then there would be the multiple smells and odours coming from the open engine-room skylight, like the waft of peat reek, timelessly evocative.

The stowed sail abaft the ventilator is almost an anachronism, a throwback to the days of proceeding by kind permission of, "the Almighty's ain win' and no' wi' the Devil's fire and brimstane". The dark-painted lifeboat neatly resting in its chocks is secured to the radial davits by traditional rope falls.

Below: North-bound off the Horse of Burravoe during the colourful pre-war years when the *Earl* was looking her best. She certainly makes a handsome sight as she surges along with distinctive wash, and funnel streaming smoke. There are the characteristic canvas dodgers at the foredeck and aft which helped the well-being of travellers. The blurred slightly undulating line at the top of the photograph will be the Out Skerries coast.

Chrissie Mann

Gordon Donaldson

THE BEGINNING OF AN END ...

From Christmas 1937 the womenfolk who shopped at Burravoe frequently found that expected goods were not there. This meant a return walk in hope, the next day or so. It happened too often with the result that Bertha Lethbridge, for long a school teacher in Burravoe and public-spirited, mentioned in a letter to the press the inconvenience if the steamer could not linger long enough to unload many essentials. Much of the cargo from Lerwick was perishable and if the ship bypassed Burravoe to land goods at Mid Yell to the north then a lorry had to be hired to bring these over. Additional expense for travellers was another factor.

It could be assumed that the non-appearance of the steamer on occasion was a reflection of road development, by 1937 an integral part of the island scene. The eight miles or so by lorry would not seem much of an inconvenience to the Earl's men when they had other priorities. Curiously enough the inconsistency of the visits to Burravoe was a corollary to the pressures induced by the Tuesday/Wednesday sailing in the isles initiated through purser David Gray, itself a result of the invading rivalry of the overland route.

In February 1939 another letter to the press complained, "... we, the North people were accommodated once a week but now ... Mid Yell only on a Sunday. North and South Yell passengers have to find their own conveyance, as the small buses do not run until Monday morning. If the (North Company) manager would look at the advert put out by the overland service he would observe the buses and ferries connect with each other ... in the interests of both North and South Yell. I hope the manager will see that the Earl's sailings are changed to Monday or an arrangement made with the Post Office to send their mail buses to connect with the steamer every Sunday."

Time tabling for March 1938 confirmed the reasons for the criticisms: "... every Sunday for Whalsay, Mid Yell and Uyeasound." Eventually another acknowledged the need — from a Burravoe point of view at least — when a 1939 shipping notice stated: "Earl of Zetland from Lerwick every Sunday at 2pm to Whalsay, Burravoe, Mid Yell, Brough Lodge and Uyeasound." The seemingly spontaneous alterations due to complaints were symptomatic of the prolonged period of transition from sea-dependence to land monopoly of transport, yet meanwhile the aged Earl retained her own special focal-point status.

But the wind of change was blowing steadily. A Zetland County Council discussion in February 1938 led to a letter of request to the North Company for a replacement for the 61 year old Earl of Zetland. Meanwhile she traversed her familiar route. James L. Smith, the new manager of the North Company, was making a first voyage north to Scalloway — the St Clair was on her summer west-side schedule — in June 1938 and, although he experienced at first hand the quality of the hospitality, he would be aware of the Earl's outdated facilities which would, of course, contrast those of any new and modern ship. Be that as it may, "da auld Earl" had carried big numbers of visitors by the end of the 1938 holiday season who had responded to that peculiar and particular atmosphere, not easily defined, which was life on board, scene of personalities and a multitude of events supervised by successive skippers and ably continued by Tom Gifford.

In the September the steamer transported a large group to Symbister for the annual regatta and football match between Lerwick and Whalsay. It was a drawn game with a goal each. The weather had been in agreeable mood with sunshine, shadow and a lively wind which was all in contrast to the severity of a December gale which pinned down the Earl during a North Isles Thursday run. She had been late in leaving Lerwick at 10am, made fairly heavy weather of it up to Whalsay, failed to call at Burravoe, often a difficult port in heavy seas at the mouth of Yell Sound, and finally ran to Mid Yell where Tom Gifford decided to lie until the Saturday. He risked the exposed coast — the gale was a south-easter — up to Baltasound that afternoon but was storm-stayed until the Monday morning. Ultimately a return was made to Lerwick at 3.30pm the same day. The New Year of 1939 was then imminent.

It was a fateful year for the planet; a year in which a dictator called his hand for global domination; a year when free nations were forced to make decisions; a year of awesome changes and challenges for all peoples. In general, little in the world could remain untouched; in particular, with the United Kingdom everything was affected. As the little Earl of Zetland lived out her last official weeks no-one could visualise that she would ultimately have a role to play in the destiny of a Jewish people in achieving

their "Promised Land." Neither could anyone envisage that the peerie steamer would have another six years of service to Shetland as the fates of war brought about emergency reorganisation.

The summer came. June and July dragged past. Europe was descending into turmoil. The British government watched apprehensively. The weeks slipped along and despite disconcerting news reaching Shetland, folk still talked about matters of the moment. What would the new ship be like? The old Earl would be going. A deep-seated attachment found expression in Baltasound public hall on Friday evening, 4th August, 1939. Tom Gifford had brought his well-loved steamer north on her routine call, moored at the familiar pier and gone with his crew to join a crowded audience in the hall already decorated with the colourful bunting from the Earl. There were people from all the North Isles communities.

Major H. W. L. Hunter spoke warmly of the ship and her achievements then introduced eminent Unst man Fordyce Clark: "This is an occasion of more than passing interest. We are about to say farewell to an old friend and contemplate the breaking of a tie ... and although we do not sorrow as those who have no hope — for we believe a new and better era is about to dawn — yet we cannot witness the passing of such a familiar friend as the Earl of Zetland without a sigh of regret.

"... sailing those northern waters in all weathers since the oldest among us were boys ... she has brought both gladness and sorrow to our homes ... she has helped to keep us all alive by bringing to our doors the necessities of life ... and she has carried away to the markets of the world our island produce, our sheep, our ponies and cattle ... indispensable to the life of the islands.

"Yet when some of us have entrusted ourselves to her tender mercies she has at times treated us rather unkindly. Of course we should on those

Isobel Manson

Above: William Spence had followed captains Gifford (William) and Burgess who had piloted the Earl in World War One, as skipper in 1919. Having had a colourful career in world-wide shipping he assiduously guided his beloved steamer for 17 years until his retiral in 1937. His successor was his mate Thomas (Tom) Gifford whose tenure on the venerable ship was coincidentally brief, lasting two years. But only a week after his appointment Tom Gifford took his old Earl to the southern approaches of Bressay Sound to meet, and bid welcome to the second St Clair, a product of the Hall, Russell yard at Aberdeen and a coal-burning vessel of 1637 tons. He was destined to captain her.

PASSENGERS AND CARGO ARE CARRIED SUBJECT TO THE CONDITIONS INCORPORATED IN THE COMPANY'S SAILING BILLS.

The North of Scotland and Orkney and Shetland Steam Navigation Company Limited.

(HEAD OFFICE: MATTHEWS' QUAY, ABERDEEN.)

PLEASE REFER TO

IN YOUR REPLY.

Telephone No 43.

Telegraphic Address "STEPHEN, LERWICK"

FIRST CLASS STEAMSHIPS

LEITH, ABERDEEN, CAITHNESS, ORKNEY & SHETLAND.

(Carrying H.M. Mails)

S.S. Earl of Zetland

Lerwick 30th April 1937

To whom this may concern. I do here by Certify that the Bearer Mr Thomas Gifford has served as First Mate on board the above named vessel from the 3rd day of October 1931. to the 30th day of April 1937. and during that time under my command five years and seven months and I always found him sober willing and obliging Also a good seaman that always could be relied on to do his various duties and well worth the highest position in his profession. And I am sure that he will render entire satisfaction to any one requiring his services

Wm Spence - Master.

to day Retiring

Below: A painting by the author, owned by Dennis Coutts of Lerwick, depicts the *Earl* in tide lumps and silhouetted by a low horizon light from the east. The stretch of water in mind at the time was between Burravoe and Mid Yell with the ship off East Yell, coming up into Colgrave Sound and looking out into the open sea between Skerries and Fetlar. The wind would be from the south east, with the *Earl* northbound.

occasions have blamed the weather, but it relieved our lacerated feelings to have a grouse at the old *Earl*. In later years she has brought our mails and that has made her arrival more of an event than ever. In short she has become an integral part of the life of these islands … she has a warm spot in all our hearts."

Fordyce Clark looked back to the era of Captain William Nicolson; the genial purser David Gray; and engineer Sammy Harrison due to join the replacement ship.

Then the parish minister Rev James Binnie reminisced: "In this age of machinery and mass production when romance and poetry are apt to be banished from our lives, this meeting is proof that feelings still exist. It is not usual for us to lavish our affections on the merely material, but next to wives and sweethearts, small boats and ships, especially in these islands, claim our attentions … the North of Scotland steamers are all Saints. The *Earl* is no saint but she is no sinner. The New Testament word for sin means really to miss the mark! The *Earl* never missed the mark; she has always reached her goal, has never run ashore. What, never? In the words of Gilbert and Sullivan's Opera — well, hardly ever! I am credibly informed that no life has ever been lost from the *Earl*. She surely has earned her right to canonisation and the title of Saint …

"Looking back … names: Captain Spence, Tom Moffat, Jamie Garriock, John Fraser, Colin Henry and Jamie Jamieson … one remembers the hospitality … the really good cup of tea on the *Earl* and the crisp yellow fried haddocks, tails in mouths, served between Whalsay, Skerries and Mid Yell …"

The Unst member on the Shetland County Council, Andy Irvine, found it difficult to express in words what he really felt; the good old ship had become so much part of life … a real and well-known friend to each islander. Her significance had been brought home to him one Monday when despite a southerly gale he saw the *Earl* "shouldering aside the billows of a raging south tide in Bluemull Sound on her way to Cullivoe," and he felt so glad at seeing her he expressed his depth of feeling in a poem which he sent to the press.

Written originally on the back of an envelope during the tenure of Willie Spence, reputedly the indefatigable mariner had the newspaper version framed and honourably placed in his peerie cabin below the bridge. Furthermore the crew were so impressed by this spontaneous tribute to their steamer that when Andy Irvine was next on the *Earl*, purser Davie Gray said, "No fare Andy." That intrepid commentator and satirist of the island scene remarked it was the only poem that ever paid!

It brought vigorous applause that evening in 1939, then 33 years later, in 1972, it was to stir similar memories on the retiral of Captain Willie Sinclair from the second *Earl* when he specially asked for the famous poem in the self-same hall at Baltasound.

Adam Robson 1982

Dennis Coutts

"DA *EARL*'S TOOT"

Da simmer and da hairst is past
An' winter comes in surly blast,
Wi wind an' rain an' hail an' sleet,
Da grund is just wan slush o' weet.
Up here inta dis Northern Isles,
Frae news and cities miles and miles,
Dere's just wan thing at helps wis oot,
We ken we'll hear da *Earl's* toot.

Tro darkness, wind and rain an' hail,
Shu comes twice weekly wi wir mail,
Shu brings wis up wir Christmas drams,
For Unst, like 'Lerwick Then and Now'
Is weet and dry by turns, I trow.
She carries doon my bit o' rhymes,
She taks wis up da "Shetland Times"
Shu brings wis claes an' maet frae sooth,
At warms wir backs and fills wir mooths,
An' folk could never get aboot,
If it wisna for da *Earl's* toot.

Shu's been troo muckle strain and stress,
Shu's backit in frae Muness Ness,
Shu's had her rudder split in twa,
Shu's been on Robbie Ramsay 's baa,
An' ae time apun her roond
She brook in twa at Baltasoond,
Dey raised da ends, shoved in a middle,
An dere she was as fit as fiddle,
Even sinkin' could na knock her oot,
Shu still could gie her cheery toot.

An whin da *Earl* gangs awa,
We miss her — yea, baith ane and a'.
We daurna ship wir stock to sell,
We get wir mails ower land frae Yell,
We canna blame da onken men
Da "Road ta da Isles" dey dunna ken,
But when da *Earl* comes ageen
We greet her, yae, lak some auld freend
An' we a' houp, week in week oot,
Shu lang may gie her cheery toot.

Andy Irvine went on to conclude: "The *Earl's* toot will soon be heard no more in the islands but her memory will linger on with the people for many a year. I can think of no more fitting place with which to close than just to say to her: 'Well done thou good and faithful servant'."

Major Hunter addressed Tom Gifford, thanking him for his seamanship, courtesy and kindness to all who travelled on the steamer. Amid deafening applause the captain rose to reply; "On behalf of the officers and crew and myself, I wish to thank you for the kind thought that prompted you to arrange this gathering here tonight and for the kind invitation extended to us through our good friend William Hunter. I also thank you for the many kind things said tonight. It is very gratifying to know that the little bit we do is so well appreciated and I can only say that in the future, as in the past, we shall endeavour to give you our best. I feel confident that when the new ship comes you will have a worthy successor to the old one."

Major Hunter brought in David Gray: "The last time you entertained us was the farewell to Captain Spence … tonight is the farewell to the old ship. I have been connected with the *Earl* since I left school … I am as pleased to tell you she is not going out of service in disgrace. Why I say this is because on 29th July she did Symbister Bay to abreast the Lerwick Fish Market in one hour, which is a record. But tonight I would like to say something about the new *Earl*; and the reason we are having this most up-to-date ship in the company.

"Mr Smith, our present manager, has, I think, made only one trip to the North Isles … he saw the necessity for better accommodation, also speed, for people of the North Isles who comprise over 25 per cent of the Shetland population. All that is required now is your co-operation to give the new *Earl of Zetland* facilities at the ports of call …"

He was inferring the lack of berthing, Baltasound apart, at North Isles ports and optimistically anticipating progress. He was not to know that a six-year war would pass plus many post-war years before anything was done at several obvious ports, although the developments came too late for the highway of the sea. Thus David Gray emerged as something of a visionary but …

William Hunter summed up: "And so we pass from the old to the new, but whatever ship may come to this northern isle of Unst we shall always remember the old *Earl*."

Wholeheartedly the audience rose to sing:

"So goodbye old ship o' mine,
And for the sake of auld lang syne,
Your name will live on till the day is gone,
Goodbye old ship o' mine."

The gathering dispersed in thoughtful and reflective mood into the August darkness, then at six o'clock on the Saturday morning, the birth of a new day, many came to the pier, some awoke and others stirred in their sleep as Captain Gifford tugged the whistle lanyard and the *Earl* sounded a farewell — and her thanks — when she turned south at Balta Isle for what they thought was her final visit to Baltasound.

Throughout the first half of August the routine run continued with Tom Gifford in command. The old *Earl* had Uyeasound as terminal twice, Yell Sound — Ollaberry — once, and Baltasound another five occasions. It was

Above: Mate Tom Gifford and purser Davie Gray in official mode below the bridge, both seen in welcoming passengers aboard at Lerwick. It would appear that Davie has tickets in hand … this in the great days of the steamer in the early 1930s.

on the fourth of these on Saturday, 19th August, that Willie Spence came back and witnessed the speeches on the *St Magnus* in favour of his former charge as well as skippering her into Lerwick.

The approbation had been remarkable and possibly unique. Neighbourhood and personal tributes abounded. Could any coastal steamer in any community in the universal sense have made a similar impact? The new ship had received a generous welcome while the ancient forerunner received plaudits in profusion. In the wide range of comments James L. Smith, Aberdeen manager, spelled out the intricacy: "She might tell us she sailed Shetland waters for a million miles; carried safely half a million passengers; almost half a million packets of His Majesty's mails; 200,000 ponies, cattle and lambs. That is not a bad record.

"She has carried Shetland people in health and she has carried them in sickness. She has served her owners; she has served her masters. She has known these masters. She has had their confidence. She has shared their anxieties. She has been officered by men who cared for her, and she has been kept ship-shape by seamen. She has been well engineered and she has had firemen. She has had stewards, she has had pursers. All are typical of a type of man and seaman second to none in this world …"

James L. Smith then asked the captains present, William Spence, Donald McMillan and Tom Gifford to be associated with the cheque for £100 as a memento of the *Earl* in a gift to the Gilbert Bain Hospital. Sheriff Wallace, who had made many trips on her, gratefully accepted this on behalf of the hospital board.

It was a moment of warm sentiment on the *St Magnus*. In addition to speakers already quoted, Mr R. J. H. Ganson, vice convener of Zetland County Council, replied to Mitchell Williamson's toast to "The Old Rock" and remarked that books could be written about the old *Earl* … he was very glad that they had retained the honourable old name *Earl of Zetland* in spite of the controversy that raged in the press. In the plethora of toasts

Mr J. W. H. Dickson in toasting "Town and Trade of Lerwick" confirmed that the warmest tribute the North Company could pay them was this ship. Bailie Magnus Shearer, who replied, spoke of the awareness of the links with Aberdeen and the company which had presented them with such a magnificent ship.

If the old to the new meant the beginning of the end it could only be attributed to progress, yet the exceptional poignancy had one final flourish. The old *Earl's* saloon proved to be a setting of singular value. She had come back after her North Isles "final flourish" from the Sunday into the Monday, 21st August, when she berthed at 2.40 pm alongside Victoria Pier. It was the final scene before the curtain rang down.

Lerwick Harbour Trust and their chairman Billy Tulloch, a familiar figure in Shetland, invited members of the shipping company and Captains John Scott, Spence and Gifford to the compact saloon. They gathered as soon as the steamer docked and were caught up in nostalgia. Captain

Below: A port bow aspect emphasises the sturdy construction of the old steamer, her plating well defined. The vitally essential anchors are sharply etched and in an extraordinary way the starboard anchor neatly replaces the head of a passer-by, while above possibly one of the crew leaning out over the stem takes up a stance not unlike a figurehead! With the fo'c'sle canvas dodger removed details of the deck arrangement can be noted. Another man seems about to go below at the hatch by the anchor windlass. Meanwhile, others stand in the well-deck apparently looking out into the harbour.

For reasons unknown the *Earl* is berthed alongside Albert Quay at right angles to her normal haven of Victoria Pier. Astern of the steamer is one of the old wooden stages, long since demolished, and the spectators there would suggest a special occasion, probably confirmed by the bunting brought alive by a breeze. The 'pilot on board' flies at her flag halyard above the bridge with its canvas dodger partially raised. Again, the year is 1938, although a possibility in 1939 when the second *Earl* came to Shetland. What a pity such a photograph could not be in colour!

Isobel Manson

Halcrow rose and surveyed the men grouped round the old bogey stove which had provided warmth for generations. He addressed Willie Spence "It is wonderful … service without a single fatal mishap … imagine the way successive commanders have woven themselves into the texture of public affection and memory. Indeed, I do not know what will linger longest in island memories the ship or her crews … for decades … the fine reputation she has. Some have joined the great majority …"

The intimate atmosphere of the saloon had its effect. James Smith, the Aberdeen manager indicating the immaculate black stove said, "As I have sat looking at the stove I have just been wondering how many stories have been told round here — some true and some not so true! It symbolises the history of the ship and her fine stature … I give you a toast, "Farewell to the *Earl of Zetland*." The company rose and drank.

An hour later, at 6pm the esteemed vessel led her successor and the *St Magnus* out into Bressay Sound. Off the lighthouse the new *Earl* dipped her ensign and turned back, a mere hint of diesel fumes atop the compact buff funnel, contrasting the dark streaming smoke emerging from the old

Earl's tall smoke stack. The low sunshine cast an ideal gleam on them. The booming sirens again echoed round the township, beaches, rock-faces and hills. A final parting. For a time the *St Magnus* kept company until her superior speed took her away to the southward beyond Mousa and the little old *Earl* was left ploughing along on the big expanse of sea beyond the Knab from which men, women and children watched her out of sight and bound for Aberdeen.

Above: Judging by the one pair of oars this could be the Whalsay flit-boat – not a soul in sight! Perhaps she is self-propelled! It is fortunate that the day is calm because, as was the case with many a cargo, freeboard was minimal. What would the Board of Trade have made of this?

Left top: The appearance of the bow of the *Earl* on the right shows how far her berth encroached into the Lerwick town centre near the Market Cross, helping her to be very much a focal point in community life. Lying at the Albert Wharf is a Swedish line-fishing vessel, with her small boat alongside.

Gas lamps are a feature and indicative of the pre-electicity period – power came to Lerwick only in 1930 – while the styling of vehicles and clothing suggests the early 1920s.

To mark the opening of the Victoria Pier in 1886 the Marquis of Zetland gifted an ornamental gas lamp to the harbour authority, to be known as the "Dundas Lamp" from the family name. The actual lamp is standing to the left of the *Earl's* stem and silhouetted against the water, but unfortunately it was eventually lost in pier layout alterations. The famous Diana Fountain stands in the lower left foreground.

Left middle: A wet and misty day in Lerwick, suggesting steady rain in windless conditions. The steamer is framed neatly between the town's rooftops. It is difficult to observe if she is going ahead or astern, but the wisp of smoke at her funnel and a hint of propeller wash at her stern suggests that she is leaving her berth. Just visible on the extreme right is a large funnel, probably that of the third *St Magnus* built in 1924, at 1591 tons the biggest vessel of the North of Scotland, Orkney and Shetland Steam Navigation Company. At the time of this scene she would be on the indirect run.

Left bottom: A view of the wheel-deck and bridge during a transitional era when the rails below had been sealed off from the inside with teak boarding and those above were tightly covered by what looks like canvas. As a minor concession to comfort a door was fitted at the after end of the catwalk as seen here. However these 'improvements' were little more than token. It all remained uncomfortably exposed; in fact, almost unbelievably, it remained that way until the years of the Second World War when a wheelhouse and bridge wing shelters were fixed. It was said that Willie Spence was known to come off the bridge with lips cracked and bleeding after a bad time of bitter wind and flying spume.

Here, however, the sun casts a benign light with the vessel under way off Yell, Donald McMillan in command. It is 15th July, 1924. The rather stylish ladies are enjoying the moment. Presumably the lifebelts on the bridge are red painted, then the funnel is still of a narrow version which could only be improved upon – and was in due course.

49

FROM THE OLD TO THE NEW – AND WAR

James L. Smith's formal attendance in Shetland back in June 1938 was, in essence, an official acknowledgement that the North of Scotland and Orkney and Shetland Steam Navigation Company Limited had accepted the view of the islands council that a new vessel for the inter-island service was not only desirable but vital. He had seen for himself the inadequacy of the old steamer, despite her abundant innate character as a friendly ship. It would now be a challenge for the designers of a replacement to come up with something comparable in atmosphere but modern in styling.

Meanwhile the new concept was appearing on the drawing boards in the premises of Hall, Russell and Company Limited at Aberdeen following an official order number of 749, and entered in the order book by hand in stylish copperplate writing. It was a personal touch in an era when technology was developing fast, though hardly at the computer stage! With the date of the order given as 1st December, 1938, the transference from design stage to building was in evidence as the keel was laid and plating began to rise rapidly to what would be port and starboard of the new ship. Throughout the early spring of 1939 the hull rose steadily plate by plate, just as had happened in the new weeks of 1877 when the first *Earl* was being created. There was a big slice of human life-time in between …

Even as the "new" arose to well-deck, then main deck, and bridge level, the "old" left Lerwick for Aberdeen and overhaul on 13th May, 1939. Tom Gifford had added the suffix "II" to the name and presently he wrote further in the "scrap" log: "Thursday, 18th May, went on a pontoon at Fish Market. 10am — left berth. 10.45am — on pontoon. 19th May at 10.34am — came off pontoon. Coaling at back berth."

Remarkably, a day later a few hundred yards from the pontoon, the brand new *Earl of Zetland* took the water in style.

The Aberdeen *Press and Journal* featured the occasion in the issue of 22nd May, 1939: "An appeal to Aberdeen people to visit the North Isles and support Aberdeen ships was made at the launch … from the yard of Messrs Hall, Russell and Company Limited, ship-builders and engineers, Footdee, Aberdeen on Saturday afternoon … the new ship is the first passenger motor vessel to be constructed at Aberdeen. Her progress down the slips was watched by large crowds. As she moved off, the ship was named *Earl of Zetland* …"

History was made, and echoed. Just as, "… Mr Fullerton entertained a select company in Merksworth House to cake and wine" so, "At a cake and wine banquet … Mr A. Hall Wilson presided …" 62 years later. Amid a variety of toasts Mr J. H. F. Gordon, a North Company director, whose wife had elegantly named the ship, said: "We all regret the passing of the old *Earl* — particularly Mr Smith, Provost of Lerwick, and the people of

Shetland who are very much in love with her — but I am sure they will be enamoured of the new vessel …"

Technicalities followed as noted in the schedule books: "Inclining. 5th July, '39: All tanks empty. Generators to go on. 2nd August, '39: Vessel undocked. 7th August, '39: Tanks full except forepeak and trimming tanks. 14th August, '39: Vessel on trials. Tanks full except forepeak and trimming tanks. Lubricating oil 5½ tons. Oil fuel 5 tons. Expectancy was high and was met in faultless trials off Aberdeen.

Sometimes comparisons between the old and the new are invidious. Here were two ships of different eras serving people of different generations with differing expectations, which were inevitable in the development of progress. But what the old *Earl* lacked in facilities she made up for in atmosphere; the new *Earl* would clearly have the desirable accommodation and equipment, but only time could serve to establish that indefinable ambience.

Although peace was now under serious threat in the summer of 1939 the veneer of normality had to continue and in the eyes of Shetlanders nothing was going to detract from the celebrations for the arrival of the successor.

The description of the interior gives a clear image of quality and taste: "On the main deck aft in a smoke-room, panelled in English elm and burr and Australian walnut, with chairs upholstered in green. Adjoining the smoke-room is a large dining-saloon, the main entrance to which is panelled in Nigerian cherry. The woodwork within the saloon is of maple, sapeli and sycamore … the chairs are of mahogany, covered in blue moquette to match the curtains and the flooring.

"Down the companionway between the smoke-room and dining-saloon are the first-class staterooms on the lower decks. Most of these are two-berth … also four-berth … a total of 38 berths in first-class. The second-class accommodation forward is in keeping with the general excellent appointments; the crew are also in the f'o'csle.

"On the main deck under the bridge is a large deck shelter, well lit with windows and furnished with basket chairs.

"The bridge has the most modern of equipment, including an echo-sounding meter and a 'Clear View' screen in one of the windows which permits an unobscured view being obtained even with heavy rain or snow. The steering gear is controlled by motor from the bridge."

The description added: "… a radiogram is installed in the saloon, from which music can be relayed by loudspeaker to various parts of the ship. Leading off the dining-saloon are the galley and the pantry, with up-to-date equipment, including a large Esse Major cooking stove."

The stage was then set for Shetlanders to see for themselves; the transition from the best of the present in tangible form. Initially this shaped

Aberdeen City Archives

ORDER BOOK.

NAME.	DESCRIPTION.	AMOUNT.	DATE OF ORDER.	WHEN FINISHED.

Left: The beautifully hand-written entry in the order book of Hall, Russell and Company Limited, dated 1st December, 1938, with the new ship priced at £52,500. It can be noted that the mv *Earl of Zetland* was launched less than six months later on 20th May, 1939, then within twelve weeks was on sea trials off Aberdeen.

Left: The very substantial rivetted plating of the hull makes an admirable clean-cut backdrop as Mrs J. H. F. Gordon, wife of one of the North Company directors, prepares to make the formal contact with the launch bottle. Hidden behind her forearm is a young member of the family while, accompanying her are Mr A. Hall Wilson and Lord Provost Mitchell.

Aberdeen City Archives

Right: A marvellous moment in time as the *Earl of Zetland* surges proudly into her natural element at the Hall, Russell slipway at Aberdeen. It is the culmination of months of designing, planning, implementing, constructing and furnishing; a ship come to life.

To her will fall part of the continuation of a zealous tradition in coastal shipping around Britain but with a focus on Shetland and Orkney which have from time immemorial been particularly dependent on sea links; and always will be so.

Aberdeen City Archives

Aberdeen City Archives

Left: Part of a big crowd of well-wishers, and the curious, on the historic day of 20th May, 1939. Like her predecessor the *Earl of Zetland* "… reached the water and floated successfully."

The Aberdeen harbour tugs take the strain, the *St Fotin* at the bow and *St Machar* behind. They were owned by the Aberdeen Steam Tug Company Limited, the *St Fotin* of 1902 vintage and the *St Machar* of 1898.

Sunshine blesses the occasion as a proud hull lies compactly in the water.

up in an unusual, maybe unique manner. It had been announced in April 1939 by the North Company that their new — first-ever — motor ship would bear the time-honoured name, *Earl of Zetland* and application had been made to the Board of Trade to place the suffix "II" after the name of the existing ship, then Tom Gifford had written accordingly "… Ship's name changed to *Earl of Zetland II*."

Although on nothing like the same scale as back in 1876-1877 there was some renewed comment about the name: "… it should include *Yarl* … here are a few of the names suggested: *Yarl Olaf; Yarl Harold; Yarl Eric; Nordland Yarl* — the latter being considered by many as very suitable for an exclusively North Isles boat … the *Yarl* itself would be quite suitable … just as today people refer to the present ship as the *Earl*". In fact the writer was not far wrong; seldom, if ever in Shetland was each ship known as other than "the *Earl*".

Thus it came about on Saturday, 19th August, 1939, *Earl II* sailed out of Lerwick to meet the new *Earl*. It was a poignant yet joyous moment, and unforgettable, for four North Company skippers. Willie Spence had come out of retirement to command the old *Earl* and she and the lovely white-hulled second *St Sunniva*, skippered by William Gifford, eased away from Victoria Pier to head down towards Mousa to greet the new *Earl of Zetland* from Aberdeen and the big third *St Magnus* out of Kirkwall, captained by Tom Gifford and Donald McMillan respectively.

For the first, and only, occasion four North boats rendezvoused. If not perfect, the day was cloudy/bright with a gentle breeze. The spectacle stirred the imagination, since it was symbolic of so much history and progress. The four vessels came up in line-ahead through the middle of Bressay Sound, each ablaze with colour, dressed overall, with the old *Earl* in the lead followed by her successor, then the *St Magnus* and *St Sunniva*.

There was another great surge of people from the Knab — like in 1877 when the old *Earl* came — anxious to witness the simultaneous arrival of four North Company vessels. Fittingly the entire scene became sunlit, accentuating the white flurry of steam at the funnel of each of the steamships, visual evidence of the booming sirens which echoed round the shores and into the hills.

An hour after the arrival of the "fleet", the newcomer carried the directors and guests on the afternoon cruise, prior to dinner in the *St Magnus*. Local public figures and businessmen had been invited. Mr J. H.

F. Gordon, chairman of the directors presided over a company of about 60. The toast to "the new *Earl*" was proposed by William (Billy) A. A. Tulloch, chairman of the Lerwick Harbour Trust who said, "… and I trust that the ship will be loyally supported by the public and continue to run as long as her predecessor …" Mitchell Williamson of Aberdeen Chamber of Commerce added, "… the old *Earl* is something of a chip off The Old Rock (Shetland) and the new *Earl* has much to live up to …"

In the evening of recollection, sentiment and optimism for the future, Captain Halcrow of Lerwick Harbour Trust toasted the builders. Mr C. S. Maclay, Hall, Russell shipyard manager, replied. He was very gratified at the interest being shown in the new ship. The trial trip earlier in the week had been very satisfactory …

On Sunday, 20th August, the arrival celebration continued. Uniquely both North Isles ships sailed out of "da nort mooth", the "old" setting out on her final voyage to Baltasound and the "new" bound for Yell Sound and Ollaberry, where she lay overnight, on a directors' cruise. Finally — or it should have been — at 6pm on Monday, 21st August, the ancient steamer bade farewell to Shetland as her successor's siren signalled Godspeed for her well-being in an unknown future. And that night the "*Earl's*" berth" at Victoria Pier was occupied by the MV *Earl of Zetland*.

Many folk in the North Isles had come to Lerwick to witness the coming of the brand-new motor vessel and were immensely pleased with what they saw; a custom-built ship to serve their ports. Admittedly there had been the gradual encroachment on the routes by the overland service and passenger motor boats were operating on Yell and Bluemull Sounds; Davie Gray's holding action with his Tuesday/Wednesday sailing of the old *Earl* could only be a stop-gap. Essentially then the new *Earl's* route

Below: One of the finest of all photographs of the new ship shows her at full speed on trial off Aberdeen on 14th August, 1939. Her 850hp Polar Diesel propelling machinery, supplied by the Atlas Diesel Company Limited of London, thrusts her splendidly through the calm sea, yet the way on the *Earl* sets her flags streaming in the breeze. The ship's pennant embroidered *Earl of Zetland* is at the foremast. This flag is now in the collection of the Shetland Museum in Lerwick, a priceless memento. It was given to the author by Captain Willie Sinclair when the book *The Saga of a Ship* was published, but then passed to the museum in 1984.

Aberdeen City Archives

was curtailed compared to yesteryear — but what could the near future hold in any case?

There was the fragile and insecure peace of those final days of the August of 1939 when everyday life had to have a veneer of normality, yet not felt by anyone. Even in the spring of that fateful year there were positive hints of preparation in the island. Whatever attempts Prime Minister Chamberlain was making, a sense of inevitability and futility was an insidious infiltrator of confidence within the population. Flying boats appeared at Lerwick, while a naval presence was gradually more in evidence and yet by the early summer the appearance of the herring boats gave a semblance of peaceful human activity. It was an anomalous situation.

Yet, since by definition it was not war, then peaceful matters continued. There was no need for secrecy about the first programme of voyages amid the isles by the new ship, thus she was advertised in the Shetland press as leaving Lerwick at 2pm on Sunday. Her calls were at Whalsay, Burravoe, Mid Yell, Uyeasound and with Baltasound pier for overnight berthing. Off again at the crack of dawn on the Monday, she visited Uyeasound, Cullivoe, Brough Lodge, Mid Yell, Skerries and Whalsay en route to Lerwick. Then, unusually, she headed back towards the North Isles at 8pm on the Tuesday for Whalsay, Burravoe, Mid Yell and Brough Lodge with Uyeasound as terminus for anchoring. The return trip began at 8am on the Wednesday and was via Mid Yell, Whalsay and Lerwick. She left Victoria Pier again at 8am on the Friday to call at Whalsay, Burravoe, Mid Yell, Brough Lodge, Uyeasound and Baltasound, departing there at 6am again for Uyeasound, Cullivoe, Gutcher, Mid Yell, Burravoe and Whalsay.

Thus she was north-bound on Sundays, Tuesdays and Fridays, although fortnightly, on a Thursday, she made a voyage to Ollaberry, West Sandwick, Ulsta and Vidlin, with occasional calls at Houbie in Fetlar. Bastavoe was a fortnightly call too.

Such advertising was short-lived as far as the second *Earl* was concerned. One week it was there, the next it had gone, hingeing on that critical Sunday of 3rd September, 1939. Thereafter the ship sailed in a cloak, not so much as of secrecy, as of non-information. A veil is drawn over all movements and she presumably continued with the North Isles and Yell Sound passage in the highly uncertain first long weeks of the war.

The chances of enemy activity increased as the weeks wore on, although Tom Gifford and his new crew, including his brother Lowrie, who lived on Bressay, and Sammy Harrison the engineer of long standing, were

Below: Every age has its expectations and what is feasible for one will not necessarily be acceptable to another, especially when there is the march of progress. When the *Earl of Zetland* appeared on the scene in 1877, "… the internal fitting up has received careful attention … a large saloon and a ladies cabin in the poop, furnished in a handsome style … a poop deck which will form an excellent promenade for passengers in fine weather …"

Given that "fine weather" all was well but otherwise … what shelter? The saloon could be warm and comfortable on a poor day, yet for no one on board, crew or passengers was there real comfort. In 1877 there was no bridge; the wheel was on the open deck; everyone was in it together.

Come 1939 and there was the change of progress: "On the main deck, under the bridge, is a large deck shelter, well lit windows and furnished with basket chairs … the bridge has the most modern of equipment …" This photograph makes an eloquent comparison; perhaps, truly what you have never had you never miss.

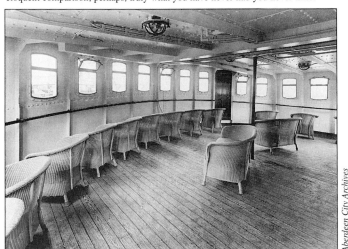

The care taken in design is illustrated by the photographs of the stair-head and smoke-room, the variety of wood veneers showing up particularly well in their varied textures.

Above: To the left and right of the companionway are the dining-saloon doors, "… in Nigerian cherry," with a central glazed panel neatly curved at top and bottom of each one.

Below: In the smoke-room here is the visual confirmation of deckhead, bulkhead, deck and seating finishes; "… panelled in English elm and burr walnut and with chairs upholstered in green."

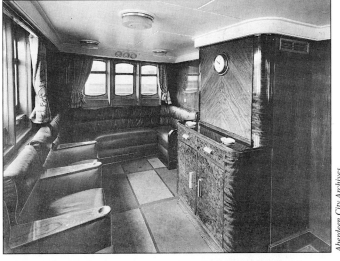

Above: A pleasant perspective of the dining saloon, specially arranged for the presentation photograph and looking immaculate. All the public rooms had been, "… decorated and furnished from designs prepared by a well-known firm of Glasgow specialists … throughout finished in a pleasant and artistic manner."

The table lower left was the "Captain's Table" for a succession of skippers like Gifford, Ramsay, Johnston, Sinclair and Gray.

Aberdeen City Archives

preoccupied enough in "breaking in" the new ship and familiarising her with the people and the port. Inescapably the harbour at Lerwick became a centre of activity and therefore more likely for German attention. With the flying boat base and aircraft lying in the North harbour local firms were commissioned to maintain supplies and Hay and Company's launch *Freefield* was active ferrying items to the anchored planes. As early as January 1939 the RAF invited local firms to apply for the agency but Hay's lost out in favour of Robertson's (Lerwick) Ltd. Yet Hay and Company's premises at Freefield, both buildings and land, were let for storage of materials and such as bomb scows, cradles and dinghies. With Shetland's strategic position in the north-east Atlantic the *Earl's* men were acutely aware of the build-up of defences; gun emplacements, jetties, landing runways and vast numbers of Nissen huts to cater for the invasion of service personnel who were ranged over the islands from Sumburgh to Saxa Vord. The frantic building of jetties and landing stages seemed a total irony to the *Earl's* crew when for decades the lack of piers in the North Isles had been a sore point with the folk; and a further ironic twist was the fact that, Baltasound apart, the ports were not of strategic importance. Yet the *Earl* herself was, in her wartime grey paint, crucial for both civilians and troops on what was the domestic front within Shetland.

Like Orkney, presently the scene of the new *Earl's* wartime activities, Shetland was practically sealed off from the rest of Britain, becoming what was known as a protected area and no one was able to enter or leave the islands without permission. Communications with the south became erratic since the steamers *St Clair, St Magnus* and *St Sunniva* were all commandeered by the Admiralty, being replaced by smaller vessels like the *St Fergus*. Furthermore, ships from Shetland had to be in convoy which meant delays for travellers, this in contrast to the *Earl's* fairly regular, though unannounced, routine throughout the Yell Sound and North Isles areas.

If the wartime pressures were building up, the autumn of 1939 was the period of the "Phoney War". Britain and France were passive externally but a turmoil internally in preparation; action was confined to dropping leaflets on German cities; there was probably a reluctance to make the first aggressive move. Meanwhile, German aircraft became increasingly active. The *St Clair* steaming north off Sumburgh Head in the October was subjected to what could be described as a "fly-past". The incredulous crew

watched in amazement as a JU88 came from astern and flashed past below mast height in a crescendo of engines and blur of shape and insignia, the gloved hand of the pilot raised in salute. Suddenly the war seemed very near.

There was an apparent anomaly in the German tactics. By 18th November, 1939, the *Scotsman* newspaper could report with truth that enemy aircraft had visited Shetland on more occasions than any other part of Britain — possibly the distance and lack of aggressive defence gave the Luftwaffe its best chances for testing capabilities of pilots and planes. Isolated bombs were harmlessly dropped, but on 13th November twenty exploded, reportedly killing a solitary rabbit, then on 22nd November six Heinkels came in low and attacked and destroyed a flying boat in Lerwick harbour … before defences were effective.

The month of December was a period of gales although German aircraft were active over Unst and at Sullom, then on 1st January, 1940, in gloriously bright sunshine, HMS *Coventry*, lying in Sullom Voe had a narrow escape from a bombing run which wrecked the New Year dinner arrangements!

With such a build-up of enemy air activity, and her almost day by day work up Shetland's east coast, the *Earl,* in essence, was "running the gauntlet". It would have been surprising had she not been raided; and further astonishing that over her many runs to the North Isles between the beginning of September 1939 and January 1940 there was only one reported attack. Since that occurred on 22nd November, 1939, it seems likely she was bombed by one of the aircraft which demolished the flying boat at Lerwick.

The ship was south-bound and according to the engine-room log had left the unlikely port of Bastavoe at 6.55am, calling at Uyeasound, Cullivoe, Mid Yell and Whalsay. She had off-loaded a few passengers and sundry items there, before leaving the anchorage at 11.22am. There was good visibility and a moderate sea running when the *Earl* was just off the Flaeshans of Sandwick at the south end of Whalsay with the mouth of Dury Voe to starboard when Tom Gifford and the helmsman became aware of the aircraft. The ship had been under way a matter of minutes from Symbister as the Heinkel swept in from a southerly direction. Fortuitously the single bomb was not well aimed, falling harmlessly in the sea, although clearly heard within the ship. Long-serving engineer Sammy Harrison noted in his log: "11.25am German aircraft appeared over the vessel; one loud report heard in engine room. 12.07pm German aircraft again passed over the vessel, when near Brethern Rocks."

It could be assumed that the Heinkel had used up bombs and ammunition in the Lerwick flying-boat incident but in any event the *Earl of Zetland* had had a narrow escape which was duly reported by Tom Gifford to the North Company. James L. Smith the Aberdeen manager, who had so recently spoken at the transference of the old to the new *Earl,* was swift in his reply, dated 23rd November, 1939: "I have to thank you for your very prompt report of the incidents which took place yesterday and am glad to know that you and your crew, and all on board, escaped any hurt. As you say I can hardly think that the enemy tried to hit you — at any rate let's hope he didn't."

If the reply was somewhat platitudinous at least it was both sympathetic and prompt, and no doubt a reassurance for the morale of the crew whose stay in Shetland waters was now known to be short-lived because they had been informed that, in January 1940, the new *Earl* would go to Orkney waters for troop movements while the old, with her roving activities over the Pentland Firth from August 1939 onwards, would come back to Shetland to traverse her familiar pathways of the sea for a time unknown. The grand indefatigable *Earl* had survived the First World War which would see the end of all global conflict and perpetual peace would ensue — at least that was the theory; meanwhile she had so very unexpectedly become embroiled in the complexities of the Second World War.

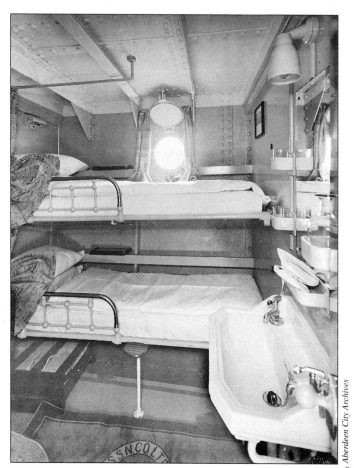

Left: A compact two-berth cabin, "modern" in its time and offering "facilities", i.e. wash-hand basin. This is in contrast to expectations of the 21st century when "facilities" often imply not only wash-hand basin but shower and toilet.

Although on the deckhead the substantial rivet-heads show, these do not detract from the neat appearance of the accommodation, while soft furnishings of patterned curtains plus the company logo on the rug enhance the satisfying effect.

Life jackets are stowed under the lower bunk and a framed diagram of how to fit is above the upper bunk. However, the single wood step for the upper bunk suggests the need for an athleticism in getting up! It could also be an awkward projection with the roll of the *Earl!*

Aberdeen City Archives

LOOKING BACK TO THE HALCYON DAYS OF THE *EARLS*
A SECOND PICTORIAL ESSAY – THE COMING OF THE SECOND *EARL*

Shetland Museum

Above: A reminder of a highly significant moment in the annals of Shetland on that Saturday, 19th August, 1939. The "old" makes way for the "new".

Isobel Manson

Left: Tom Gifford, now skipper of the new *Earl*, and mate Willie Sinclair, about 1948.

Tom Gifford effected the transition from old to new *Earl* in 1939. In April that year the North Company announced that a new motor ship would bear the same name *Earl of Zetland* and, unusually declared her predecessor would then have the suffix 'II'!

Then, in a marvellous touch of sentiment, when the new *Earl* came to Lerwick Willie Spence returned to his old charge to lead the newcomer (Captain Gifford) through 'da Sooth Mooth'. The date was Saturday, 19th August, 1939. Then came the Second World War on 3rd September that year; existence and lives were changed at a stroke. For the next six long years Thomas Gifford guided the *Earl of Zetland* in the troop movements in the Pentland Firth, while the *Earl of Zetland II* worked her familiar route in Shetland until December 1945.

Meanwhile, William Nicolson Sinclair first appeared as mate of the new *Earl*, if briefly, in 1944, but he joined Captain Gifford in December 1945 on a more or less permanent basis and they worked together as captain and mate until 1950 when Tom Gifford was given the comparatively new *St Clair*.

Willie Sinclair then was mate, mainly to Captain J. M. (Jimmy) Johnston from 1951 until 1965, when he assumed command of the MV *Earl of Zetland* in September 1965, a captaincy lasting until almost the advent of vehicle ferries in 1973.

Shetland Archives

Above: A semi-formal group on the stern of the old *Earl* during the late afternoon of the day of the coming of her successor. A full and shapely bow forms a backdrop. Back row, left to right: J. Scott MBE, second skipper of the first *Earl*; S. Harrison, chief engineer; Captain W. Spence (retired); A. B. Laurenson, clerk, Lerwick Harbour Trust; W. A. A. Tulloch, chairman, LHT; R. J. H. Ganson, LHT; L. W. Smith, LHT; Captain Thomas Gifford; L. Laurenson, LHT. Front row: centre, Captain A. Halcrow, convener, Zetland County Council; and left and right are directors of the North of Scotland and Orkney and Shetland Steam Navigation Company Limited.

Isobel Manson

Isobel Manson

Left and above: Captain Thomas (Tom) Gifford, in his shore-going clothing, has a yarn with docker James Tait at the end of Victoria Pier. The stern of what is possibly the *St Clair* (II) of 1937 is behind them, moored in the customary berth for "da sooth boat".

James Tait, popularly dubbed "Jeemie Sheeksie" was a weel kent personality around the port of Lerwick, who relished yarning about every conceivable local subject – and more forby! The second, close-up, photograph reveals a face of rare character. He had three sisters, Mary, Christina and Annie.

Another docker at Lerwick, nicknamed "Whalsay Willie" was also a character, and depicted on the foredeck of the *Earl* in another photograph. He was something of a rival to "Jeemie Sheeksie".

Right: The arrival of the new *Earl* in Lerwick on 19th August, 1939, has been well documented as this series demonstrates.

Magnus Shearer

Shetland Museum

Left: A moment in time … the old *Earl* is just berthed at the Albert Wharf and the new *Earl* is going gingerly towards her place at the Victoria Pier, observed by a solid wall of spectators. Meanwhile two lads have a good vantage point by the bows of the aged steamer and amid the barrels of fuel. Away beyond the crowd, the sturdy *St Magnus* is manoeuvering in.

Right: Here we see the incomer easing alongside, with a crowd on the pier, glimpsed through the mast, derrick, rigging and bunting of her forerunner. Lying off, but about to come in is the *St Magnus*, while the *St Sunniva* is not yet in the frame.

Magnus Shearer

Left: Donkeyman Bertie Pearson makes the most of a brilliant Shetland day at the bow bulwarks. He had had wartime experience in trawlers out of Aberdeen, thus was well versed in engines. Occasionally he sailed as second engineer on the *Earl*.

Leslie Smith

Right: A glimpse into the "inner ship" serving the "inner man"! The cook, Alec Smith from Camb, in Yell, has a look at his cooker, possibly in an off-duty moment judging by the cigarette poised between the fingers of his right hand! Steward John Rognaldson looks over the top, jug in hand.

In the heyday of the famous Snowy Owl in Fetlar in the 1960s there was a big influx of bird enthusiasts of an international flavour. They came from near and far with the result that the *Earl* was busy to the extent there were two unprecedented sittings for lunch to the discomfiture of Alec Smith who was not slow to give the bird "the bird", so to speak!

Leslie Smith

Left: A study in concentration for the task in hand. The ship is heading out of Baltasound and Willie Sinclair conns her into the sound past Balta and Huney islands. Harry Johnson is at the wheel … the immediate environment is an incredible contrast to the wheel on the open deck of the old *Earl*.

Leslie Smith

Right: Routine maintenance. Each *Earl* was scrupulously cared for both on a day by day basis and on annual surveys and overhauls. Here wire-brushing and scraping prior to re-painting are underway on the foredeck. On the left is Hughie Pottinger, accompanied by Willie Anderson. Further aft, and concentrating, is "Peerie" Robbie Tulloch from Cullivoe. The *Earl* is lying at Baltasound.

The seat/liferaft on the left looks a more comfortable design than the kind placed on the foredeck of the old *Earl*!

Left: The second *Earl*, like her predecessor, had crew who were familiar figures to folk at the ports and regular passengers. Willie Anderson from Yell stands on the left, with Tammy Laurenson (known as "Tammy O'Gorie") from the east side of Bressay. He served in the whaling industry in South Georgia during the Second World War.

This photograph was taken with the vessel north-bound amid the islands during an overcast day. Passengers stand around on the foredeck, while the bridge perspex wind-break is seen to advantage. Also the engine room telegraph looks immaculately polished.

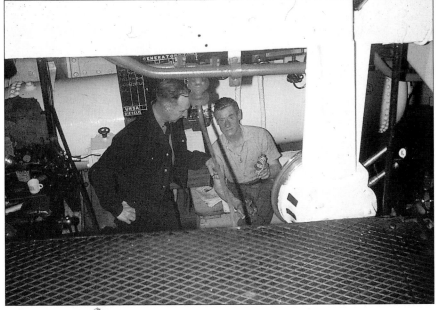

Right: An engine-room scenario. Lewis Burnett in conversation with Alexander Geddes from Buckie, who was donkeyman. He was always known as "Akie" and knew both *Earl*s.

Leslie Smith

Left: Lewis Burnett, chief engineer, from Aberdeen, awaiting orders. At a later date he emigrated to Australia.

Below: A unique view of the shaft-tunnel. This illustrates the compact access for maintenance, including safeguards from the spinning shaft. Drums of lubricating oil are in evidence under the curving frames of the ship's underwater structure at the stern.

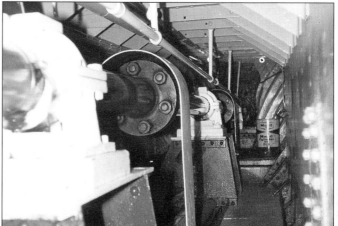

Leslie Smith

Below: The Polar diesel engine was designed to be cooled by raw salt water direct from the sea, but this had severe limitations, particularly in winter when the engine could be extremely difficult to start from cold. In fact oil rags would be put into the scavenge space below and set alight to provide some initial heat! Reputedly the *Earl* could take an hour to start up and she habitually sent perfect smoke rings up from her funnel during what could be a frustration for engine room staff. The original engine was so strongly built there was little evidence of salt water corrosion, even later in the ship's career.

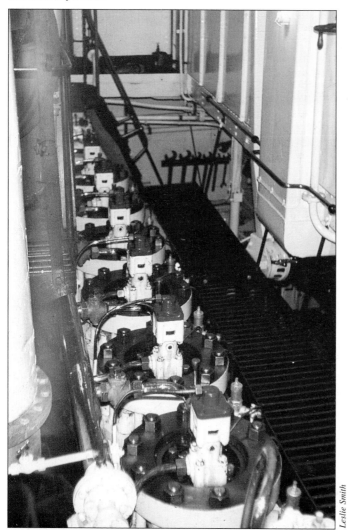

Leslie Smith

Leslie Smith

Above: A clear view of the fuel pumps. Each individual unit (cylinder) was served by its own pump, ensuring the correct measure of fuel to each injector. It can be noted that the gauges are "live", indicating that the ship is underway. Probably each vessel has some peculiarities or idiosyncracies and the *Earl* had her own – rolling was one – and on the signal "full astern" with the engine-room telegraph the engine had to be stopped and put into reverse. This meant that the propeller was idling and in a tideway it could be still turning, keeping undue way on the ship. Each skipper in turn learned to judge accordingly – Whalsay could be tricky with the tide-flow in South Voe!

Right: Nearing the end of yet another voyage to the North Isles. With her flared bow and compact shape the *Earl* always succeeded in looking purposeful when underway. Lit by afternoon sunshine she is characterised by a big bow wave, as if implying an urgency to reach the Victoria Pier at the earliest possible moment. She is nearing the north entrance with the Holm of Beosetter in the background and with her "Pilot Aboard" and "Red Duster" flags stiff in a southerly breeze. Of course she is not far from Robbie Ramsay's Baa which compromised the old *Earl* so dramatically in 1924.

Left: Arrival at Mid Yell. The figure of Willie Sinclair, then mate, casts a line towards the pier, prior to the hawser being hauled out.

Right: A superb day in winter. Heading north out of Whalsay during a spell of high pressure weather. Unusual features in this shot are the snow-covered foredeck, including the tops of the bollards, and the foreshortened aspect of the derrick with the end of it catching the sunlight. Also the sheen on the paintwork of the mast.

Seen on the port side of the mast, suspended, is the lamp cage. This was for an oil "at anchor" light. It was standard practice at overnight stops, lying at Baltasound Pier, at anchor in Uyeasound, or at Victoria Pier, to shut down completely. The ship would be without the generator, therefore without electricity, a policy which persisted well into the 1960s. However, batteries were available for cabins and some circumstances, while the *Earl* had oil-lamp fittings throughout at key places.

Shutting down was sometimes said to be a save money "penny pinching" attitude by the North Company. Certainly as noted elsewhere the inter-island ship became gradually less cost-effective.

Over the next two pages is a series of photographs depicting an amalgam of the ship and crew taken on the relatively new pier at Symbister, in May 1975, during what was her ultimate voyage there. It could be a sad moment, although the sun shines in morning light. It is a sentimental journey for former skipper Willie Sinclair.

Left: Harry Johnson operates the derrick winch. The P&O flag flutters in the southerly breeze at the bow in this strong perspective of the ship.

Right: Handling boxes of sachets of milk for Whalsay. From left: Peter Manson, Lowrie Smith, Gordon Smith (mate) and Davie Drummond.

Left: Sachets unloaded and on the pier; left is Robbie Williamson and on the right is Tammy Reid, steamer's agent at Whalsay.

Right: David Wilson, chief engineer, and Hector Strachan.

Left: Left to right: Bruce Simpson, mate; Willie Sinclair; Hance Smith, mate (retired); Hector Strachan, chief engineer (retired); and Jim Tait, captain.

Right: Most of the men in this group sailed the *Earl* south on her departure from Shetland. Back row, from left: Eddie Knight, second engineer; Bobby Scott, chief steward; Dave Drummond, able seaman; Alec Sim, assistant steward; Lowrie Smith, able seaman; Peter Manson, able seaman; Dave Wilson, chief engineer; and John Abernethy, donkeyman. Front row: Harold Young, cook; Jim Tait, captain; Harry Johnson, bosun; and Gordon Smith, mate.

Michael Gray

Above: Bright afternoon sun lights the hull and superstructure as the ship eases down and loses way in the approach to Cullivoe in Bluemull Sound. The date is 6th October, 1972.

A David Shearer container stands in the well-deck beside the hatch; the shape of things to come in sea transport. Three men by the flagstaff anticipate probably coming alongside at the pier.

The rocky stretch of coastline of Unst between the point of Hoga Ness by Belmont up to the Blue Mull also catches the warm light.

Right: An idyllic day. Morning light glints off the superstructure as the *Earl* moves effortlessly away from Victoria Pier, with Bressay and Maryfield House basking in the sunshine. A flat calm offers a lovely rhythmical reflection of the ship. This would be in the 1960s. In the background is Gardie House and the then relatively recent council houses at Voeside.

The Author

David Nisbet

Above: Another angle to calls at Yell's principal community on the shores of that particularly sheltered inlet called Mid Yell voe. In earlier days, long before the arrival and development of road transport there were, of course, three flit-boats operating. Sail is much in evidence in photographs elsewhere in this publication during the era of "da auld *Earl*", but here a motor flit-boat is snug alongside, under the flare of the "new" *Earl*'s bow. A soft wind ruffles the surface of the sea on a bright day in the early 1970s.

Below: High summer. The pale blue of the machine in the foreground complements the impeccable black of the *Earl*'s hull as she swings away from the pier at Mid Yell in 1969. The figure of Michael Gray can be discerned on the bridge and passengers are clustered along the port side and at the stern appreciating the moment of departure on a fine day. The cloud-flecked superb blue of the sky and the hillside at the Head of Hevdagarth form a beautiful backdrop, further enhanced by the clear blue of the sea.

David Nisbet

Brian Patton

This is the *Elida*, a dual-purpose creel and flit-boat, built for Sandison of Baltasound by the late Andrew and Gordon Laurenson in the early 1960s. The engine was a Lister diesel about 10 hp and air-cooled. The pipe at the stern, suitably guyed, is an upswept exhaust. The year is 1972.

Top left: The flit-boat comes in at the well-deck. Jim Johnson deals with a taut bow rope. At the controls is John Cluness, skipper, a great local character in Uyeasound. Aft, bending over may be Bill Thomson. Passengers, including Jack Renwick, recognisable by the hat, peer down at what is always a fascinating transfer of goods and people. In the background is Uyea Isle.

Above: Boxes and crates galore have been loaded. Passengers follow, assisted by John Cluness, and steward Bobby Scott.

Left: The *Elida* gets underway, her immediate task completed. She shows compact and sturdy lines as she moves away from the *Earl* to the little enclosed harbour at Uyeasound.

THOSE WAR YEARS
THE ORCADIAN SCENE

In the summer of 1919 the phrase on the lips of millions had been "the war to end all wars is over." Yet when Marshal Foch of France learned of the form of the Treaty of Versailles he commented with remarkable foresight; "This is not a Peace, it is an armistice for twenty years." Despite the creation of the League of Nations that same year and the deterrent of a dreadful sacrifice of human life in the First World War, mankind again slid into the abyss of another near-universal conflict two decades later, as implied by Marshal Foch.

In August 1939 the final days of a precarious peace were overshadowed by the rapidly deteriorating situation in Europe. Britain had resolved to stand by Poland in her hour of need, subjected as she was to bully-boy tactics by the German Third Reich, and amid the subsequent general mobilisation throughout the United Kingdom civilian shipping was subjected to immediate requisition. Vessels of the North of Scotland, Orkney and Shetland Steam Navigation Company Limited were inevitably drawn into the forefront. August dragged to a close. Neville Chamberlain, the British Prime Minister waved his futile paper of Treaty with Adolf Hitler to a sceptical British public and the Dictator promptly issued his "Directive Number One for the conduct of the War ... the date of attack on Poland, 1st September, 1939; the time of the attack 0445". Britain was committed. The mobilisation had already begun as war was declared on Germany on Sunday, 3rd September, 1939.

Amid the hectic activity nation-wide, thoughts of selling the first *Earl of Zetland* were countered by ideas that she might yet be useful and, indeed, even in the last days of that fateful August she appeared to have a roving commission. On 30th August she was at the company's Matthews Quay in Aberdeen, ready to load, with Captain Logie in command. Then on she went to Kirkwall with a full cargo, thence to Scrabster. She was there by the late afternoon of Saturday, 2nd September, and even as Neville Chamberlain announced on the Sunday morning to the Nation that we were at war with Germany, the venerable *Earl* sailed for Scapa Flow. Of course she had ended her 62-year commitment to Shetland's North Isles by Monday, 21st August, 1939, taken over by her stylish successor, and she was laid-up in Aberdeen until the 30th. Then for a time the old *Earl* assisted the first *St Ola* on the traditional Scrabster/Stromness run over the Pentland Firth. The *St Ola* had been built in 1892 by Hall, Russell and Co. of Aberdeen. She was 47 years old in 1939, thus the two vessels between them shared 109 years!

However, just to add to the remarkable diversity the *Earl* plied between Kirkwall and Aberdeen with the odd call at Wick, interspersed with being laid up again in Aberdeen in September and again for most of October and November 1939. From 27th November until 22nd January, 1940, skippered by famous Orcadian William Banks, she worked with the *St Ola* under government direction, until superseded by the second *Earl*, taking up a formal Scottish Command (Army) requisition. Thus it proved to be a very varied period in the chequered history of the two ships of the same name, *Earl of Zetland*.

Despite some 30 crossings of the capricious Pentland Firth in association with the *St Ola*, the old *Earl's* voyages were incident-free

although her limitations were obvious enough. Her cargo capacity was restricted; her passenger facilities left much to be desired; she was anything but fast and, therefore, more vulnerable to enemy attack. The answer was quite clear. There had been talk for some months amid the folk that the new *Earl* would be sailed in Orkney waters, while her predecessor would return to Shetland.

The North Company were action-minded and anxious to offer ships and personnel as the situation demanded. Certainly the old *Earl* had been involved in a hectic round of activity over the early months of the war and epitomised the spirit of co-operation expressed in a fine little booklet produced by the North Company after the war, in December 1946: "Daily — hourly — requests from the Admiralty, the Ministry of War Transport, Army and other Service departments were acted upon ... Soon the Company's ships were drawn into the maelstrom of war — the bitter unceasing struggle between merchant ships (at first ill-armed, almost defenceless) and a powerful enemy, winging the skies and lurking below heaving waters ... Widely varied was the cargo handled in the general trade to Orkney and Shetland, amounting to about half a million tons; from guns, explosives and ammunition, to vegetables, ice, clothing, hardware, fruit, motor cars, vans and ambulances, with as many as 2000 individual consignments in a single cargo. Indeed a mixed bag from the means of dealing death to the necessities of maintaining life ... As for livestock, an important part of the Company's work, 176,000 sheep, 35,000 cattle, 4500 pigs and 3000 horses were transported over the war period as well as 1,300,000 packages of HM mails. In the course of these sailings the company's vessels completed 1600 voyages, steaming about 840,000 miles — a distance equal to more than 33 times around the world."

Yet the fates were to bring infinite variety — very greatly affected by tragedy — to the lives of millions world-wide before that retrospective booklet was published in 1946. Meanwhile the first *Earl's* stay in Orkney waters was about to end. As the New Year dawned in 1940 she was still involved in her day-by-day three-hour run across the Pentland Firth, with Captain William Banks still in charge. Frequently she was in Stromness, but generally the route was between Scrabster and Scapa. Eventually she came alongside at Scrabster on Monday, 22nd January, berthing at 1.55pm, and there she awaited her own hand of fate. Thus she sailed into the unknown at 5pm the very next day, Tuesday, 23rd January, 1940, under command of Captain Adam Tait, an Aith-born Shetlander who was destined to pilot the old ship throughout the war years, serving the North Isles of Shetland. They were to prove hectic and action-packed.

The new *Earl of Zetland*, now requisitioned by Scottish Command, was used initially for troop movements from Scrabster and within Scapa Flow. She was under Military control from Stromness and for the first two months she was a regular visitor to Scapa (pier), Lyness and, occasionally, to Longhope and Flotta. Overnight lie-overs were shared between Scrabster and Stromness, although occasionally such as St Margeret's Hope was utilised, being another secure berthing place.

The "hand-over" between the two *Earls* had been a smooth, if entirely informal, transition. It was inevitable that the new motor vessel would take over from her predecessor because of the vital nature of Orkney as a strategic point in Britain's offensive and defensive structure; speed and carrying capacity in shipping would be crucial. It was, of course, being assumed that the veteran *Earl* could cope with events on the east side of Shetland; at that time, when Adam Tait sailed his new command to Lerwick, the Germans had yet to invade and occupy Norway — Bergen as near to the town as Aberdeen.

In any event the new replaced the old in Orkney waters before the end of January 1940 and even as Adam Tait recorded his inaugural voyage in his written log-book, Tom Gifford was skippering the new *Earl* in the beginning of a huge number of troop movements in support of the fortress which was Orkney. No evidence has emerged as to the likelihood of the

Anderson Manson

Left: The first *Earl*'s counterpart in Orkney, the *St Ola*, had a 59-year career serving on the Pentland Firth, although she did not have the *Earl*'s spectacular ending, being broken up at Charlestown on the Forth in 1951.

For many years the Shetland steamer relieved in Orkney during the *St Ola*'s overhauls and is in evidence here leaving the dock at Scrabster before heading to Stromness in May 1939.

two *Earls* coincidentally being seen together during that first month of 1940 in the Scrabster or Stromness areas but … the old steamer had been berthed at Scrabster by Captain Banks on 22nd January and a mere twenty-odd hours later she was en route to Shetland … the new ship, "… took up Military service between Scrabster and Stromness on 23rd January …" Could she have been in the Caithness port even as Captain Tait and his crew were preparing to set sail? Might they have passed each other? The matter is academic but interesting.

Thereafter the two vessels had divergent wartime careers. Captain Gifford and his crew fell into a fairly regular pattern of leaving the Scottish mainland about noon and crossing over to Stromness, often with a call at one of the Scapa Flow ports. The *Earl* would then head back to Scrabster, reaching port between five and six in the evening. Of course Scrabster was her "home" berth over those war years, although her Saturday sailings were generally north-bound only, giving week-ends in Stromness. Each Monday she was back on her daily routine.

The demands of troop movements were heavy, to the extent that eventually several ships were needed for the Pentland Firth connection. The aged first *St Ninian*, the other North boat involved, was joined by the *Morialta*, a new ship built in Aberdeen for Australian owners but requisitioned by the Admiralty and apparently managed by the North Company from October 1940. Then there was the first *St Ola* working the commercial service and relieved by the new *Earl* when on annual overhaul. In fact, Captain Gifford and crew had the distinction of serving naval, military and civilian operations year by year and "living dangerously" in the face of possible attack from an enemy-occupied northern Europe, as did so many other vessels.

The old *Earl*'s departure for Lerwick in January 1940 might well have been the end of her appearances in Orkney waters, yet there was a final flourish. In a rather anomalous situation, on release from military duties the new *Earl* came back to Shetland and covered the North Isles route from December 1945 until early March 1946. Her namesake had been reallocated to the Pentland Firth for general assisting work for some weeks from 20th December, 1945, and then returned briefly to the North Isles of Shetland until June 1946, before heading finally for Aberdeen and an unknown fate …

From accounts — and there are not many of them — the new *Earl*'s wartime sojourn was relatively free of hazards despite the multitude of crossings of that turbulent stretch of water named the Pentland Firth, where wind and tide in conflict could raise mountainous seas, forby the attendant risk of air or submarine attack. The stated figures of 100,000 miles and 600,000 passengers speak for themselves … it remains a telling record of consistency.

The Orkney and Shetland defence system was dubbed OSDef and the *Earl* was known as their own troopship. Regular leave rosters for services personnel were in position, while units were changed in rotation, all leading to a great deal of movement of people, not only within OSDef itself but over the United Kingdom defences. There was, for instance, a big exchange of anti-aircraft units during 1941, when some, brought to the islands in 1939 and 1940, were relieved by equivalent units from the south. Similar exchanges were made with coast-defence gunners.

Such a range of regular movement kept the *Earl* at full stretch as she ferried vast numbers of service-people to and from Scrabster, as well as links with other Orkney ports, albeit with some discomfort in traversing the sometimes awesome Pentland Firth. Like the elderly *St Ninian*, built in 1895 and notoriously prone to rolling, the *Earl* could be lively, as described elsewhere. Many a serviceman — or woman — was mightily relieved to step ashore at Scrabster, then onto the comparative calm of a troop-train on the way south from Thurso railway station. But nevertheless other vessels in the same seas could pose identical problems — not so much the ship as the sea!

The copy-letters appearing on page 68 from Movement Control in Thurso and in Stromness illustrate succinctly the value of the *Earl of Zetland* and her crew in the eyes of the military authorities; they are splendid testimonials to a ship which, despite some rough passages off such as the famous rock pillar the Old Man of Hoy, was very popular with passengers.

When the time came to return to Shetland after derequisitioning, the ship was paid tribute in the island newspaper *The Orcadian* of 29th November, 1945. Under a heading "Earl of Zetland Au Revoir", the article went on: "After being on the trans-Pentland Firth route for the past six(sic) years conveying Service personnel, the MV *Earl of Zetland* (Captain Gifford) made a final call at Stromness on Thursday … her sturdy and easily identified form entered Stromness harbour for the last time under present conditions. Having discharged her human freight and shipped a final consignment, a lot of good-natured chaff and banter took place before her departure … To the accompaniment of much siren-blowing she backed away, turned round in the harbour and sped out Hoy Sound for Scrabster. Except for RMS *St Ola*, there has been no more familiar vessel entering Stromness Harbour during the six war years than the *Earl of Zetland*. Her visits will be greatly missed and the good wishes of the townsfolk go with her on her return to the normal round in Shetland. Au revoir the *Earl*!"

The new *Earl* had sailed from Scrabster to Aberdeen for reconditioning in that November of 1945. In her final call at Stromness she was still featuring the drab wartime grey which no doubt figured in the spontaneous humour of a unique moment. No time was wasted in her refurbishment, because Shetland needed her which, in a way, would symbolise the renewed life in islands freed from the yoke of war. By early December the smart black hull, with white upperworks, had been made as good as new, while the attractive buff of the funnel set-off her appearance perfectly, thus when she sailed for Shetland from Aberdeen at 5pm on 10th December, 1945, she made a picture reminiscent of her appearance during her trial runs six long years before. *The Shetland Times* commented: "The *Earl of Zetland* arrived on Tuesday at 1pm after a smart run from Aberdeen. The vessel is in fine condition despite the large number of wartime passengers carried, and is a credit to Captain Gifford, his officers and crew."

Although there was lively interest in her appearance in Lerwick, the immaculately presented motor vessel created rather less acclaim than she had done on 19th August, 1939. She was unloaded immediately, took on cargo for Yell Sound and the North Isles and sailed from Lerwick at 4am on the Wednesday, 12th December. She left her predecessor lying forlornly alongside the innermost part of Victoria Pier, until she had steam raised for transference to the Pentland Firth — again! Eight days later, on 20th December at 4pm, she got under way, skippered by William Ramsay, yet another Yell man, with Leonard Mainland as mate. About 15 hours later they took her into the all-too familiar Stromness, her orders being to temporarily assist the *St Ola* on the run from Scrabster. Thus ended the saga of Orkney for the two ships of the same name *Earl of Zetland*. Now, relief work apart, and occasional social and sporting links, by the new ship, the Orcadian scene for both *Earls* had come and gone — it had been one of wartime necessity yet had had warm associations.

Right: It is not surprising that the old *Earl* was acknowledged as being in tip-top condition. Like her successor, the North Company ensured regular maintenance. Here is a reminder of an overhaul visit to Aberdeen for the first *Earl of Zetland*.

Movement Control,
THURSO.

Captain Thomas Gifford,
Master, M/V, Earl of Zetland.

My Dear *Cpt Gifford*

Before leaving Thurso, I must
place on record the thanks of Movement
Control, particularly myself, for all
that you have done for this Unit in
the 2 years I have been stationed here.

It has been a grand partner-
ship, and I have never known such smooth
working between a ship's company and a
"shore gang".

Your owners should be proud of
the Ship and her complement.

We have asked you to do some
almost impossible things, and you have
always tackled them with a smile and
willingly, and I for one am grateful.

I look forward to a meeting
after hostilities and to a cruise in
the "Earl" in her own home waters.

Yours very gratefully,

Captain, R.E., (99550),
Staff Captain, Q, (M),
Embarkation Commandant, Thurso.

2.3.43.

Isobel Manson

Headquarters,
Movement Control,
Osdef Ports,
Stromness

23 Nov. 45.

Dear Captain Gifford,

Lieut. Col. Sir J. R. H. Graham V.C. wishes me to offer
you and your officers and crew of M/V Earl of Zetland
the very sincere thanks from himself and Officers and
Staff of Movement Control for the magnificent spirit of
co-operation and good will which always existed between
your whole Ship's company and Movement Control in the
Orkneys and at Scrabster for so many years.

It was very hard for me to sever at such short
notice an alliance lasting only a few weeks short of four
years, and I am most grateful for the helpful collaboration
and useful advice which you were always ready to extend to
me and which helped to surmount many a difficulty.

We all wish you, your officers and crew a very
happy future and such a port as you would wish in which to
drop anchor when you retire from active Service.

Yours Sincerely,

A. C. Holmes

Captain T. Gifford, M. N.,
c/o North of Scotland & O & S Steam Navgn. Co. Ltd.,
Matthews Quay,
Aberdeen.

Isobel Manson

Left and above: Taking into account the determined attack by the German JU88 on the old *Earl* off Muness and near Skuda Sound, Unst, in Shetland, on Saturday, 4th October, 1941, it is not surprising there was at least one bombing incident involving the second *Earl*, also on the east side of Shetland. That the standing of the *Earl* and her crew was high is confirmed by two letters to Captain Tom Gifford, held by his family.

ORKNEY

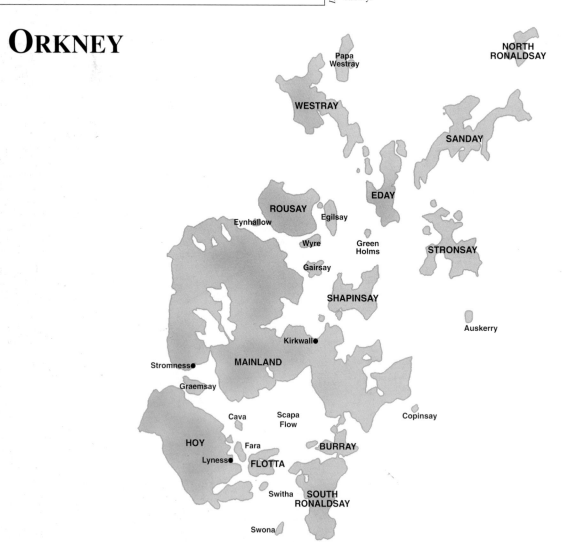

NORTH RONALDSAY

Papa Westray

WESTRAY

SANDAY

EDAY

ROUSAY

Egilsay

Eynhallow

Wyre

Green Holms

STRONSAY

Gairsay

SHAPINSAY

Auskerry

Kirkwall

MAINLAND

Stromness

Graemsay

Cava

Scapa Flow

Copinsay

HOY

Fara

BURRAY

Lyness

FLOTTA

Switha

SOUTH RONALDSAY

Swona

THOSE WAR YEARS AND THE OLD *EARL*

Captain Adam Tait had been mate to Captain William Leask sailing on the *St Clair* during her demanding schedule between Aberdeen and Lerwick, before the requisition by the Admiralty in January 1940 to become HMS *Baldur*. He was in the midst of a well-earned short leave at his home in Edinburgh at the end of the third week in January after the *Clair* had been taken over. A Sunday morning was ideal for some relaxation but his moments were rudely interrupted when the Leith agent of the North Company called. Apologetic though he was, the message was unequivocal and to the effect that the *Earl* was lying at Scrabster in urgent need of a skipper to take charge of her for the North Isles of Shetland. Adam Tait had been nominated and they were anxious for him to take her North immediately, the new *Earl* being requisitioned and just then heading to Orkney waters from Lerwick.

As the troop train trundled towards Thurso his thoughts were many and varied. They were of home and family; the *Earl* and crew; the North Isles — unknown to him; the war in relation to Shetland; the islands and their strategic importance in the Northern Approaches; the question of Norway less than 200 miles away and more than likely a German invasion there. At Thurso there was a quick overdue lunch hence over to Scrabster, given a naval order, taken down to the ship which lay alongside with steam up, introduced to Shetlanders, David Henry (a nephew of the fine seaman Colin Henry) from Gutcher in Yell, who was mate, David Gray still "part" of the steamer and purser, and John Findlay, the engineer; and given orders to clear off as quickly as possible to the east or west of Orkney.

Thus, still surprised, Adam Tait found himself on the bridge of the *Earl of Zetland II* that dark and bleak late January day, suitably clad to withstand the snow coming with a strong south-easterly wind. So the fates of combat ensured that the little steamer coursed north past Sumburgh Head — was it really 63 years since she had first come? She berthed at Victoria Pier, virtually unnoticed, on the still grey morning of 24th January.

When Adam Tait took his ship north to Uyeasound on 25th January, 1940, on the first wartime voyage by the old *Earl* to the North Isles the sole armament was a Winchester .5 repeater rifle!

This ludicrous, totally inadequate, state of affairs lasted until early July, when the *Earl* sailed alone — no convoys for her — to Aberdeen for some defensive equipment. A large kite to be flown at the end of a fine steel cable (in suitable wind conditions!), an ancient Lewis gun, and a gadget called a Holman Projector were fitted. The Holman was unique, temperamental and frequently more frightening to its users than to any enemy. The principal was simple. A Mills bomb was fired into the air to deter (or destroy) aircraft engaged in low-level attack. A length of steel piping formed a six-foot barrel which could be swung about freely and the firing power was either compressed air from a bottle, or a steam supply from the boilers. Utilised mainly by smaller vessels, the device was often only powerful enough to spit out the bomb uncomfortably close to the hull. All the weapons on the *Earl* were tried out off Sumburgh Head on the return voyage. They successfully projected one Mills bomb a respectable distance, fired off 20 rounds with the Lewis gun and flew the kite for 5 hours in a moderate easterly wind.

Variety had been a feature of the old *Earl's* peacetime existence, especially in the days of sailing vessels, and inevitably the risks of war created incidents as well as those from other factors. The steamer continued her conspicuous series of salvage episodes within weeks of her return to Shetland.

Winter darkness had reluctantly given way to grey daylight on 6th February, 1940. A west-bound depression ensured discomfort on land and danger at sea. The scattered dwellings on Unst were obscured by driving, icy rain; the wind-torn waters in the voe at Baltasound, slate grey and punctuated by white crests, indicated the state of the sea outside. It seemed likely that the *Earl*, due that evening, would have sheltered somewhere, maybe at Mid Yell. No other vessel was expected.

The ship was inside Balta Isle before she was noted, a shadowy form in the gloom, steadily moving into the voe, a slab-sided hull riding high, acquiring more definition as she neared. Those on shore watched with curiosity as the big three-island steamer with the tall vertical funnel amidships kept moving further into the voe beyond the pier; she would be aground if she ventured that far ... there were ballast heaps; even the *Earl* had struck one about 40 years before. From the pier the anonymous steamer loomed large against the low-lying land at the far side of the voe

as a cloud of rust dust on her fo'c'sle indicated at least one anchor down. She swung bows on to the increasing gale.

Severe overnight gusts blasted the unknown vessel and she had dragged in the blackness of the night; by dawn she was aground on sand and shingle at the top of a spring tide, white water breaking round her. After daybreak Charles Sandison of Hamar, Baltasound and the Coast Prevention Officer boarded the vessel from the lee side by the proffered rope ladder. In broken English her master explained she was the *Vahva* from Tallinn in Estonia in ballast to an English port. He insisted on a tow to get his ship afloat.

As anticipated, Adam Tait had sheltered in Mid Yell on 6th February. On the next day he logged: "Strong SSE wind. Overcast. Rain at times. Rough sea and heavy swell on passage to Baltasound. Boats having difficulty in coming off at ports of call." Once alongside the only pier in the North Isles Adam Tait met Charles Sandison, acting on behalf of Garriock, Lloyd's agent in Lerwick. Presently the North Company Limited telegraphed: "Attempt salvage of ss *Vahva* at own discretion."

David Henry and John Findlay boarded the Estonian and found a worried captain: "It is blowing strong. I am in despair if the wind rises any more." Soundings around the steamer indicated that she would float, assuming tanks pumped out. On the morning of the 8th Adam Tait wrote: "7.30am. Left pier. Strong SE wind, overcast, raining." Then 75 fathoms of the *Vahva's* eight-inch manila rope were linked to a bridle of 2-45 fathom lengths of the *Earl's* five-inch rope, the ends attached to the bow and stern of the grounded vessel. The North Isles steamer was anchored to windward which was the only possible position; the *Vahva* had her anchors raised. It was 9am and ballast tanks had been emptied.

The water churned white under the *Earl's* stern. Inch by inch the tide

Below: Captain Adam Tait.

Jessie Irvine

rose round the Estonian's hull until after 45 minutes of tension she budged slightly, then was freed from the sea bed. And slowly, very slowly, the *Earl* dragged the 3655 ton bulk of the *Vahva* until by 10.30am she was afloat with enough water under her keel. The old North Isles ship had been rather more successful than she had been with the *Maella* in Lerwick back in 1922!

With the *Vahva* cleared and anchored the episode should have ended

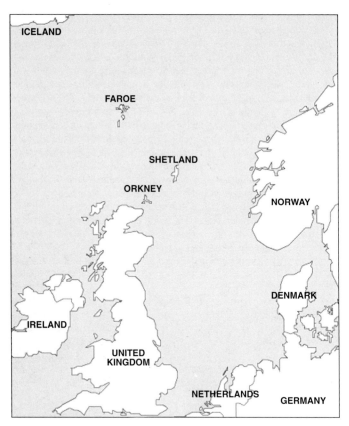

Below: A fascinating perspective shows the bridge-wing shelters and wheelhouse as effectively as could be wished. Why they were not fitted years previously will never be known. Could it be assumed there was a theory that the fresh sea air kept skipper and helmsman alert; or to prevent them falling asleep?

The old ship is in a transitional phase. It is 1946 and she is being "decommissioned" from wartime status. Here Willie Sinclair, mate at the time, rests his forearms on the canvas dodger and above is the ship's identification board *Earl of Zetland II*.

Shetland Museum

but the naval commandant at Kirkwall had learned of the stranding and ordered HM Rescue tug *St Mellons* to Unst, not appreciating that the *Earl* was already coping successfully. The tug was hurriedly bunkered and left at 4pm on the 7th. The skipper noted, "Proceeded out of harbour through SE gale; high, dangerous sea ..." At 8am on the 8th he logged: "Arrived Baltasound; contacted SS *Vahva*; vessel lying broadside on to rocky shore and aground fore and aft, strong SE wind and high ground swell. Vessel resting on shore. Island mail steamer trying to tow her off but unable to do so."

This was an astonishing interpretation of the situation, because Aldis communication between the *Earl* and *St Mellons* confirmed that the two ships would take the *Vahva* to a secure anchorage further out in the voe. And curiously enough there was no other mention of the *Earl* in the log of the St *Mellons* apart from a note of her departure.

There was a touch of irony in subsequent events. The powerful *St Mellons* transferred a rope to the stern of the Tallinn vessel while Adam Tait held her in the relatively safe position, ready to coax their charge out past the pier. Unfortunately the *St Mellons* tow rope was not controlling the stern which began to swing to leeward making the possibility of crashing into the pier with its interested group of locals observing the rust streaked hull with much of the rudder and screw out of the water. The seabed halted the drift, the *Vahva* was aground again. The onlookers breathed again!

Adam Tait had lost schedule time but the day was far spent and he anchored overnight. He left Baltasound early on 9th February, leaving the *St Mellons* with a not too difficult task, only a portion of the hull being aground. On the 10th the log of the tug recorded: "1400/10 *St Mellons* and *Vahva* arrived safely in Lerwick. *Vahva* handed over to charge of N.O.I.C.; safely anchored in harbour."

A compromise situation resulted. Legally the *Earl's* efforts had merited a direct, successful salvage claim. Yet the *St Mellons* log implied failure. The *Vahva's* owners were reluctant to co-operate and the issue went to arbitration. A sum of £3000 resulted in August 1940, £2480 of which went to the Admiralty, leaving £520 to be disbursed to master and crew of the tug! Adam Tait had made the incident quite clear to the North Company, who contacted the Salvage Association and negotiations resulted in an award summarised by James L. Smith: "Naturally we had to put up a fight to get a sufficient amount, but we considered the circumstances justified a reasonable payment, and that the good work undertaken by yourself and your crew deserved a generous part of the total paid."

The *Vahva* affair was a milestone for the *Earl's* crew; it had tested their teamwork, given considerable satisfaction and brought about a not unwelcome financial windfall. Routine followed. Week by week the steamer worked the Yell Sound and North Isles ports including Skerries, beyond which lay the threat over the horizon of Nazi aims in annexing Norway. Hitler had made the decision in mid-December 1939: " ... I am informed that the English (sic) intend to be there and I want to be there before them." The German propaganda machine had already declared that: "To Norway will be restored the Northern Isles (Orkney and Shetland) as 'living space' when they have been liberated from the yoke of Britain." By April 1940, a "cat and mouse" game developed. The British laid mines off Narvik which aroused strong protests in the Norwegian government, little aware of a drastic invasion of their territorial rights by a very severe enemy. The Germans struck at a variety of targets like Oslo, Trondheim, and Narvik in the north, with sea and air forces, including paratroops. Hitler had indeed come first, with vastly superior numbers. Norway was, essentially, an enemy stronghold and Shetland in the vulnerable position of being next door.

Short of an attack nothing could have brought the news of Norway's downfall to Adam Tait and his crew more tellingly than the arrival of the seaplane. They were northbound from Mid Yell to Uyeasound when the drone of an aircraft penetrated the noises of a ship at sea. They looked in wonder as the plane banked and curved downwards — no sign of aggression; then astonishment as it touched the sea's surface and settled in a great swathe of white foam. Adam Tait rang down, "Stop engines" and the seaplane taxied over. Her crew confirmed in English: "We just managed to get out. When we left the base the Germans were coming into Bergen." The plane's crewmen were the first of many refugees encountered by the *Earl of Zetland*. It was 9th April, 1940.

The Germans claimed a master-stroke in outwitting the British, who launched a major attack on a coastline for so long only associated with the colonising Vikings but, although there was an exacting toll on Nazi fighting ships, the attack proved to be abortive. Now the struggle in

Norway became introverted, yet such had been the British commitment at sea the enemy surface ships were essentially nullified for aggression. But Norway was firmly in German hands.

Since the *Earl* covered more than 45 miles of the exposed east coast almost day by day, she was often a welcome sight to beleaguered escapers from the long western seaboard of their besieged homeland. Norway had been physically overcome but not subdued in spirit. Through the introverted war they fought back and the immortal story of "The Shetland Bus" gradually emerged, the movements being a painful thorn in the German flesh. The island voes echoed to the familiar "tonk-tonk-tonk" of the two stroke, often Wichmann, engines of the Norwegian fishing boats with famous names like *Aksel, Arthur, Bergholm,* and *Sandöy.* This amazing saga of the spirit and the seas was immortalised by David Howarth in his superb book "The Shetland Bus" first published in 1951 and printed and published again in 1998 by *The Shetland Times.*

The refugees came in all manner of craft from small open boats to big fishing vessels. One 43-footer was eventually bought by George Leslie of Sumburgh. She came on the Shetland fishing boat register in 1942, listed as having been built in Norway in 1915. Named *Duen* she was used for fishing after the war. The *Erkna* was a much bigger vessel. Originally she was employed in fish transport from ports in north Norway to Trondheim and she was commandeered by the Germans. In early November 1941 she lay at Stokmarknes in the Lofoten Islands needing engine repairs and her owner, one Mathias Myklebust learned through the Norwegian Resistance in Alesund that the *Erkna* would be ideal to take a group to Shetland. Could he arrange for her to be "stolen"? The repairs were done, and the co-operative Myklebust then "abandoned" the boat in the hope that the scheme would work out in the ignorance of the enemy and the *Erkna* would win through to Shetland. Time would tell.

In the darkness of the night of 16th November two men, a skipper and an engineer, both members of the resistance, slipped the moorings for a stealthy short run to nearby Ulsteinvik. Nothing else moved. They half expected a German reaction but no patrol emerged and after nightfall boatloads of men climbed over *Erkna's* bulwarks. The final boat brought the total up to 60 personnel with the craft now ready for the clandestine voyage to Shetland and freedom.

At 0130 the next night she abandoned her moorings and headed out into the inhospitable North Sea, swaying westwards in conditions gradually worsening in visibility and sea form, which gave added security should the alarm have been raised. Daylight came and went then by 0500 on 19th November they knew a coastline would be in the offing, probably that of Unst. By early afternoon it was known they were somewhere between Fetlar and Skerries, still lurching violently in the near-gale. Two watchers on board spotted a vessel amid the merging grey of sea and sky but only just because she was also grey. They sensed she was an inter-island steamer, possibly bound for Lerwick — she looked friendly. It was providential they thought; contact seemed sensible.

Several hundred yards separated the vessels when two things happened. Simultaneously from each ship there was noted a dark shape swivelling, dipping into the troughs, lifting to the crests of the waves. Also, coincidentally the *Erkna's* engine stuttered then faded completely with compression trouble and she swung broadside, rolling heavily within a few boat lengths of the shape — now identified as a mine.

For the *Earl* — inevitably it was the *Earl* — the mine was a first priority. They had already proved a hazard by exploding on the Shetland coastline and by 1941 the *Earl* had disposed of thirteen. Crewman Magnie Fraser from Papa Stour had proved a crack shot with the steamer's rifle and armour piercing bullets, so the crackle of gunfire wafted in the wind and the mine sank.

Adam Tait and his mate, Davie Henry, had assumed that the drifting fishing boat of Norwegian appearance was another escape effort. A large number on board judging by figures at her bulwarks. They surmised she could have been destroyed by the mine. Time now to consider what to do about the strange vessel. The gap between narrowed.

Captain Tait indicated a tow, acknowledged by a wave of the hand from the *Erkna,* thus a line was passed, hawser attached and, with the Norwegian yawing about, they made slow progress up to the lee of Whalsay. There, Olsen, one of three Norwegian security officers working in rotation on the *Earl* boarded the refugee boat and came back with the advice to leave the 60 people where they were until both ships reached Lerwick. No chances to be taken he maintained.

Still the wind kept the sea up, meaning a slow uncomfortable passage through an area of water known for its rock hazards, thus Adam Tait was markedly relieved to hand his "guests" over to the naval patrol guarding the North Mouth, in the November twilight, his second wartime salvage securely completed.

The captain's report elicited an immediate response from Aberdeen. Manager J. L. Smith wrote, " … I congratulate you and your crew on this accomplishment …"

Early in the December Smith sought details of the *Erkna* … salvage claims were imminent. The subject was debated at high governmental level, not without disagreement, but it was not until April 1943 that the *Earl's* men had recompense for their labours … the North Company received £250, Captain Tait £13, Davie Henry, mate and John Findlay, engineer £6.15/- each. Davie Gray, as purser, Magnie Fraser, Robbie Robertson, Lowrie Gifford and Jimmy Grains, as seamen, Bill Knights and Andrew Cormack as firemen, Robbie Gray, as steward, and John Sutherland, as cook picked up £2.15/- each. Leask, the boy, had a single pound and 10 shillings! Wrote Mr Smith: "I trust that you and your crew will consider the result to be satisfactory in the circumstances." Their reaction was never recorded. In terms of risks amounting to danger, judgement in seamanship and responsibility for a ship in distress, it added up to a paltry award.

THE OLD *EARL* SOLDIERS ON

Such relatively meagre returns were characteristic, given reluctantly by owners of disabled or stranded vessels. This occurred again in 17 eventful months of the *Earl's* war. The location was the Unicorn Reef lying offshore in that infamous stretch of water between Whalsay and Lerwick's north entrance. The victim was the 80-ton Norwegian motor vessel *Haugen* more kindly treated by the jagged reef than the warship *Unicorn* of 1567 which was lured to a drastic end as she tore out her underside under full sail, in pursuit of a quarry. Her name was given to the hidden reef.

A moderate south-south-west wind had created a ground swell, the sky growing overcast as the *Earl* dipped her bows southwards into the undulating surface off Whalsay on 21st April, 1943. Adam Tait noted

Below: A crewman makes adjustments to the mainmast high above the aft guns fitted during the Second World War.

Shetland Museum

routinely in the log: "6.56pm Passed Mull of Eswick lighthouse". Fifteen minutes later Davie Henry observed a vessel: "That fellow's going to be in trouble if he's not careful."

They watched as the other ship, unaware of the danger, lurched onto the Unicorn, was held, and ground against the unyielding gneiss. The *Earl* was manoeuvred carefully in with a hawser passed and, eventually, at 8.10pm the *Earl's* log recorded: "M/V refloated. Engines in working order, but unable to steer owing to loss of rudder. Vessel leaking badly. Shortened tow rope and commenced towing towards harbour." Even services personnel on the *Earl* were enlisted to help keep the water level at bay on the Royal Norwegian Navy vessel which was berthed by another Norwegian with pumps available.

There was more interesting correspondence to the *Earl's* master from the North Company: " ... war circumstances seem to have resulted in salvage opportunities coming your way and I trust that the effective services rendered by yourself and your crew will be recognised in due course ..." And later, " ... We have found by experience difficulty in arranging matters with the Norwegian authorities ..." By mid-September (the incident was on 21st April) the confirmation of payment reached Adam Tait. "Our (the North Company) usual procedure is to apportion the total award, after deduction of expenses one quarter to crew and three-quarters to the owners ..."

Adam Tait did rather better than he had done with the *Erkna*, receiving £20. Davie Henry and John Findlay lifted £9.10/- each. The rest of the crew shared £36. It was the *Earl's* ultimate salvage adventure — the end of an impressive record of assistance to shipping in danger, given in the grand tradition of the sea, bringing the best out of a ship and her crew.

The catalogue of German aggression expanded. In Aberdeen the North Company offices had records destroyed in an air raid, while Shetland itself experienced some 240 alerts over the war years. Bombs were dropped in 27 attacks but without major destruction. What stirred up anger was the German habit of indiscriminating forays on defenceless people. School children in the country districts learned to dive for a ditch; wives of two lighthouse keepers lost their lives in calculated machine-gunning; a man had his arms smashed.

With such callous disregard for humanity the *Earl's* men knew their risk. Yet, for months after her return to Shetland in late January 1940 the *Earl*, although sighting German planes almost daily, was ignored, unlike the new motor vessel which had had the encounter with a Heinkel in November 1939. What is surprising — but fortunate — is that neither ship appeared to be seen in the lifeline context by the enemy and how if either or both had been lost, the effect on morale in both Shetland and Orkney would have been serious. Perhaps then the air raid on the old *Earl* was not unexpected and she had a narrow shave.

She had slipped her moorings at Baltasound in the early morning of Saturday, 4th October, 1941, a grey overcast day of moderate sea and reasonable visibility. An hour later she was due to alter course into Skuda Sound and with a call at Uyeasound. The lookout called: "Aircraft off port bow, heading south-west." It was 7.40am. The plane was far enough away to make identification difficult. It was then lost in the overcast. Fourteen minutes later the skipper scribbled in the scrap log: "7.54am. Crew ordered to action stations. Unidentified plane bearing south at approximately 4000 feet, distant 1/2 mile, heading westwards. Vessel rounding Ness of Ramnageo and heading NW x W".

Seconds later no one was in any doubt. In a rising crescendo of engines the JU88 banked steeply and came at the *Earl* from dead ahead. In a long moment of waiting, the crew, services personnel and a sprinkling of civilians, were painfully aware of possible destruction. That the German meant business became clear as five black objects detached from the plane's underside and plummeted at the ship. Any one of the five missiles could have meant the end for the *Earl of Zetland* and all onboard.

The whistle of the falling bombs was lost in the chatter of Lewis guns from fo'c'sle and bridge. The erratic Holman Projector immediately developed a leak in the air valve and was useless. Personnel on the bridge watched momentarily then flattened themselves behind the half-inch teak boarding where they doubtless prayed for salvation. Their escape could be regarded as a Godsend. Adam Tait glanced up as the bombs came straight in line but seconds later the beam wind providentially blew them off course.

When the detonations came Chief Findlay, below in the engine room, felt the staggering shock of the missiles which had struck the sea about 90 feet from the starboard side. The old steamer listed violently in the blast;

Above: A scraperboard impression by the author as the JU88 unleashed its potentially lethal load and banked away.

Grains and Cormack, the firemen, grabbed what they could to avoid being flung about. They wondered what to expect next, but the engines picked up the rhythm and the *Earl* sailed on.

Captain Tait commented: "That attack was a close call." Even then the result was sensational and petrifying. As the JU88 roared overhead, its guns spitting a shower of tracer a vast wall of water arose, blotting out the coast of Unst and Ramnageo in cascades of white which slowly subsided. The deck canted alarmingly in the blast before the *Earl* came back onto an even keel. Pursued by return fire the JU88 banked and was swallowed up by cloud to the south-east.

A quick scrutiny revealed that the sure hand of Fullerton, the Paisley builders, had made a strong ship. Not a rivet had sprung — only two coupling bolts at the tail end of the propeller shaft had broken. The funnel had bullet holes in it and there was evidence of bullet damage elsewhere.

The JU88 had escaped, as had its intended victim; although German radio reported otherwise. That same day, as they headed towards Lerwick, Lord Haw-Haw, in one of his "Gairmany calling" broadcasts announced that "a large troop transport" had been sunk on the east side of the Shetland Islands. The captain and crew of the *Earl of Zetland* took the liberty of assuming that they were the subject of the broadcast!

Headquarters, Shetland Defences, responded to the report of the incident. "The defence commander has asked me to write to you (Captain Tait) and convey his congratulations on your narrow escape in Skuda Sound on Saturday morning.

"He feels sure that the saving of the *Earl of Zetland* and her passengers must be accredited to your able handling. The quick action of your crew in answering the enemy's fire is a pleasing sign and it is hoped that, if the occasion should ever arise again, a 'bull' will be registered.

"The commander further hopes that the *Earl of Zetland* and her captain will continue to run the service between the outer isles and the mainland for many days to come, in spite of the Nazi's efforts. He wishes you and your crew the best of luck in future encounters with the enemy — may there be none!"

And there was none! But a contrasting and tragic episode created a great sadness amongst the crew just five months later. As the ship closed in on Out Skerries from Lerwick on Saturday, 1st February, 1942, a twin-engined plane caused "action stations." A slow-moving Blenheim fighter bomber was identified. As the *Earl* swung round towards the north-east entrance at Skerries the aircraft banked about a mile off Bound Skerry on which the lighthouse stood, and to the horror of the onlookers nose-dived into the rock pile. There was a grinding crunch, a flash and an immediate belch of fire-tinged purple smoke.

Within ten minutes of the crash the steamer was hove-to off the lighthouse boat-slip and Davie Gray went ashore in charge of a boat's party. He reported: "Three of the crew and myself went ashore … regret that death must have been instantaneous on impact. I assume it was the rear gunner who was thrown clear. The other two were burning in the wreckage … exploding ammunition and the heat was terrific, so we could not approach too near. But we made a careful check to make sure there were no more than three in the wreckage." A disconsolate group rowed back to the steamer, now anchored with the Skerries flit-boat alongside; behind them an enormous pall of dark smoke towered heavenwards, a funeral pyre for men who had run the gauntlet of German anti-aircraft fire in Norway.

Adam Tait's reminiscences are colourful and varied. Armaments were woefully inadequate early in the war; it is astonishing that even two years into the struggle — in 1941 — the *Earl's* weapons were so limited; elderly Lewis guns and an unreliable Holman Projector plus an unlikely "kite". So-called "J" Rockets replaced the Holman, although even those had a "Heath Robinson" flavour. Not long after installation they were inadvertently released by a curious visiting officer at Out Skerries who had pulled a lever "just to see if they worked"; they, the crew, did, scattering instantly to action stations! Long wires attached to parachutes drifted away over Bound Skerry. Only once were they used in anger in passage to the North Isles when a plane came at the *Earl* with seeming aggressive intent. The skipper held on until the last moment and fired the packages which seemed to work because the aircraft had to take quick evasive action! Only it proved to be a Blenheim. Yet British aircraft were instructed never to fly in close to friendly shipping — there was an RAF apology after the reported incident.

Effective armaments came too late. Near the war's end Colt Brownings with shields, mounted to port and starboard on a platform abaft the funnel and over the engine room skylight were capable of terrific fire power and even augmented by a powerful Oerliken on a stern emplacement as seen in the photograph on this page. The *Earl* would have been a prickly customer with which to deal but the guns were never used in anger and they contrasted the virtually unarmed second *Earl of Zetland* running in Orkney waters. Perhaps it was assumed the land and other weapons in Orkney were adequate cover … but when the JU88 assailed the old *Earl,* a couple of Brownings and an Oerliken would have offered real fire-power. The German may not have lived to fight another day!

There had been another occasion when they might have brought arms to bear although an old-fashioned ramming would also have been a possibility. They had left Baltasound in very early morning darkness, keeping well out past the Vere reef and giving the Baas of Muness a wide berth in a strong south-south-east wind, when the lookout reported a small light away to starboard and inshore. Davie Henry had remarked, "That might be some fellow in difficulty. It could be a ship's boat." Certainly with a rocky lee shore and breaking seas there could be a problem for someone. Of course the *Earl* was sailing blacked-out as was customary and with permission of Naval control, thus was well hidden in the darkness.

Adam Tait had turned her stern on to the seas and they progressed for

Below: It is the end of the Second World War and the drab, featureless uniform grey paint has been obliterated in favour of the familiar black hull and funnel, with buff masts and white lifeboats and rails. Perhaps appropriately the sun shines on the *Earl's* transformation. Yet an uncertain wartime is being replaced by, simply, an uncertain future … the old *Earl* is about to be offered for sale. A purchaser? The ship-breakers?

Meanwhile workers are aloft on the foremast apparently suspended precariously at different levels. Long overdue wing shelters are visible on the bridge, offering at least a modicum of shelter compared to the totally exposed bridge of well over 60 years previously. Such weaknesses in work conditions would not be tolerated in this 21st century.

The shrouded Colt Browning machine guns abaft the funnel and the Oerlikon emplacement at the stern are reminders of living dangerously in northern waters. Life-belts are in abundant supply on the rails!

Shetland Museum

Above: The old *Earl* forging ahead in Orkney waters.

Below: A cheerful John Findlay, engineer during the years of the Second World War. He also served on other North boats.

half a mile or so towards the mysterious light moving vertically in the water. Abruptly they were aware of the conning tower of a submarine, a dark rectangular shape, and her lookouts must have been startled enough because there was a tremendous flurry of water as she crash-dived close by the *Earl's* stem and was gone.

The affair was mentioned in Uyeasound and information passed to Naval Control in Lerwick, who confirmed there were no British submarines in the area. U-boats had, of course, dodged around the Shetland coastline during the First World War — Whalfirth being a case in point — and during the early stages of the Second World War a submarine had been noted in Bluemull Sound on a moonlit night running on the surface while, in fact, on 9th January, 1940, the Greek steamer *Torris Chandris* ran onto the same Vere reef when fleeing from a U-boat. She sank, taking her cargo of iron ore from Norway with her, not directly by enemy action, but in the act of escape. Perhaps she was claimed by Lord Haw-Haw too!

All the *Earl's* skippers had awkward moments with bad weather and Adam Tait recalled a tricky situation at Out Skerries: "One day in winter it was a relief to escape from a heavy sea into Skerries which was quite well land-locked and we worked cargo and passengers in reasonable comfort. But as we lay there the wind shifted round to the north-east and blew up directly into the entrance, blowing smoke very quickly.

"I said to chief Findlay; 'We've got to get out because she can't hold here very much longer, not with the wind in this direction' ... I had heard about the narrow north-east way into Skerries and how it could be a problem ... we had to go. The wheel needed three men. It was all manual. If she lost way and her bow caught the wind she could be in pieces; there was no room to manoeuvre.

"She staggered — I can see her yet — butted her way through and gradually ... we were clear. The sea was just like snow drifting. For hours we battled to get through to Mid Yell. It was bad but she just took her own good time. We were relieved to get there, went well in, put down both anchors and that was us for the night."

Adam Tait's command was rather shorter than it might have been. After an unexpected appointment in 1940 he had had responsibility in circumstances far more dangerous than any of his illustrious predecessors; probably the JU88's bombs summed up the risk — a fortuitous waft of wind, or maybe the Lord's guidance, stood between existence or eternity. At least by 1944 the Germans were wilting; in the islands movements were nearer normal. In September that year Adam Tait was appointed to lead the staff at the Leith Nautical College based in the ship *Dolphin*. It was a task he relished despite a reluctance to depart from ship and crew for which he had a real affection. But he took with him the goodwill of a community which had been under siege.

The natural successor was Captain David Henry from Gutcher in Yell, a fine fiddle player, who as mate had supported his skipper throughout the worst and uncertain days of the struggle. Now it was his task to pilot the *Earl of Zetland* through what were to be her last months in Shetland. He had been on her since May 1939, was well versed in her idiosyncrasies and knew the North Isles like the back of his hand.

Throughout the autumn of 1944 the old grey-painted steamer continued in her diversity of work and domestic circulation of the ports. Evidence of the recession in German power showed when the Shetland Home Guard was stood down before Christmas, while the Earl transported units of the forces away from the North Isles. Now there was nothing to fear from the enemy by air or by sea.

Clearly it had become a matter of time before German defeat and when the announcement came in Britain, on Monday, 7th May, 1945, the entire country rejoiced and celebrated. On the Tuesday, in company with communities throughout the United Kingdom, all Shetland exulted. Bunting flew stiffly before a strong breeze along the Lerwick waterfront. The *Earl* appeared, the brightness of her flags contrasting with the neutral over-all battleship grey of her hull, funnel and masts. It was the final opportunity, the last time the aged steamer would be dressed overall — and yet two years later she would be flying flags and displaying banners in a totally unexpected, even bizarre, circumstance.

The war had given the old *Earl* a reprieve that could not last, although the North Company maintained careful overhauls. Davie Henry took her away to Aberdeen for her final survey between 9th and 19th April, 1945. *The Shetland Times* recorded further transition on Friday 22nd June, with a heading: "Old *Earl* Discards War Paint", and a paragraph: "People in the North Isles will be pleased to welcome the old *Earl* (*Earl of Zetland II*) in

Anderson Manson

Shetland Museum

her peacetime paint again when she arrives today (Friday). Painting was done by the crew, with extra helpers, so that the transformation should be as complete as possible."

In Aberdeen plans were made for her disposal. The directors resolved to attempt a sale rather than commit the 68-year-old ship to the indignity of the breakers hammer — at least not yet. No one on board could then even begin to imagine the extraordinary manner in which she outlived her time, and brought life to bear on a cause of life.

David Henry guided her fortunes for several more months. Still the routine. No longer the threats, apart from questions posed by the weather. In July 1945 Captain Henry left the North Company for pastures new and Captain William Ramsay, another Yell man, took over. With the awful time for humanity ended the summer and autumn of 1945 passed peacefully; the lights of Lerwick and shipping were once more reflected in the waters of Bressay Sound and the island scene had been returned to its serenity of living.

The communities had been deprived of their new-found comparative luxury of transport on the highway of the sea when the new *Earl* went away after only four months in Shetland, albeit in wartime restriction and risk; now was the hour of her come-back after the prolonged departure of her namesake.

Curiously enough the old *Earl's* timing coincided with the passing of two men who between them had given yeoman service to trade and travel in Shetland. In mid-December 1945, the intimate atmosphere of the well-used dining saloon was the setting for a retiral presentation to the long-serving David Gray, who had devoted 40 years of his life to the North Company, 30 of which had been on the veteran steamer. Davie was given

a wallet of treasury notes subscribed by the *Earl's* crew, the Lerwick office staff and workers at Victoria Pier. Only 57 years of age, this outstanding character was forced to take a shore job through ill-health and became factor to the Garth Estate. Sadly, only months after taking leave of his beloved ship, he collapsed and died suddenly on 2nd March, 1946.

Less than a year previously it was the same Davie Gray who had penned a tribute to his former skipper, Willie Spence, who had died in April 1945. " ... Shetland has lost a man of physical strength and courage ... kindly ... obliging ... always minimising his accomplishments rather than magnifying them." If the slightly built purser did not have the physical strength, most of the remarks about Spence could have been applied to Gray himself.

In the autumn of 1945 the second *Earl* had, to all intents and purposes, taken over, but, astonishingly for the old there was one final foray in Shetland. Right after the war the Orkney agricultural economy expanded fast. The North Company had a new ship the *St Clement* on the stocks, but the Aberdeen - Kirkwall run needed shipping space and speed. The answer was simple; they would bring the new *Earl* south yet again. At least it was appreciated the arrangement would be very temporary when William Ramsay brought the age-old steamer back to Shetland — not for a week or two but for four months. This was met with resignation in the North Isles!

Finally — and it was finally — the *Earl of Zetland II* made her way to Aberdeen on 21st June, 1946, to be put on view for interested parties in response to the circular publicising the sale. Captain William Ramsay had the privilege of taking her south. He had as his mate William Nicolson (Willie) Sinclair, grand-nephew of William Nicolson, first skipper of the *Earl* who had watched her being built near enough 70 years before, and as

Magnus Shearer

Above: A reminder of the peacetime scene. This low angle reveals the attractive texture of the granite paving setts of yesteryear at the head of Victoria Pier. They were practical for horse-drawn traffic, although a new era has dawned; an Austin car of 1938 vintage stands below the bridge of the *Earl* and across the pier the big third *St Magnus* works cargo, while dressed overall; as is the inter-island steamer.

The fountain on the left, still carefully preserved today at the same location, was erected in 1890 by the brother of ship's surgeon Edward Smith in his memory. He sailed on the whaler *Diana*, wrecked in 1869 near the mouth of the River Humber. It was the end of the 13th voyage to the whaling. The first trip to the Davis Straits was in 1856.

Shetland Museum

Right: Another recollection of happy days. Getting underway for the North Isles in a summer dawn in the 1920s. Not only steam-up with the stoker hard at work below, but the saloon and cabin crew have the bogey stove going, the smoke wafting away in an early morning air.

The *Earl's* screw churns the water as she turns to port away from her berth. In the background is the silhouette of the Widow's Homes with the barely discernible Ward Hill on Bressay beyond.

The Old Haa Trust, Burravoe

Above: William Ramsay from North Sandwick, by Gutcher in Yell, went to sea near the end of the First World War in 1917 and eventually joined the North Company in 1937. He sailed for a time as mate with Willie Spence on the *Earl* and it fell to Captain Ramsay to skipper the old steamer to Aberdeen in 1946. He later emigrated to South Africa where he died.

his engineer Peter Johnson, son of another noted commander in the early years of the 20th century. The other coincidence featured the bo'sun who was the long-serving Lowrie Gifford whose brother Tom had captained the old *Earl* and was now destined to play a significant part in the North Company.

There was little to do in Aberdeen. They had sailed empty and berthed her beside the North Company offices at Matthews Quay in the lower harbour where she remained overnight. Captain Ramsay was called away next day, thus it fell to William Sinclair to take his great-uncle's ship through the harbour and up to Regent's Quay. It was a fitting touch of sentiment through a family connection, for her life in Shetland had been all about the family of the community. Her crew were paid off on 24th June, 1946, and the original *Earl of Zetland* was left to her fate. As she lay below Aberdeen's bustling Union and Market Streets, silent and lifeless, few people gave her more than a passing glance, knowing nothing of the pulsating life of her existence in Shetland. Within a year she was destined to lie similarly abandoned amongst a motley collection of ships in the distant port of Haifa, ultimately to be discarded and fated to be broken up. There would be no more reprieves.

As she awaited disposal throughout the months of July and August 1946, the repercussions of the Nazi disregard for all that is right and proper were reverberating round a world seeking stability in such a recent peace. That the timeworn steamer could conceivably have an influence on any aspect of it would seem utterly remote and any association with strange names like "Haganah", "Mossad", "Yishuv" and "Yehuda Halevy" highly unlikely. Nevertheless, she was to become part — a tiny microcosm — of a history-making project which arose partly from a deep-seated belief in a promised land for the Jews of the world and partly from a people — a vast community — desperate to escape all the evidence of a ravaged Europe.

But there was one rather poignant domestic touch to come. Freddie Pottinger of the *Earl's* crew and Willie Keir of the North Company's staff in Aberdeen had the invidious task of making an inventory of all the contents and fittings. Young Pottinger had joined as a cabin boy in 1932, and was subsequently catering manager of the North Company, but now there was the realisation that the beat of engines and propeller below the saloon would no longer set the crested crockery rattling on the dining tables; that the lilt of Shetland voices mingling with the bleating of sheep and lowing of cattle would no longer fill the air; that the clank and rattle of steam winch beside the open doors of the well-deck at a port would no longer be heard. Sentiment and sadness abounded. They removed all the evidence of human touch from barometer to basins — all taken to store, although old, somewhat stained framed photographs of Shetland scenes in the dining saloon and fitted to the wooden panelling were left. The ship gradually took on an anonymous quality as North Company items disappeared, but unmistakably, and proudly, there was the clearly carved name *Earl of Zetland* on the teak casing of her rudder quadrant at the stern. It was to remain her identification, as if refusing to lose all of her original character, right through to her demolition.

Tom Anderson

THE FINAL VOYAGING

The *Earl* had cost over £7000 when built; she was on offer for £6000 through Glasgow ship-brokers, Thomas McLaren and Company; she sold for £2650, ostensibly to the Anal Compania Provential SA of Panama through a Greek gentleman, Simon Pilides. In the agreement the signature of James L. Smith, manager of the North Company, was witnessed by Robert C. Mackie and that of Simon Pilides witnessed by W. H. Cunningham of T. W. Tamplin and Company Limited, ship-brokers, London.

In the background to the purchase there was the powerful influence of the Mossad and Haganah organisations, both dedicated to the creation and sustenance of a formal State of Israel and the *Earl* was destined to be drawn into the great fleet of Jewish illegal immigrant vessels; her former owners the North of Scotland and Orkney and Shetland Steam Navigation Company had assumed their steamer would be trading conventionally but little did they know …

In any event, the deal completed, by late November 1946 appropriate freshening up had been done, with the new name *Anal* on bow and stern; "Aberdeen" obliterated as port of registry, and "Panama" painted on her counter. Her new owner had seemed satisfied with progress and events, had appointed a mysterious Greek captain and an ad hoc crew, and a week before Christmas the steamer, laden with bunker coal, slipped unobtrusively down the harbour at Aberdeen past the North Company's offices at Matthews Quay and the *St Clair* lying alongside prior to her Thursday run to Lerwick. She was a mute witness of the former *Earl's* exit.

The *Anal's* arrival at the River Tyne on 20th December, and her departure the next day had been recorded. Three days later, on Christmas Eve she was noted in the Port of London where she lay until 10th January, 1947. By the 18th she had reached Brest for a week's stay and some provisioning.

The Bay of Biscay then proved to be a major obstacle when a severe gale tested her and the makeshift crew during a week of hard steaming which greatly reduced the supply of bunker coal. Gibraltar seemed a haven of rest to the sea-weary crew as the *Anal* slipped virtually unnoticed into the sheltered harbour below the massive rock-pile, a nondescript coastal vessel looking rather the worse of wear. She lay there from 1st February for almost three weeks. On the 20th of the month the former *Earl of Zetland* had entered the Mediterranean, bunkered and provisioned further.

It was the last lap of her voyage from Scotland prior to arrival and fitting-out at Marseilles. The coastal trip up the eastern seaboard of Spain had proved to be much less exacting than the open Atlantic with the land in close proximity and Almeria, Cartagena and Alicante appeared to port in quick succession, followed by low-lying Formentera and then Ibiza to starboard. Inconspicuously the *Anal* had slipped into the harbour entrance at Marseilles to berth at the ship chandlers quay set aside from the regular berths at the ancient seaport. And there she was to lie until the end of April undergoing what was to be the biggest change externally and internally since the ancient steamship had been lengthened in Aberdeen 63 years before.

Mossad representatives in Paris were reportedly encouraged by the deal done with Pilides, the Greek, although it was reckoned he had not lost on the transaction. The vital factor was the acquisition of a vessel which was well-found, seaworthy and with proven reliable machinery. The men recruited by Haganah set about the reconstruction task with zest and purpose, although it became obvious the work would take longer than expected despite the fact that the call had already gone out to the people, the Zionists, from Morocco, Algeria and Tunisia who were due to gather at a camp on the Algerian coast to anxiously await the arrival of their vessel. Nothing could be speeded up at Marseilles due to limited resources available, so by the end of March 1947 the occupants of the camp somewhat inappropriately named "Calm and Health," were considerably discomfited.

Their presence in the tented "village" near a town named Ténès, 200 kilometres west of Algiers, was the result of dedicated missionary zeal by one Ephraim Friedman, who persuaded the Mossad that there were, indeed, the numbers in this area of North Africa to justify a ship. The people there had given Friedman tremendous support in towns like Mostaganem, Sétif and Tizi Ouzou in Algeria, Casablanca, Marrakech and Tangier in Morocco, and Beja, Grombalia and Sfax in Tunisia; amid these and many other communities the Zionist committee, with Rephael Chemel and Yani Ostrowsky supporting Friedman, spread the gospel. This co-

ordinating committee co-opted a young Tunisian Jew, Nadia Franco, who did much to ensure notification to every potential immigrant, yet seeking confidentiality because the operation of leaving by ship in this way would be technically illegal.

Furtive though meetings in towns, villages and hamlets had to be, the concepts of Zionism divulged raised the highest aspirations in the minds of the would-be immigrants, thoughts of idealism in the best tradition of one Yehuda Halevi, a Jewish poet who was inspirational to those North African Zionists. He was born in Northern Spain near the end of the eleventh century, had great natural gifts in creative writing and a basic belief in the rights of Jews to their Promised Land. There were the Biblical proclamations: "And I will plant them upon their land, and they shall be no more pulled up out of their land which I have given them saith the Lord thy God … and they shall dwell in it even then, and their children and their children's children for ever." Motivated by this God-given incentive Halevi himself was drawn to Palestine and expressed this through his timeless evocation: "Doves who flock in distant lands — whose wings droop — rise up! Yours is not a place of rest. Your home is troubled."

Throughout the Diaspora — the dispersion of the Jews after the Babylonian and Roman conquests of Palestine; the Jewish people and communities outside Israel — there was desperation and an ardent desire to flood the land of Palestine with their people, exacerbated by the appalling Nazi genocide of the Jews of Europe during the Second World War. The unspeakable crimes became fully evident through the autumn of 1944 and spring of 1945. It was the attempted destruction of a race of human beings; a third of the Jewish world population exterminated. With such a background, the great upsurge of Jews in the Diaspora to attain unity, security and, hopefully, a lasting peace by the creation of the State of Israel, was so entirely understandable. It was the ultimate of incentives.

The situation was further compounded by the 1921 League of Nations mandate to the British for the control of immigration by Jews into Palestine, an invidious task for the British Government, especially when

---

20 years later a White Paper of 1939 decreed a cut back on immigration and purchase of land by the Jewish community. This brought burning and bitter criticism which led Jewish Prime Minister Ben Gurion to declare: "We shall fight side by side with Britain in our war against Hitler as if there were no White Paper, and we shall fight the White Paper as if there were no war."

Come in the Haganah (organisation for Jewish defence, founded back in 1920) with their policy statement declared on a publicity poster: "They are coming. Driven by the suffering they have taken, the one way of light for Jews in this world — the road to Israel. The world and the nations' hearts are closed to them. Only one hope exists — homeland. Only one heart is open — that is of the Yishuv (the Jewish population of the land), the heart of brothers. Cruel laws will not stop them, barbed wire will not frighten nor bayonets deter them; if denied, their spirit will not break. They come and they will continue to come to their homeland, the land of Israel." Come in the great motley fleet of immigrant vessels sailing mainly from a wide variety of ports around Europe. Come in the *Anal*, alias *Earl of Zetland*.

Back in Marseilles the steamer was gradually altered; the well-deck, so familiar to Shetlanders as a focal point, disappeared; between the wing shelters the bridge remained open but a large deckhouse engulfed the wheelhouse below and incorporated three latrines on each side. Two large cowled ventilators sprouted through the roof of the deckhouse; another deckhouse appeared abaft the mainmast. The Mossad paid close attention to safety. There had been loss of life with earlier immigrant ships in 1940

and 1942. The two boats which had served the ship for so long, the adequacy of which had been questioned away back in 1912 after the Lunna Holm stranding, were augmented by two more, one on top of each of the originals, with extended davits. Life-rafts were stacked on available roof and deck space — 15 in number.

Below, in every available corner, wooden three-tiered bunks were hammered into place; ladders fixed firmly through the former for'ard hatch space, leading to more cramped and claustrophobic sleeping quarters; a large fresh-water tank went into the forepeak near the anchor chain locker. Space had also to be found to maximise bunker coal supplies. Perhaps no port would be prepared to bunker a suspicious-looking vessel. Further, there could be delays due to bad weather. Even in April and May a Mediterranean storm could be vicious.

Such eventualities had to be considered by the Haganah team, two of whom, Palestinian Jews, Israel Kharkovsky and Eytan Sapodznikov were key figures in the reconstruction; indeed Kharkovsky was to command the *Anal* on her forthcoming mission.

The prolonged refit was at the finishing stage by the end of the third week of April. Provisioning and bunkering were organised, a mainly Spanish exiles crew recruited, the engines run after steam was raised. The well-worn power unit, so tenderly cared for by such men as Sammy Harrison and John Findlay was unlikely to fail now, even after so many years. The hull was as strong and secure as the best of the immigrant fleet. She was still a well-found steamer, ready for sea. At break of day on 28th April the *Anal* probed out into the Mediterranean.

THE VOYAGE OF THE *ANAL*
(LATER TO BE KNOWN AS IMMIGRANT SHIP *YEHUDA HALEVY*)

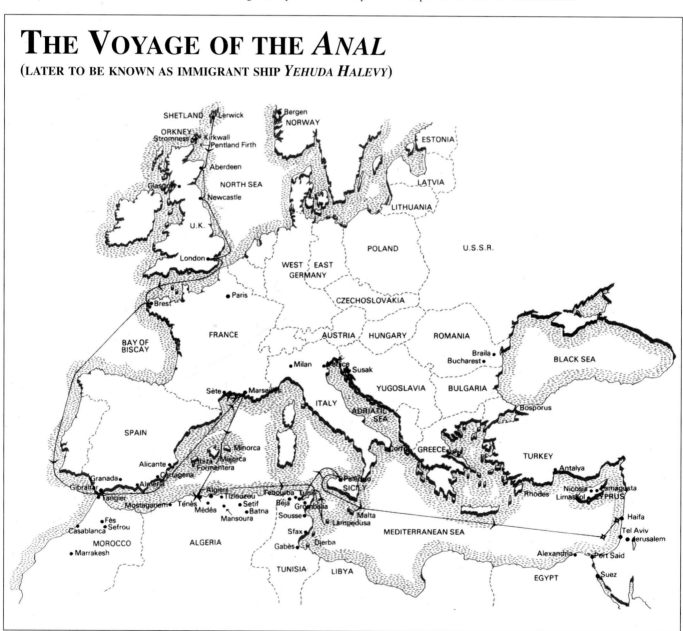

POLITICAL PRESSURES

The immigrant ships were a serious difficulty for the British in their long-standing problematical mandate, complicated by the White Paper. The Zionist Armada invaded the Mediterranean, forcing Britain to commit large numbers of ships and personnel in maintaining a vigil and keeping a blockade throughout the area. There was embarrassment in the actions and discomfiture in political and diplomatic circles in those post-war years.

It was further revealed because Zionist leaders had abandoned faith — even hope — in the British Government as a means of relief, and had looked to Washington for real support ... paradoxically the two wartime allies, in harmony over Europe were in conflict over Palestine; the issue became a "hot potato".

The Arab factor was another political, diplomatic and human problem which has penetrated through, often devastatingly, into the 21st century. In 1939 that controversial White Paper had taken the sting out of their natural acute sense of grievance at the disruption of their life and lands by Jewish aspirations. Antipathy towards Britain did diminish and anti-British agitation eased-off temporarily.

Thus with such a background of political fragments the British post-war Labour government, and its Foreign Secretary Ernest Bevin, followed a path fraught with disenchantment and exasperation in what seemed to them Arab obstinacy and Jewish perversity compounded by American involvement. Astonishingly, as early as November 1942 an American Palestine Committee issued a statement in denouncing the White Paper. Two years later — the Nazi "final solution" having become painfully apparent — the Americans reacted further: " ... resolved that the United States shall urge its good offices to the end that the doors of Palestine shall be opened for free entry of Jews to that country ... so that the Jewish people may ultimately reconstitute Palestine as a free and democratic Jewish commonwealth." President Roosevelt, in attempts to reconcile a polarised situation had tried to encourage both sides. At a convention of American Zionists — a powerful movement — in 1944, he commented: "I know how long and ardently the Jewish people have worked and prayed for the establishment of Israel ..." Yet in 1945 he reaffirmed in a personal letter to Arabian King Ibn Sa'ud: "Your Majesty will doubtless recall ... I assured you that I would take no action, in my capacity as Chief of the Executive Branch of this government, which might prove hostile to the Arab people."

After the death of Roosevelt the new president, Truman, felt he had to continue to be seen to be supporting both sides, but from 1945 till 15th May, 1948, when the State of Israel was formally established, he pursued two simple principles: that the United States must not be involved in any Palestine strife, and that action must be taken with the object of giving a chance of a new life to as many as possible of the survivors of Nazi barbarism. Meanwhile the British were on the receiving end of coping with what to all intents and purposes was a "no win" circumstance. And ironically a British ship, the former *Earl of Zetland* had a role to play in the unfolding drama which was counter to the White Paper.

The former Shetland steamer passed down between Minorca and Majorca heading south throughout day and night towards Ténès and the so-called camp "Calm and Health", where she was anxiously and eagerly awaited by a community vastly different to those she had served for six decades.

Responses to the missionary passion of Ephraim Friedman and Nadia Franco and committee had been beyond expectations; there were 640 men, women and children. The question arose as to the ability of the expected ship to cope. As it was, resources were badly stretched at the camp set up on a rocky and secluded hillside above a bay; food and water were becoming problematical; there was bartering with local Arabs; they had suspicions as to the authenticity of this camp "Calm and Health". There was evidence of French police interest. It was becoming worrying, and the committee worked hard at maintaining morale.

By the first days of May they could assure the people that the arrival of the ship was imminent. With flagging spirits revived the immigrants turned thoughts into inspiration with quoting and reciting from the widespread poetry of Yehuda Halevi; while their previous elation had found expression in making two 20-feet long banners of white material, each with lettering

Above: A ship of hope somewhere in the Mediterranean Sea. It looks a day of promise as sunlight glints on the ancient hull of the *Anal* and her Panamanian flag lifts in the breeze. As if to complement it, there is the domestic touch of laundry hung out to dry high between the bridge and the funnel, while people appear to be at leisure on deck.

But she has already been under surveillance by the British Navy patrol sloop, HMS *Whitesand Bay*. Ostensibly she is a trading coaster carrying labourers to Port Said for the Suez Canal Company, but questions are there to be asked. "What ship are you, where bound and why?" comes from the sloop. Israel Kharkovsky, skipper of the *Anal* responds appropriately; and then, "Are you under full power?" "No, but we are saving fuel".

"Thank you *Anal*", comes the non-committal answer and *Whitesand Bay* pulls away from the now identified vessel on 24th May, 1947. The questioning is not of much significance to many immigrants; they are too preoccupied but the crew of the "illegal" know that the rather transparent explanation is unlikely to convince the commanding officer of the intercepting ship. She remains in attendance about a mile away.

Conditions on the *Anal* are problematical. She had been at sea for a fortnight and had encountered the gale off Lampedusa which has led to deteriorating sanitary conditions. The herding of men, women and children into very confined spaces for long periods with extremely limited facilities means, in effect, that the ship sails in an invisible cloud of pollution. And to compound the issue care must still be taken to try to convince the British, with their powerful binoculars, that the ship does carry a complement of labourers ...

two-feet high. One proclaimed in Hebrew and the other in English, "Haganah Ship Yehuda Halevy", choosing to spell the surname with a "y" instead of an "i". It mattered none what the ship might have been named before. To them she would be the *Yehuda Halevy*.

The first week of May dragged past. Arab suspicions had brought about a desultory visit by the French police but they had gone and not come back. Dawn on the 10th was normal for a North African sunrise; then the heat of the day. Around noon a group of immigrants on the rocky foreshore were aware of a speck on the horizon to the north. Could it be? Assuredly, yes. On came the vessel until they could discern a small, flush-decked coastal steamer with a black hull and funnel which the committee confirmed was the *Anal* from Marseilles, but she remained well offshore, now parallel to the coastline.

Smoke by day and a fire by night — there had been a bonfire each evening for camp socialising — were to be confirmation for skipper Israel Kharkovsky, thus he knew the situation and at nightfall he came close inshore to anchor by a coastline devoid of piers. They were all set for their passengers. Careful training was part of the preparation, thus everyone from oldest to youngest knew the drill.

While the Jews prepared the Arabs were not idle. Such a vessel with its collection of boats and life-rafts aroused concern; they worried about the security of their own village. For a second time they informed the French police.

In keeping with the studied preliminaries vehicles had been arranged to take older Jews to the embarkation point. Younger and fitter people would go on foot. The movement began. Nadia Franco supervised loading at the camp; Ephraim Friedman and Shimson Sarfati, a committee member, checked vehicles on each run; Yani Ostrowsky and Rephael Chemel were at the embarkation place.

More than two thirds of the immigrants had reached the shore when police activity erupted at the vehicle convoy and there was chaos, although no violence. Sarfati had charged into scrubland, evaded the torch-flashing police, dashed to the shore and raised the alarm in the still, dark night. Well over 300 persons had boarded the *Anal* from a fleet of life-rafts by that time; Kharkovsky had to make a decision. He rang down for "full-ahead", aware of the misfortune to committee and would-be immigrants alike. Eventually at the embarkation point the police found only the remnants of possessions. It had been a narrow escape for the steamer and her complement, tempered by despair that so many — even close relatives — had been left behind. No one was to know then that another ship *Shivat Zion* (Return to Zion) would call for the forsaken in mid-July 1947. Theirs is another episode.

Right: An intercepting warship. Here is seen HMS *Talybont* in the English Channel. She was a unit of the Third Destroyer Flotilla and had been launched in February 1943, displaced 1087 tons, could raise 25 knots and required a crew of 158. At the time of the encounter with the former "*Earl*" she was on general interception duties in the eastern Mediterranean and had already been involved in incidents with illegal immigrant vessels.

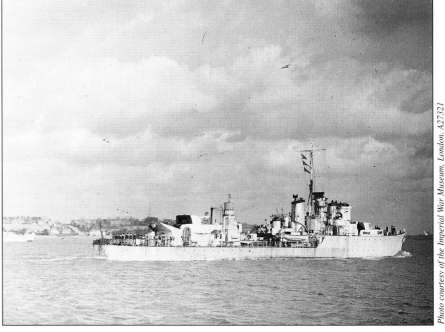

Photo courtesy of the Imperial War Museum, London. A27321

Photo courtesy of the Imperial War Museum, London. A30695

Left: HMS *Peacock*, an escort sloop of the modified Black Swan type, depicted here possibly at Portsmouth and barely underway. She was attached to the 5th Escort Flotilla and had been launched in December 1943 with a tonnage of 1350, had a speed of 20 knots and was manned by 192 men.

She acted in concert with HMS *Talybont* in arresting the *Anal* off the shores of the then Palestine. The third Royal Navy ship in the action was a minesweeper of the Algerine class, HMS *Skipjack*, also commissioned in 1943. She weighed 850 tons, had a moderate capacity of 16½ knots and carried 85 crew. Also a close up of her stern appears in a photograph as she tows the *Yehuda Halevy*.

Of course the other warship involved was HMS *Whitesand Bay*, a "Bay" class escort sloop completed after the end of the war. Her task was to "shadow" illegals.

VOYAGE OF HOPE

By noon on 11th May the *Anal* was well to the seaward off Algiers with her folk settling in for the 2000-mile voyage to Palestine. What they discovered on board was primitive and basic, especially felt when Israel Kharkovsky made it clear that only a limited number could be on deck at the same time. The ship had to appear to be sailing legally. This need was unexpectedly highlighted when, only hours out, a fast French patrol launch swept alongside the slow-moving steamer with questions about name, origin, destination and cargo. Her crew seemed to be satisfied with the response … "*Anal*. Panama. Port Said. Labourers. Suez Company." It was thought the launch call emanated from the gendarmes visit at the embarkation point.

Shipboard life began to develop a pattern. The skipper called a meeting of key figures on board; a close-knit discipline would be needed; help in the engine-room, stoking duties, cleaning of living quarters and sanitary facilities, preparing and cooking food, washing-up … men, women and the 26 children on board were all co-operative. This was invaluable to other leaders on board like Moshe Amir and Jacob Melnitzer, radio operator, who had dubbed the old ship "The Grandmother", such was her apparent vintage.

With 550 miles logged and the *Anal* north of Tunis there was a threatening wind shift which blew up into a full gale and the ancient hull was put through all manner of gyrations. Israel Kharkovsky discovered that the *Anal* did not have the power to cope with the wind and sea and he resorted to "tacking", a gambit so often used in bygone years. He elected to run south for shelter at the island of Lampedusa, which was only partially successful in that his passengers were in a state of seasickness in cramped accommodation and inadequate ventilation. The stench of vomit permeated the ship and the victims wished they were anywhere but on this old tub at this time; there was no letting-up; the gale persisted. In desperation, and in due consideration for his charges, Kharkovsky put into Tunis to allow a let-up and a clean-up, which was problematical because he could not afford to allow passengers on deck in numbers in port. All immigrants were forced to remain in the sour-smelling confinement out of sight of port authorities, while without a bill of lading *Anal* had to sail or be arrested.

They put to sea in greatly improved weather, headed towards the western tip of Sicily and Palermo for coaling — with luck. Jacob Melnitzer had radio contact with Mossad agents in Milan; 40 tons of coal could be bought at Palermo, enough to see them to Haifa. But they ran foul of British influence when the Italian coal-suppliers had a directive to unload, which caused consternation. Curses were directed at the White Paper, Bevin, the British Government and British Intelligence Agents who would probably have information about an illegal immigrant ship. It was Kharkovsky himself who salvaged the situation by using his "emergency fund" to bribe the suppliers to leave 20 tons secreted away and, hopefully, enough to see them into Palestine waters at much reduced speed. On 19th May, fuelled, though only just, and provisioned, the careworn steamer moved slowly away from Palermo on her ultimate voyage. It was the

Tom Anderson

Above: They knew there could be no easy way; at the very least they could count on some discomfort; more than likely privation. There would inevitably be uncertainty, including a high-risk factor amounting to danger. Yet they were prepared to chance all in their determination to escape from the modern Diaspora (originally the dispersion of Jews after the Babylonian conquest of 587 BC and, again, after that of the Romans, finally by 135 AD) and to help to pioneer the planned State of Israel. In their eyes it was an enormous incentive.

Thus the Jews had come from communities large and small in North Africa – from Algeria, Morocco and Tunisia, with little of their worldly goods but an abundance of spiritual fervour. They awaited the unknown vessel which would provide them with a means to an end near the little town of Ténès, 200 kilometres west of Algiers. When she came there was disappointment; she looked so small. But they crowded on board, men, women and children alike, to discover confined and cramped facilities with crudely formed bunks throughout.

This illustration offers an idea of what had been done when the old *Earl* was fitted out at Marseilles after 24th February, 1947, when she arrived there. This is the scene below at the after-hatch, with a roughly formed companionway to the right. The photograph seems to be taken from an actual bunk … the immigrants could count on some discomfort!

beginning of her end but, blessedly for her people merely the end of the beginning.

Meanwhile, HMS *Whitesand Bay* was patrolling on "immigration interception" in the eastern approaches of the Malta channel. There was information about a possible illegal in her area. On the morning of the 21st a smear of smoke was seen on the horizon and *Whitesand Bay* gradually neared the stranger. In the boredom of patrol her appearance was not unwelcome and she looked to be a small coaster, maybe 250 tons.

Within hailing distance a check was made as illustrated on page 79 and the warship simply shadowed mile after mile at the *Anal's* pace, barely under way. Steering a course slightly south of east the coaster did seem to be heading for Port Said. As day gave way to night on the 24th immigrants climbed out of the stifling, sour depths. If the fo'c'sle, 'tween decks, cabins aft and saloon had a modicum of air circulating, the hold was a cesspit of perspiring bodies, reek of inadequate sanitation plus the aftermath of seasickness; the purity of sea air was a revelation. Sadly, the youngest on board, a two-year old child, died and was buried at sea away from the prying eyes of the crew of HMS *Whitesand Bay*. The loss meant gloom amid the immigrants, tempered by the excitement of anticipation as Palestinian waters drew ever nearer, albeit slowly.

Kharkovsky, Melnitzer, Amir, Sarfati and others met in conference and discussed plans. Guidance by the Mossad was clear to the Haganah men. Ideally, the ship would be run ashore under cover of darkness. Alternatively, should she be intercepted, the main valve of the engine would be ditched to ensure the unthinkable could not happen — to return whence she came. Common to both possibilities was the destruction of the ship's papers, while Israel Kharkovksy would melt into the crowd. At a given time the ensign the Star of David, brand new, would be unfurled.

Meanwhile the destroyer *Talybont* and sloop *Peacock* had returned to Haifa just before the end of May to await further orders. On the 28th *Whitesand Bay* signalled Naval Command at Haifa to confirm continued shadowing and that the suspect had altered course away from Port Said.

At 0001 hours on the 30th *Peacock* left Haifa. She worked up to her full speed of 20 knots, heading 255° for a point about 150 miles out and by 0830 she had taken up station to starboard of the *Anal*. With a fresh north-easterly breeze the warship was downwind of the steamer and the crew of the sloop were frequently subjected to the pungent smell. During the late afternoon *Talybont* joined the little fleet, while *Whitesand Bay* sailed astern. She was covering the chance that highly motivated immigrants would try to swim for it!

About 1800 *Peacock* closed in and the disembodied voice of her commander addressed a message: "Good evening. You must understand it will be futile for you to attempt to enter harbour or run your vessel ashore. If you try either of these I have instructions to board your ship … You should now steer 042° towards Haifa. Please acknowledge." Out of courtesy Israel Kharkovsky picked up the loud hailer; he agreed to make towards Haifa but was non-committal about stopping.

With fuel supplies down to a couple of days steaming slowly, the victim set the pace — and was in a position, tactically, to do so, although futility was inevitable. Day faded into night — the 21st of the voyage — then at 2040 a minesweeper, HMS *Skipjack,* appeared to take up station ahead of the *Anal*. Her later task, all being well, would be to tow the illegal into port. At 2110 the commanding officer of *Peacock* radioed his counterparts to the effect, if need be, boarding would be the "sandwich" method, as dramatically shown in the photographs. For the immigrants there was excitement, anticipation and apprehension bordering on fear as their little vessel edged ever nearer to the Promised Land. They talked and sang the night away, and over 500 British sailors heard patriotic Jewish songs wafting through the night air, then an agonising moment came for Kharkovsky's people; the Palestinian coast south of Haifa, the sweep of the low-lying beaches with the Plain of Sharon behind them; the hills rising afar off in which nestled the hallowed places like Nazareth and the Sea of Galilee. To the south-east lay the sacred city of Jerusalem, the centre of the Jewish universe …

On board that microcosm of Israeli desires — unbelievably, the *Earl of Zetland* — feeling ran high on the morning of 31st May, 1947. Emotional reaction led to aggressive intent, part of which almost led to disaster as the now declared *Yehuda Halevy* cut across the bows of each warship in turn.

Israel Kharkovsky's resistance with his ship could only be token, although in a lost immediate cause he had tried to make his point. Having had a foray of each of the flanking British ships he rang down "stop engines" and the *Yehuda Halevy* drifted to a halt just over two miles offshore. Reality faced them all now. The game was up. His next task, as had been discussed, was to remove the main valve from the engine-room, a matter he found distasteful because he had built up a certain affection for his charge. The deed done, the hapless, immobilised, antiquated vessel lay completely at the mercy of her adversaries. They had been aware of the splash in the sea and, rightly, supposed it to be an engine part so that the illegal could not be sent anywhere.

The voyage-end was not unexpected for the likes of Shimson Sarfati,

C. A. Thompson

Above: A fleet in microcosm. The old *Earl* was one of a massive fleet of over 140 illegal immigrant ships (between 1934 and 1948) in the Jewish assault on the principles of the Balfour Declaration of 1917, and White Paper of 1939 which restricted Jewish immigration into Palestine to 1500 a month. In their eyes this was totally inadequate, hence the "illegals" – and a brief stay of execution for the venerable *Earl* …

There were some 20 vessels either docked, intercepted and towed, or beached in or near Haifa during 1947. These were: February 9th, *Merica*; 17th, *San Miguel*; 28th, *Ulua*; March 9th, *Abril*; 12th, *Susannah*; 31st, *San Filipo*; April 14th, *Guardian*; 22nd, *Galata*; May 17th, *Trade Winds*; 24th, *Orietta*; 31st, *Anal* (alias *Yehuda Halevy*); July 18th, *President Warfield* (alias *Exodus*); 28th, *Luciano* and *Bruna*; September 27th, *Farida* (alias *LCT 441*); October 2nd, *Paducah* (alias *Geulah*) and *Northlands* (alias *Jewish State*); November 16th, *Aliyah*, *Rafaellucia* and *Kadiman*.

The fate of numerous "illegals" is typified by this example of *Anal* – about to be declared *Yehuda Halevy* – flanked by HMS *Peacock* to starboard and HMS *Talybont* to port, still shadowing at this stage. The superstructure and bridge of *Talybont* thrusts above the former *Earl of Zetland's* profile. Her ultimate voyage is nearing an inevitable and sad fate – and yet she carries a complement of optimistic immigrants, serving people to the end.

Right: Closing in on their prey. The stalking is over and the warships are committed to the interception of an antagonistic victim. What is happening would be beyond the bounds of credulity back in Shetland. The old *Earl* laden with over 390 aggressive passengers who are there with the incentive to establish a new nation and with water jets directed at them. Impossible! Yet there is the evidence.

The *Earl of Zetland*, alias *Anal*, alias *Yehuda Halevy*, has ignored the command to stop and here she is, her packed decks bristling with a mass of angry, yet anxious, Jewish immigrants, still doing about four knots.

HMS *Peacock* directs three jets of water at the starboard side of "the illegal". To port, HMS *Talybont* bides her time with the fire hoses, but gradually the two British warships close the gap. It is a fine clear morning off Haifa.

H. G. Fuller

Below: Near a fateful moment. At 0845 on 31st May, 1947, the log of HMS *Peacock* noted: "Closing on territorial waters. Illegal vessel *Anal* warned of futility of resistance. Informed immigrants that they will be ordered to stop". Yet here is the ship defiantly underway, a single hose playing on a solitary confrontational passenger, but the force of the water from the hoses has served its purpose. The stern is cleared of people.

It was inevitably a forlorn hope by the British that the *Anal* – the name in their eyes – would be hove-to outwith the three-mile zone, for they were dealing with a national fanaticism. In fact, as the former *Earl of Zetland* slipped into the ad hoc territorial waters, leader Shimson Sarfati went to the foremast with the blue and white flag, Star of David, which had been so carefully husbanded since the ship was fitted-out back in far-off Marseilles.

Momentarily the assembled multitude on board the *Yehuda Halevy* – for this was the name chosen – fell silent, then as the flag broke out at the yardarm fitted to the foremast there was wild emotional cheering, immediately followed by the Hatikva (The Hope) sung with fervour and volume which carried far in the still morning air. At the same time a banner was raised at each mast bearing the word "Haganah Ship Yehuda Halevy".

This banner can be seen here at the mainmast as the steamer remains underway, with her bridge in particular a mass of humanity probably symbolising a psychological moment of feeling in control of the situation.

H. G. Fuller

Top and middle: A potential suicide. The illegal immigrant ship abruptly changes course and cuts dangerously into the path of the still-moving HMS *Talybont*, and the weight of the destroyer threatens to capsize her. For those immigrants below decks, especially the women and children, it is a moment of near panic. Their screams and wails carry up to the decks of the British ships. Fortuitously the *Yehuda Halevy* veers off and regains an even keel.

On the horizon is the coast north of Haifa, for the aspiring Israelites so near and yet so far. To the right is part of the superstructure of HMS *Peacock*, her crew awaiting events. It is noticeable that *Peacock*'s boarding party is on the port side, below *Yehuda Halevy*'s funnel!

Below: Now it is the turn of HMS *Peacock*. The *Yehuda Halevy* is keeling over having swung to starboard into the path of the warship and again she is severely at risk in a second futile token resistance. Momentarily the would-be immigrants will feel a point is being made under the flair of *Peacock*'s bow.

The banner, in Hebrew, proclaiming "Haganah ship ..." is noticeable at the foremast, with the Star of David flag at the yardarm.

Later, the commander of HMS *Talybont* wrote in his subsequent report: "Her (*Anal*'s) tactics of increasing speed and altering course into the approaching ships were extremely hazardous, and both *Peacock* and *Talybont* struck her fairly hard and listed the ship over considerably."

who wrote in his diary: "On the decks of another two destroyers we could see British soldiers armed with guns, sticks and gas masks. The time was eight o'clock in the morning. With grief and tears in our eyes we could see the coast of our land behind us. We had all looked with loving eyes towards this land, the land of our Fathers about which we had dreamt with all our families …"

Kharkovsky and Melnitzer had melted into the mass of immigrants, although the radio operator had maintained contact with the Mossad HQ. Even as the invading sailors were set to enter the radio shack behind the bridge he immobilised the set and escaped through an interior specially-made hatch into the deck below and the anonymous crowd.

Few, if any British sailors or soldiers regarded the immigrants with any animosity. Authority encouraged them to see the pathetic crowd on each ship as attempting illegal entry and, therefore, political detainees, but many of them were young National Servicemen, teenagers, and often not unaware of the disaster to Jewry. Petty Officer G. A. Neale of HMS *Talybout* confirmed such attitudes: " … you could not help feeling sorry for these people. They had suffered so much and were huddled together on board like cattle, and when they did finally reach Haifa, only to be shipped to Cyprus to be interned, you could understand their bid for freedom … There was no feeling of hate, in fact we had more a feeling of pity for them." Chief Petty Officer Cyril Martin of HMS *Peacock* commented on the physical (and mental) hardship for the *Yehuda Halevy's* people: " … a complete shambles. The middle deck below was in such a state of filth and

the stench beyond description that it left me bewildered as to how any human being could survive such a horrifying voyage …"

Sarfeti subsequently chronicled events through Jewish eyes: " … There was great excitement. At last we approached but we were told that we must leave the *Yehuda Halevy* … and transfer to a British ship to camp in Cyprus … We all wept when our feet touched our beloved land and we kissed the quay … After we had been sprayed with disinfectant like some diseased animals we were directed to a large, broad ship … a very high fence and barbed wire … we were told in Hebrew that in keeping with British law we would be transferred to Cyprus. The voyage of the ship *Yehuda Halevy* … from North Africa to Israel had not ended as we had hoped, yet we had still arrived …"

And so it was. Collectively they did it. A year later on 14th May, 1948, Ben Gurion, like a 20th century Moses, delivered his oration in Tel Aviv. "Therefore by virtue of the natural and historic right of the Jewish people to be a nation as other nations and of the Resolution of the General Assembly of the United Nations, we hereby proclaim the establishment of the Jewish Nation in Palestine to be called Medinat Yisrael : The State of Israel."

Meanwhile, despite the extreme misfortune of a totally unwanted sojourn in Cyprus, at least the *Yehuda Halevy's* people knew that their destiny lay in their homeland and in the fullness of time, given the drastically restrictive nature of the 1939 White Paper, they would be accepted and integrated into Israel to live in the chequered and precarious

H. G. Fuller

Above: The stern of "the illegal", having been cleared of immigrants by the powerful water jets, is now invaded by the British. The approach to boarding required special techniques. Warships and men were carefully prepared. Each destroyer or escort sloop was fitted with heavy metal mesh screens on the fo'c'sle as a protection against missiles hurled by irate immigrants – and these could fly thick and fast on occasion! Stout coir and rubber fenders were suspended over the bows and along the forepart of the hull, invaluable when there was a severe dunt as had happened moments before this boarding scenario.

Through experience it was discovered that the most effective method of boarding was by means of specially fitted adjustable and numbered ramps, each projecting about 15 feet at different levels, hinged at the hull and lowered depending on the height of the stern of an immigrant vessel. This avoided the very real risk of anyone falling into the sea between the ships and gave more scope for strength in numbers across the width of an illegal's stern, cleared of people by the fire hose water jets.

Ramp number 1 is in use here. A couple of men stand on ramp 2 watching the advance in width and depth as if in a rugby maul. Some of the boarding party are already on the top of the deckhouse by the mainmast. Crew members look on impassively and Lieutenant Commander D. L. Satterford DSC, Captain of HMS *Peacock*, controls the situation from the bridge.

C. A. Thompson

Left: A line is attached to the minesweeper HMS *Skipjack* and a British serviceman, wearing the standard white helmet and gaiters of boarding parties, tends to it aboard the illegal, totally surrounded by a mass of resigned onlookers. More marines are grouped around some structure at the foremast, dutifully ensuring order amid the would-be immigrants.

There are Carley Floats or life-rafts in abundance, confirming that the authorities in Marseilles, where the steamer was fitted out, were taking the safety of so many passengers seriously.

The old *Earl* blows off steam for the last time, while just visible to the right of the funnel is the bridge of HMS *Talybont*, her immediate task ended. As a striking contrast to former days the hull of the venerable steamer is badly stained and discoloured; also the well-deck, so much a focal point in Shetland, has been replaced by welded plates, although the door hinges are still prominent and thrown into relief by the morning light.

C. A. Thompson

Left: The subseqent report from HMS *Peacock* was a travesty of the human situation: "At 0922 on 31st May, 1947, *Skipjack* was ordered to take *Anal* in tow and by 0930 the tow had been passed and the ships were going ahead. A very prompt and able (sic) evolution. *Skipjack* towed *Anal* to the harbour entrance where she was taken over by tugs and berthed. Boarding took place in position 32°50'15"N, 34°54'06"E."

A hawser made fast, the minesweeper HMS *Skipjack* gets underway, the former old *Earl* wallowing astern still, surprisingly, with a wisp of smoke at her funnel. She is scrutinised by an officer of the watch, by the flagstaff, and crew of *Skipjack*. Her White Ensign fluttering in the breeze is defiantly matched by the Star of David flag at the *Yehuda Halevy*'s foremast. In the background, standing off, is the lean profile of HMS *Talbont*, her immediate brief completed.

Tom Anderson

Left: The now-immobilised *Yehuda Halevy* lies deep in the water with her huge cargo of humanity, all awaiting an unknown fate, although not in any danger from the British. The antagonism is one-sided. Any uncertainty hinges around just when the people from the Jewish Diaspora will achieve their objective of attaining the long-awaited Promised Land.

But for the old ship which had brought them within close sight of another world, time is running out. No more will smoke be seen at the *Earl*'s funnel; no more the beat of her screw reverberating through her frame; no more the wake creaming astern.

This view shows how the two-tiered lifeboats had been fitted. White-helmeted marines are grouped by the funnel; the situation seems under control. The banner proclaiming "Haganah Ship Yehuda Halevy" at the mainmast billows in the morning breeze and atop the bridge-wing shelter a solitary figure stands aloof. Meanwhile a British-manned harbour tug awaits events, her crew casually observing the unfolding drama, one man finding a davit of the tug's port lifeboat an idea vantage point.

By a truly incredible coincidence, Tom Anderson, a Shetlander and a nephew of Captain Adam Tait, was a member of the 6th Airborne Division in Palestine. He chanced to be on duty at Haifa at the time of the arrival of the former *Earl of Zetland*, recognised the very familiar profile despite the alterations, and took the historic photographs from the tug and of the old *Earl* lying, abandoned, amid the discarded ships of the immigrant fleet.

existence of all nations in the second half of the 20th century and beyond. For the vessel which had been fated to provide them with a means to an end there was no future; in the nature of things her time had run out.

For some ships there was a stay of execution. Several were patched up and later incorporated into the Israeli Navy, others were refitted and utilised to carry legal immigrants after the tiresome Mandate; others were unfit for any practical purpose, too small to be of value, of insufficient power, slow and of inadequate bunker capacity. Into the last category came the *Yehuda Halevy*. The Port Authority of the Mandatory government had sealed her fate. Only the Haogen Co-operative Boatyard maintained an interest by checking moorings and keeping watch on the discarded vessels arrayed along the sea wall of Haifa. The fugitive steamer finally faded into

obscurity when, months later, she was towed to the Shemen beach by Haifa, driven ashore, and lay in the shallows as an ad hoc breakers firm took apart the craftsmanship of John Fullerton and Company.

A Shetland goodwill audience had expressed their feelings about the old *Earl of Zetland* on 4th August, 1939, prior to her "retiral" from the islands; it proved to be the penultimate farewell; now it was the ultimate goodbye. The *Earl of Zetland* name lives on; the *Yehuda Halevy* name lives on:

> *"So goodbye, old ship o' mine*
> *And for the sake of auld lang syne,*
> *Your name will live on till the day is gone,*
> *Goodbye auld ship o' mine."*

On 1st June, 1947, the day after the incident, the English language newspaper *Palestine Post* carried the story of the old *Earl's* epic voyage. It was headlined "*Yehuda Halevy* dodged warships for ten days". A slightly inaccurate account followed: "The latest prize of the Royal Navy, 399 ragged Oriental Jews on a 300 ton tramp steamer, whom four warships had dogged for ten days before preventing them from entering Palestine, was handed over to the army at Haifa Port late this sabbath morning. Their number would have been 400, but a two-year-old child had died at sea during the 21-day journey from an unknown port.

"The immigrants had proudly named their dingy little boat after the great Hebrew poet of the 12th century Yehuda Halevy, described as 'the foremost poet since the bible', whose Songs of Zion were nostalgic with longing for the ancient homeland ('My heart is in the east and I am in the uttermost west') and who himself set out from Spain through Egypt to Palestine. The steamer, originally the *Anal* and before that the *Earl of Zetland*, flew a smoke-blackened Panama flag and bright, clean Zionist colours – the banners proclaimed that she was a Haganah ship.

"It did not take the military long to complete their part of the joint operation and transfer the people to the *Ocean Vigour* for deportation to Cyprus.

"The newcomers said after being followed for ten days by four warships their boat was boarded yesterday morning while south of Haifa, and tear gas (sic) was used by the navy as a preventive measure, although there was no indication of resistance. The majority of them are young men, very pale and thin faced, with dark, curly hair. The children looked undernourished. Few of the people had more than just the clothes on their backs and such things as they had would need to be discarded as soon as possible because sanitary conditions on the boat were very bad. The soldiers detailed to searching bundles had little work to do.

"Now and then one of the men would resent being moved around by a soldier as they were hastened down the gangplank, but altogether the routine went off without incident and in silence …"

For all the erstwhile crew and passengers on the now abandoned old *Earl* it had been a love/hate relationship. She could not have been ignored. They felt a deep appreciation for the fact that she had been available at all, a well-found and seaworthy vessel, old, but with all the evidence of care and maintenance. They sensed a profoundly deep dislike of the primitive layout and makeshift sanitation which had become desperately bad, and a hatred of close confinement which had seemed endless in its acute discomfort. In time, perhaps, she would be remembered with some affection because, above all else she had provided them with an opportunity which was of their own choosing, but for their ship there was no choice.

Tom Anderson

Tom Anderson

Tom Anderson

Top: As if convicted, a large number "28" has been crudely painted on her starboard bow immediately abaft the chain of the lowered anchor which lies on the sea bed for the last of a myriad of occasions … the grouping of vessels along the seawall at Haifa shows the sheer diversity of ships gathered by the Mossad L'Aliya Bet (B), the organisation for illegal immigration which succeeded in eventually conveying a multitude of people to the promised land.

Middle: The old travel-strained steamer is dwarfed by the towering funnel and bridge of the so-called *Hatiquva*, formerly the United States Coastguard Vessel *Tradewinds*, which had brought nearly 1500 immigrants to Palestine only a fortnight before the *Yehuda Halevy* appeared with her weary, yet uplifted, contingent.

Left: A poignant reminder to an enduring past, even if now about to be consigned to eternity through the unthinking, unfeeling stroke of the breaker's hammer. On board the timeworn steamer the sole remaining specific evidence of the Shetland connection is the artistically carved lettering on the steering gear casing at the stern. Fashioned by a Paisley craftsman of a bygone era, the words "Earl of Zetland" stand out defiantly, as if declaring an identity to the bitter end.

SHIPS OF THE PEOPLE – CONTRASTS IN ARRIVALS

C. A. Thompson

Above: Initially it is difficult to ascertain just where on the ship this is, but more than likely at the bow where the members of the British boarding party have adopted a commanding stance. Bemused and resigned acceptance shows on the faces of the immigrants, who now appear to be completely passive as they face an uncertain future. Their immediate fate will be transfer ashore at Haifa and shipping to Cyprus, there to await transport back to Palestine. The Balfour Declaration and White Paper of 1939 permitted only 1500 Jewish immigrants a month and the British, as mandatory power, had the unenviable responsibility to administer this.

Shetland Museum

Above: An arrival of the new *Earl of Zetland* at Lerwick in her heyday of the 1950s.

POST-WAR AND THE NEW *EARL* IN SHETLAND

The huge upsurge in morale and optimism at the end of the Second World War was reflected in every phase of life throughout the country; freedom had been fought for and freedom had prevailed. A dictator had been disposed of, but at incalculable expense in terms of humanity. No community remained unaffected in a global sense. VE day had been celebrated, followed by VJ day — for the world of war had seen Japan as a key opponent — and heartfelt tributes were made to the fallen who had given all. Their memory lives on in perpetuity into this 21st century; their names on the war memorials.

While Shetland rejoiced in victory, her deprivation of young manhood was poignantly remembered, then there were the negatives and the positives, firstly of wartime losses added to by insidious depopulation which, ironically, yet acceptably, swelled the numbers in Shetland Associations around the world, then, secondly, the plus factors of domestic improvements throughout the islands like a systematic electricity network and water schemes, the two-wheeled "Iron Horse" for ploughing, subsequently replaced by the four-wheeled tractors … bathrooms and kitchens into the houses …

It was into this kind of scenario that the second *Earl of Zetland* arrived. She, of course, had been so keenly anticipated not far short of a decade before, thus when in 1946 she was becoming firmly established her appearances in the Yell Sound and North Isles ports were further morale-boosters for the folk. She was bigger, better and faster; much as the old had been loved. Folk still spoke about her, often in comparison, but also in affection. It was known she had likely gone to the Mediterranean; no one knew for what purpose.

Even in the time of the old *Earl* the lack of island piers had been a focus for criticism. It was fortuitous, and fortunate that one existed at Baltasound

from the early years of the 20th century, and privately owned at that. In the late 1940s, with the coming of a modern ship, the expectancy of people grew and questions began to be asked; not only berthing facilities, but there was concern about the poor state of the road system.

During her domestic programme in 1946 the pier problem was often a topic of discussion, even argument, on the *Earl*. By 1947 the issue was beginning to be debated through the newspapers. Linkshouse at Mid Yell was a prime subject. It was said that there were two old flit-boats at Mid Yell … "These boats are over 80 years of age … when they collapse (sic) the people in the south end (of Yell) will be cut off". An official had appeared and turned down a ship pier; too much sand and a pier would silt up. Yet Adam Tait, former skipper in the old *Earl* had never encountered any siltage and only blue clay came up on the anchor.

That little progress was being made showed when a year later, in July 1948, the same Adam Tait arrived from Leith with a 36-feet long former naval harbour launch to act as a flit-boat. She was fitted with a 15 hp Kelvin engine. "… islanders will be very pleased to hear that the continued absence of a pier will not mean being cut off from the *Earl*'s services." The flit-boat was named the *John Tulloch* in memory of the father of Mr A. I. Tulloch, of Messers Tulloch of Shetland, who had bought the former naval launch for Mid Yell.

Meanwhile another aspect jumped into the news, when Charles Brown protested regarding the delay about a proposed pier at Hal, Fetlar … it was quite a while since the site had been surveyed. On the plus side there had been an extension to the Cullivoe pier completed for £540, although an anomalous situation seemed to exist judging by County Council reports of 1948: "Cullivoe: One flit-boat at present out of use, but a smaller one is available. The pier can be used under favourable conditions of weather and tide; Gutcher: M/B *Viking* available; Sellafirth: Boat available; Aywick: No boat available; suggest engaging boat *Eva* to transport goods from Mid

Above: The end of yet another visit to the north isles, back in the era of Captain James Johnston who had command of the *Earl* for over 15 years. He is seen on the bridge wing, with mate William Sinclair about to supervise the bow rope. The ship drifts gently into her customary spot at Victoria Pier in a scene with no evidence of shipping movement on a day of quiet hazy sunshine.

Above: Gradually the old oar-propelled flit-boats were replaced by motorised craft which did not always match the double-ended practical elegance of the former sixareens. This snapshot, taken on an idyllic flat-calm summer day reveals the square stern and ribbed near-vertical sides of an unknown flit-boat. In the immediate foreground, back to camera, is the *Earl*'s crew member Jimmy McLeod.

Above: A remarkable coincidental angle where the derrick of the old *Earl* follows the line of the massive Noup of Noss during a round-Bressay trip. The ship is hove-to, lying close in where the cliff-face plummets down into deep water and those on board can absorb the magnificence at leisure, and from a vantage viewpoint.

The popularity of Noss with seabirds was, and is, largely due to the geological structure. The towering east-facing sandstone rock-face has from time immemorial been eroded by many a south-east gale into a multitude of ledges and niches, providing perfect nesting situations for the variety of birds which find rich feeding in Shetland waters.

The first gannet (solan goose) colony had been established in 1911 and by 1937, when this photograph would be taken, the population was expanding rapidly, until today it is in excess of 5500 nests. It is not known what month this snap occured, but if it chanced to be in late June the passengers might just be observing puffins (tammy nories), guillemots, kittiwakes and razorbills, all there in fine profusion.

Yell; Burravoe: Boat available; Ulsta and West Sandwick: No boats available; suggest *Earl of Zetland* carry a boat for these ports, as she did last year." This was an apparent innovation in a 1947 emergency, as no record existed of the old *Earl* carrying other than her lifeboats! The report of 1948 went further: "… Mid Yell: There are two very old flit-boats here, and the boat belonging to the agent is so far gone that it might become unusable at any time." What is not clear is whether or not the comment applied to the craft brought from Leith by Adam Tait, and encountering a southerly gale on the way! Amazingly in a *Shetland News* paragraph in March 1948 it was stated: "… It was now over 12 years since the public (sic) had made application for a steamer's pier (at Mid Yell) and, although various grants had been obtained, it would seem that the County Council did not appreciate the seriousness … because nothing had been done."

Cullivoe was then characteristically innovative; a pier committee of nine was set up to look after interests and to attend generally to the management and maintenance of the pier. Robert Spence, the agent, had informed the council that he was quite prepared to collect dues on goods landed from the *Earl of Zetland,* but could not undertake to collect from fishing vessels.

A hint from Out Skerries, again in 1948, was sidelined. All catches had to be transported from fishing boats to shore, and from shore to steamer, by boat. A jetty had disappeared through age and decay … if a pier could be built for the *Earl* to call at, the fishermen could use it too. A remark was

Above: The ship eases alongside at Victoria Pier in 1947 after one of the first post-war Inter-county sporting events in Orkney. A north-westerly breeze sets the flags flying. Shetland had had success hinted at by the group standing on the monkey island with a cup being flourished and the obviously big crowd on the pier.

Willie Sinclair, then mate, supervises the bow lines, while Captain Tom Gifford, behind the bridge canvas-dodger, keeps an eye on the fenders. Unusually the cargo-handling derrick is in the stowed position. At a later date the old-style dodger was replaced by angled perspex sheets.

Above: The "new" *Earl* in August 1946. Working cargo at Cullivoe, with the ness enclosing the sheltered inlet seen in the background and the ridge of the south end of Valla Field on Unst just visible beyond. The bridge has the canvas dodger of the immediate post-war years. A young Willie Sinclair is at the cargo winch. Of course Tom Gifford is skippering, although within four years he will move to take command of the second *St Clair.*

made in committee; "That would take a long time," followed by, "Yes, it would take 10 or 20 years … the hope of a big pier for the *Earl* must be far in the distance. Look at Mid Yell — it is as far back today as it was seven or eight years ago."

The Shetland Times featured more debate: "Scarcely a County Council meeting comes along without the all-important question of piers cropping up. Tuesday's meeting showed business as usual, with the emphasis on the problems of Whalsay, Burra Isle and Tofts Voe."

Of course Tofts Voe accentuated another issue, that of the ever-expanding Overland, probing more and more into the very existence of the *Earl*. It was proving a complex situation. In the short term the *Earl* needed piers especially at some key points; in the equally short term the vehicle routes through Shetland required serious upgrading. The Mossbank jetty was obsolete and dangerous for ferry motor-boat passengers. Tofts Voe would be a safe place for the Yell Sound crossing — plans and specifications had been sent to "the Department some time ago …" That the Overland was firmly established was confirmed by an offer from the North Isles Ferry Company Limited that they were willing to pay 15% of the construction of a pier at Tofts Voe, while Yell Sound Ferry Company wished to pay £20 per annum for the lease of Ulsta pier as from 1st January, 1949.

Burra Isle emphasised a Shetland need, apart from routes of the *Earl* and the Overland, although common to all factors was the immediate post-war state of the roads in Shetland. Water bound — almost a contradiction in terms — routes were described as "a mass of potholes" and "a continuous water splash," by the increasing numbers of motorists. Some 150 miles of roads were in poor shape. A major part of the roads meant, " … when dry weather came the fine stuff blew away, or was driven away by vehicles — and nothing was left but the stones, with the result that when driving along in a car it was like a machine gun clattering the whole time!"

Thus post-war transport matters amid the islands continued to exercise

minds and energies, although not with immediate results! Indeed in 1950 a correspondent observed: " … a glance at the present Mid Yell pier should suffice. I have often wondered why their main pier should be in such a state of disrepair … Thanks to the skill of Captain Gifford, it is now almost a weekly occurrence to see the *Earl* tied up at the Cullivoe pier, and with the necessary extension it would certainly be a weekly visit …"

Another writer noted the roads: " … The same applies to lots of tourists travelling all over the mainland of Shetland, where the water-bound roads and mud tracks are stopping a lot of tourists from travelling.

"These roads have deteriorated badly during the last few years and it is a fact that people with false teeth have to take them out when travelling in a car — surely this is no attraction for tourists!"

The piers and roads debate rumbled on for some years but at least the *Earl of Zetland* was being very well received and accepted. A succinct post-war timetable spelled out her routes:

North Isles of Shetland
Thrice weekly between Lerwick and the North Isles.
Leaving Monday 8am — Terminus Uyeasound
Returning Tuesday Forenoon.
Leaving Wednesday 8am — Returning Afternoon — One Day Trip
making the round of the Islands
Leaving Friday 8am — Terminus Baltasound
Returning Saturday Forenoon.

In parallel with the regular sailings the North Company set out to maximise the use of their inter-island vessel and from 1946 ambitious excursions were publicised, although there proved to be trips of a different nature come the next year.

Left: A pen and ink sketch by the author reveals the flimsy nature of the pier at Cullivoe at the end of the 1950s. The *Reliance*, then owned by Danny Anderson, is at the far side, while the *St Vincent* lies at the end of the pier. Latterly in the *Earl*'s time the *St Vincent* stood in as a flit-boat on occasion, although, given a reasonable state of the tide the motor vessel could touch on the pier. It was said, however, in taking the *Earl*'s bow line it was safer to get down on hands and knees to avoid being flung down if she gave the shaky structure a bad dunt!

The Author

Right: A good profile of the *Earl* with her anchor chain angled out from the bow and silhouetted figures at the open doors of the well-deck. The exposed nature of the anchorage at Brough Lodge, Fetlar, is evident with the Yell shoreline a couple of miles away and open water to the north and south.

Fetlar men Lowrie Thomason (left) and Davy Anderson pull hard at the oars of the flit-boat in the face of a slightly choppy sea. The year is 1947 and the *Earl* is not long into her North Isles routine after the wartime hazards of the Pentland Firth.

The larger port lifeboat has not enhanced the look of the ship compared with its predecessor, while it was reckoned that the additional weight on each side did not favour the *Earl*'s sea-keeping qualities.

Fetlar Museum Trust

WINTER IN THE SPRING OF 1947 – AND ONWARDS

With the advent of 1947 the islands had been subjected to a week of blustery winds often reaching gale force. The seas were raised as high as had been witnessed in recent years; shipping was badly disrupted; mail was dislocated. On Friday, 3rd January, the wind gusted to 75 mph and blew hard day after day with sleet and snow developing on the Tuesday. Bressay people in Lerwick for shopping that Friday were isolated and had to stay in Lerwick, such was the ferocity of the harbour waters.

The first flurry of snow for the season turned to driven sleet but with no abatement of wind, resulting in havoc to sailings. Such as the *St Clair* (II) was four hours late in arriving in Aberdeen out of Lerwick on Saturday, 4th January, while the indirect boat, *St Magnus* (III), left Lerwick on the Thursday, sheltered in Kirkwall on the Friday and reached Aberdeen late on the Saturday night. She was unable to continue to Leith.

That same first Friday of 1947 the *Earl* was obliged to remain at Victoria pier, although she forced her way northwards next day only to discover that not all the flit-boats could be worked. She was tied up at Baltasound until Wednesday, 8th January, then struggled back to Lerwick by 3pm — still having to miss two of her calls.

Meanwhile the volatile elements of the national press pontificated about bread, flour and oatmeal being exhausted in Whalsay: " … the 1000 inhabitants are forced to eat potatoes with their meals three times a day … the situation is serious." Islanders responded … "grossly exaggerated" … "a lot of rubbish".

Yet the storm was prolonged. On Friday, 10th January, the *Earl* still remained with her schedule disjointed, while part of the sea road was washed away at Lerwick.

The Shetland Times of 17th January reported; "nine full days of gales …" and, " … many dramatic episodes have been enacted in the islands waters." North Isles ports had again been deprived of steamer calls.

Shetland had a reprieve at the end of January and into February whereas mainland Britain had heavy snowfalls, but between 7th and 14th February the snow began to escalate in the islands; frost posed problems on the roads; drifts began to accumulate. This was the start of weeks of chaos. By the end of February the islands were snowbound and emergencies multiplied. Heavy snow came on Saturday, 22nd February, and overnight into the Sunday. Transport on land was drastically curtailed by drifting. An American specialist snow plough, the Snogo, attacked the problem and fought through to Brae and Voe from Mossbank. Ten-foot drifts were a formidable obstacle. The Lerwick lifeboat made an emergency visit to Sumburgh bringing milk and mails to Lerwick. A fishing boat, the *Margaret Reid,* brought fish from Scalloway round Fitful and Sumburgh Heads on the same Saturday, then returned from Lerwick on the Sunday with supplies. The sea had to become the highway as it had been from time immemorial until the roads developed. Certainly land conditions were the worst for half a century.

Inevitably the *Earl* had a premier role to play. The Snogo broke down leaving the problem to teams of men in back-breakingly slow snow removal, thus the land difficulties were exacerbated. It was, however, eventually repaired. The emphasis had to be on sea transport — at least an alternative. The drifter *Lord Curzon* circumnavigated the Shetland mainland with supplies for the country districts, while the *Earl* joined in, turning the clock back, to prior days as she visited Vidlin, Mossbank, Ollaberry, North Roe and West Sandwick. On the trip for Wednesday, 5th March, she left Lerwick at the crack of dawn with nearly 20 tons of foodstuffs including cattle feed, in addition to mail for the five extra calls beyond normal North Isles ports. There was also the unprecedented step of carrying a small boat for unloading cargo at ports — the *Earl* supplied the flit-boat! Then emergency lifeboat calls reached double figures; a 12 year old Walls girl suffering from appendicitis; an elderly man also from Walls, needing hospital attention; a lass of eight requiring specialist treatment in Glasgow taken by sea from Lerwick to Sumburgh for the flight south. The land-based fight against the all-pervading snow almost ground to a halt.

Isobel Manson

Andrew Anderson, one of Ganson's bus firm drivers was stranded at Sandness for two weeks!

A *Shetland Times* report on Friday, 21st March, indicated; "Road clearing plans as thaw begins". The need for sea transport the previous week had been much less but once again the *Earl* had done a good job with another round trip of the mainland on Tuesday and Wednesday. By Saturday, 29th March, the deep drifts blocking roads throughout the islands had been largely swept away — ending two months of hardship. Lerwick observatory noted that for the month of March snow lay on the ground throughout and there was frost for 21 days. The cost of the snow removal operation had been £4500.

There was praise from the Shetland Council for the co-operation of the "North of Scotland Company". The gratitude of the whole of the people of Shetland was due to those who had organised emergency sea communications. If there were inevitable problems, the *Earl* had been made readily available for numerous circumnavigation voyages with provisions and the skipper Tom Gifford and crew had coped admirably with all circumstances thrown at them.

The extreme situation and the enthusiastic and efficient manner of the response by the *Earl's* men gave the ship high standing in the eyes of the community, so that in subsequent rounds of the ports there was much favourable comment, plus the historic nature of the *Earl* calling at places long abandoned because road transport was dealing with what would have been the *Earl's* cargo, and some of the travelling public.

Tom Gifford was piloting the new *Earl* in those immediate post-war years, having experienced the trauma of wartime service. By 1949 he had already skippered the motor vessel for more than a decade, and amid all the psychological difficulties of day by day risk in the Pentland Firth, where anything could have happened from air attack to a submarine's torpedo. Ironically when an attack had come it was back in November 1939 and had been half-hearted as described, and in Shetland waters. As it was he was on board the second *St Magnus* when she was torpedoed off Rattray Head in 1918.

Willie Sinclair from Northhouse, Whiteness, had joined Gifford as mate on 20th January, 1944, having been at sea since 1926 when he joined a ship named *Allwera*. His experience was wide-ranging — from coasting, to South America, to the Far East. In September 1940 he was with HMS *Explorer* out of Leith, then sailed as second mate with the *St Rognvald* and *St Magnus* until he was linked with the *Earl*. In fact he had taken the *Earl of Zetland II* up the harbour in Aberdeen after William Ramsay had departed, following the old *Earl's* demise finally from Shetland in June 1946, thus technically he commanded both *Earls* since he eventually became captain of the new *Earl* in September 1965.

While over the colourful life-spans of both *Earls* Willie Spence was the longest serving captain with his 17 years, nevertheless there were several with long tenures. In 1950 Tom Gifford was promoted to the *St Clair* after 13 years then James Magnus Johnston succeeded.

Like Adam Tait, Jimmy Johnston was from Aith, born on the croft of Ayres. He began his seafaring life in 1928, joining a ship named *Mandy Hill*. Later in his career, during the Second World War, he was on a steamer *Loch Maddy*, which was torpedoed off Copinsay on the east side of Orkney. He became mate, with Adam Tait as skipper, on the old *Earl* in 1941, then moved on to the second version, being with her until he was transferred to other North boats, rounding off his time as last Commodore of the actual North Company. Thus he covered a period from 1950 until 1965 with the new *Earl*, a long and quietly efficient service to the North Isles and, like his predecessors' work, much appreciated.

It was Jimmy Johnston who saw the bulk of the intensive marketing of excursions by the shipping firm, thus routine runs apart, he took the ship on a variety of outings. Of course the old *Earl* had had a very significant role to play in the social life of the islands; her replacement likewise.

Inevitably the full success of the trips hinged on the elements. It was near the end of Tom Gifford's captaincy, in 1948, that a North Isles outing spilled over into the next day! Fog was the drawback for 165 trippers — instead of arriving back home about 10pm they came into Lerwick at two in the morning. The excursionists had dropped off at intermediate ports but a considerable number found the encroaching fog at the July Uyeasound regatta where visibility dropped to about 50 yards; widespread throughout the isles from Flugga to Sumburgh. Even the newly developing BEA services into and out of Sumburgh Airport were cancelled for the first time in the summer schedule.

Still with the full-blown now outdated and somewhat cumbersome title

of the North of Scotland, and Orkney and Shetland Steam Navigation Company Limited the excursion promotion continued in the newspapers through into the 1950s.

Adverts were run in the Aberdeen newspapers even under "Sailing Excursions to Edinburgh," illustrating the desire to expand. In parallel with these, notices appeared in the Shetland press in remarkable proximity, considering the tight domestic sailing schedule of the *Earl*. There was a day trip on offer to Foula "provided … conditions allow," on Sunday, 15th July, 1951, followed by another to the North Isles (Whalsay, Brough Lodge, Mid Yell, Uyeasound) on Wednesday, 18th July. Boating at Foula would cost one shilling and sixpence extra; for the North Isles it was listed as " … where necessary, additional." This, of course, was everywhere on that schedule — not a "steamer" pier in sight!

By 1953 the programme was in "full-flight". The Monday holiday of 22nd June was typical. The weather proved to be fine and warm when the ship headed north with 130 on board, taking in Whalsay, Mid Yell, Brough Lodge and Uyeasound, and returning via Houbie and Skerries to Whalsay for a dance there. Jim Cameron and his band played to a crowded and hugely enjoyed occasion, the *Earl* sailing from Symbister at 1am.

The next Sunday, 28th June, the ship carried about 60 passengers to Fair Isle. A press article the following Friday prefaced the description with, "… grey mist over the face of the sea and a grey dawn breaking" — shades of John Masefield's writing — and the sail had been over a placid sea. Highlights had been … Mousa Sound … the cavorting of a basking shark … the rattle of the anchor chain in the North Entrance … the motor-boat ashore … the folk spreading out … hospitality of pancakes, bannocks and kirned butter … bird life of puffins, razorbills, shearwaters, maalies, guillemot; then high tea back on board by chief steward McLeod, and the fascination of the *Earl's* radar demonstrated by the skipper Jimmy Johnston and mate Willie Sinclair.

Another excursion, to Foula a fortnight later, saw different fortunes. The sea's surface was not so placid. The *Earl* stopped off Spiggie after a lively movement round Sumburgh Head, and edging the Roost with its strong tides, which were too much for a few passengers — they disembarked! Twenty-eight came aboard, making a party of about a hundred to head towards the magnificent, craggy Foula over 20 miles offshore. Landing was feasible at the peerie voe at Ham but the change of

Above: Captain James Magnus Johnston. After 46 years of sea-going he received a gift of a fishing rod and tackle, given on behalf of the North Company by Mr Eric Turner, operations manager, on Tuesday, 25th June, 1974, on board the *St Clair*. He had served the company for 33 years, 15 of which had been on the *Earl*.

Douglas Sinclair

Above: A still, grey and overcast moment as the *Earl* lies alongside the pier at Baltasound. The broad smiles belie the kind of day and a brief pause in the ongoing work on board. Lowrie Gifford, bo'sun stands in front of the oil storage tanks on shore; on Lowrie's left, behind, is Tom Laurenson from Bressay (known as "Tammy o' Gorie"). Tom was relief mate on the *Earl* and, on occasion, second mate on the *St Clair*. In front is Robbie Tulloch, a Cullivoe man who served on the *Earl* for years. The tall crewmember is Andy Abernethy, a Whiteness man, while, looking a touch camera-shy but with a grin is Hughie Pottinger. Missing from the group is Willie Anderson; possibly he is the photographer.

Jimmy Winchester

Above: Jimmy Winchester, the cook, at the gangway. Jimmy served on the ship for ten years.

Fetlar Museum Trust

Above: There are many side profiles of both *Earl*s, yet each with its distinctive nature. This photograph is no exception, the second *Earl*, her anchor chain angled out, waiting off Houbie on Fetlar. With her derrick in the non-working position, which is unusual, it is thought her visit coincides with the coronation of Queen Elizabeth in 1953. Certainly she is carrying maximum of bunting, fully dressed overall, while passengers seem to find the well-deck catwalk a particular vantage point.

Sandra Sales

Above: As if specially posed for the photograph she lies motionless in a near flat-calm off the Bressay banks and her bunting hangs limp in the windless conditions. There is evidence of some passengers on the foredeck but only two stand at the stern. The photograph is probably unique because of the *Earl*'s static position and the locality. It may have been taken about the time of her arrival in Shetland in 1939. Noticeable is the agreeable proportion of the port lifeboat to the size of the ship. Bigger lifeboats were fitted at a later date.

tide could make a return to the ship difficult and unlikely; yet one or two intrepid people went ashore to explore and stay for a day or two and await the next mail-boat run to Walls.

Captain Johnston took his ship south-about, passing close in by the massive precipices of the Kame of Foula and raising the seabirds in their thousands in agitated clamour with a blast on the siren, then rounding the north of the isle with the second highest cliffs in Britain — only surpassed by St Kilda — and taking farewell of a remote isle past the marvel of the amazing arch of the Gaada Stack. By way of compensation at failure to land, the skipper took his passengers in past Vaila on the mainland to enjoy what is splendid rock scenery en route to Lerwick via Spiggie.

Coincidentally Jimmy Johnston was party to the 75th anniversary of the first visit to Foula by William Nicolson's *Earl of Zetland* in 1878 — 75 years; where had they gone!

Also, 1953 was the first year when all three — Fair Isle, Foula and Muckle Flugga — summer excursions happened as planned. The Flugga outing was offered with imaginative variety, leaving Lerwick at 9am; Uyeasound at 12.30pm; Bluemull Sound along the west side of Unst;

around Muckle Flugga, to Baltasound around 3pm … leave via Uyeasound (if required) 5.30pm; back in Lerwick about 9pm, all at twenty-five shillings, including high tea.

Seventy-five years and 75 passengers — the recorded number for the Flugga voyage — and a circumnavigation of Unst for good measure! It proved to be a fabulous Sunday of weather and experience: " … a boiling ebb tide with us, we sweep through Bluemull Sound at a spanking rate, one lovely view following the other … Cullivoe was surely at its loveliest, Gloup and Blue Mull showing their heights to great advantage … on to the pièce de resistance of the trip, Muckle Flugga … much was the wonderment at the achievement of the building of the lighthouse — on such an inaccessible and towering height. Yet withal it is recorded that seas, not merely spume but a weight of solid water, have swept over that great rock … more than 200 feet up, to pour in an irresistible cataract carrying everything loose before it down the other side.

"On Sunday the rock and lighthouse looked out on an ocean serene, and to waving signals exchanged between passengers and the lightkeepers we rounded the tip of Unst, with nothing between us and the North Pole but

Jan Mayen Island, hundreds of miles away … we took farewell of Flugga with a strident blast on the siren to the evident alarm and annoyance of seabirds …

"As we left Baltasound dark, lowering clouds gathered and with remarkable swiftness a thunderstorm developed, which as quickly after a few reverberating peals, passed over … in steadily improving weather we reached Lerwick via Whalsay at 10pm — the end of a … well nigh perfect day."

Innovation was the byword of the North Company, by 1953 changed to the North of Scotland, Orkney and Shetland Shipping Company (their first motor vessel, the new *Earl* had been a catalyst for the name alteration), and every opportunity was taken to promote their Shetland interior shipping routes. The year 1954 was "trip-intensive". Adverts proliferated: on Wednesday, 23rd June, an evening cruise round Bressay; on Sunday, 27th June, an excursion to Fair Isle; on Wednesday, 30th June, a unique outing to experience the eclipse of the sun!

This was due on the afternoon of the Wednesday when the eclipse was anticipated to be total from a point some 40 miles north of Muckle Flugga, therefore the north ends of Unst and Yell were going to be the finest viewpoints in Britain. So there appeared the one-off notice in the Shetland newspapers: "Eclipse of the sun. Sailing of MV *Earl of Zetland* on Wednesday, 30th June, 1954 …"

The *Earl* and Leask's overland service were inundated by a host of astronomers, scientists, press-men, photographers and others. Most of the people aimed for Unst as the best option but others opted for Yell. Three American astronomers from Pennsylvania had their observation post at Gutcher, with equipment reckoned to be insured for £10,000. The *Earl* had set off from Lerwick at 7am, called at Whalsay, Brough Lodge, Mid Yell and Uyeasound and reached Baltasound in good time for the eclipse. She had on board school parties from Lerwick Central School and Brough School, Whalsay.

Inadvertently there was an indirect comment on the state of the roads. The American astronomers had brought their instruments by vehicle and, " … the lorry had to be padded and the driver moved along at little more than a walking pace." They might have been well-advised to try the *Earl*!

Nature could have been more kind to the assembled multitude and it was summed up in a national newspaper heading: "Three seconds we can never forget." … "We saw it. It was the merest glimpse through the dark, driving clouds. But for perhaps three seconds, we saw the total eclipse, probably as much as any observer in Europe this side of Sweden."

"It was a near thing. Half an hour after the excursion steamer (sic) *Earl of Zetland,* then four hours out from Lerwick, tied up at the pier at Baltasound, a wall (sic) of cloud blew over the sky." The report was accompanied by a photograph of Captain James Johnston showing Mary Hunter of Scalloway the Azimuth Mirror, seen on this page.

In his fine book "The Second St Ola" by that natural, indeed obsessive, North boats enthusiast, the late Alastair McRobb, published in 1977, he makes frequent reference to the relationship between the Orkney ship and the second *Earl*. Regularly the old *Earl* had covered for both the steamer *St Olaf* of 1882 and her successor *St Ola* (1) of 1892.

Although the *St Ola* (II) was built by A. Hall and Company Limited (as distinct from Hall, Russell and Company Ltd) nearly ten years after the *Earl*, in 1948 she had remarkably similar proportions, although with no well-deck and having two lifeboats on each side.

When the *St Ola* departed for her first overhaul in January 1952 Jimmy Johnston took his ship away to relieve her, while — almost a tradition — the *St Clement* (II) covered the Shetland North Isles. Her predecessor had

Elma Groat

Above: Jimmy Johnston on the bridge, showing stylishly-clad passenger, Mary Hunter (now Mrs Houston), some of the basic elements of handling an Azimuth Mirror. The instrument held by her was a device fitted on top of the compass bowl and was used, firstly, to take bearings of the sun/moon/stars to ascertain the compass error and, secondly, to take bearings of prominent points of land (or objects on shore such as a lighthouse) to fix the ship's position when involved in coastal navigation. Detachable as required, the Azimuth Mirror had a small hand wheel with an arrow attached to the prism, and when pointing upwards was positioned for heavenly bodies, and downwards for land bearings. Judging by the angle of the derrick, cargo is being worked.

Elma Groat

Left: The *Earl* lies at anchor off the north-east haven at Fair Isle during a visit on a fine sunlit summer's day in the early sixties for what might well be a National Trust for Scotland occasion. The ship displays her bunting at the foremast, as the afternoon sunlight glances off the bridge.

Two boatloads of visitors appear to have embarked for the run back aboard, both boats heavily laden and people apparently unconcerned about safety! A knot of wellwishers is gathered on the pier, today obliterated by modern harbour works and screened from northern gales by a solid breakwater stretching from the skerry to the banks on the right.

Above: Young men in the old days, because 1959 is no longer just yesterday! Bobby Scott, saloon steward, Jimmy Winchester, cook, and Archie Thomson, galley boy, seen at what was often a favourite corner for photographs.

Like her predecessor the second *Earl* always was given fastidious attention in maintenance and kept in sound working condition. Locations for upkeep varied but often she was slipped at Hall, Russell & Co. in Aberdeen, indeed where she had been built. These box-camera snapshots were taken in the 1950s by Jimmy Winchester. **Above:** Bill Coull, a crewman, leaning at the stern prior to the ship being taken out of the water. **Below:** The *Earl* coming off the slip after the work done on her. Back view of an unknown deckhand and onlooker Bobby Scott, steward. The bow of an Aberdeen trawler appears, awaiting slipping.

done so too. Then the *St Ola* came to Shetland regularly in the mid-1950s when the *Earl* was on refit, thus a reciprocal arrangement was made year by year. The duration of this kind of interchange would be about three weeks, with an unexpected extension of a fortnight when the *Earl of Zetland* was discovered to have a cracked tail shaft in 1968.

There was a mild irony in two instances when over her years in service the Orkney vessel had remained trouble free and unscathed, and suddenly, on Saturday, 26th November, 1960, in leaving Aberdeen for Lerwick to replace the *Earl,* she developed mechanical problems and had to turn back. Meanwhile the Shetland vessel had already left Lerwick that same Saturday for the overhaul and was too far into her voyage to return. The Monday/Tuesday run to the North Isles was a non-starter!

Secondly, back in 1964, the *St Ola* had a glancing blow from an underwater rock at the north entrance of Lerwick harbour when bound for the isles and was obliged to return to Victoria Pier for inspection. There was no damage of consequence, while it was never confirmed if she had touched on Robbie Ramsay's Baa, the scene of a much more serious mishap in 1924, some 40 years previously.

The old *Earl* had had more than her fair share of misfortune but the immense difference in power and marine technology meant that her now illustrious successor was never going to be at anything like the same risk, albeit she had had her moments during the war and infrequent peacetime mechanical malfunction, the odd mishap, and the heavy seas of a Shetland winter — even summer.

Today, beside the splendid Boat Haven at Norwick on Unst there is the unexpected evidence of a remedy against any (further) mishap. Outside, as a permanent feature, is a large encrusted anchor which had been salvaged from the sea-bed during the Baltasound harbour development at the end of the 20th century. It was realised that this anchor was, in fact, used by the *Earl.*

The explanation is that the ship had given herself and the pier a severe dunt during a nasty south-east gale in 1951. The simple solution to avoid further risk had been to lay the anchor on a convenient shoal with a chain laid into the pier, enabling the skipper to haul her off if need be.

Saturday, 1st February, 1953, was a further case in point. Captain Johnston had brought the ship back from the North Isles amid increasing northerly wind gusts and vicious rain squalls. In the north harbour of Lerwick the short, steep seas had their tops whipped off and the surface was beginning to "smoke" in a seething mass of spindrift. The north-facing side of the Victoria Pier was untenable, leaving no choice for the *Earl* other than running and attempting to ride it out between the Knab and the Bressay Light.

She was forced to dodge, keeping just enough holding power and bows on as consistently as possible in the face of a mean wind speed of 76 mph at 10.30am, heightened by a gust of 100 mph at 11.20am. The crew had a long, weary night in their containing action, until by 8.30am on the Sunday the wind and sea eased and the ship could be berthed at her usual place, when harm became evident — fortunately not to the *Earl.*

The hurricane — for it was so — produced the worst seas ever seen in the harbour; two launches and a haddock boat sunk; destruction at piers; the pier up at Symbister demolished; tragically two Nesting brothers, Harold and Harry Gear, were drowned when out setting haddock lines; there was damage to buildings in Fort Charlotte; electricity and telephone lines were disrupted … the lanes of Lerwick, Commercial Street and even the Hillhead were littered with sand, grit and debris.

Orkney suffered too. A counterpart of the Shetland North Isles vessel, the *Earl Thorfinn,* was caught on passage and had, like the *Earl,* to run but into the open sea east of Orkney. She had no radio and apparently disappeared although after surviving frighteningly mountainous seas she eventually turned up in Aberdeen after a nightmare experience.

Even in June 1953 poor weather disrupted events on the Queen's Coronation day. Activities and games for the children were cancelled as were Monday and Wednesday special trips round Bressay by the *Earl.*

However, the marine climate and its vagaries notwithstanding, the North Company persevered with the principle of excursion sailings until economic and financial pressures decreed otherwise, while two other factors rumbled on, firstly the pier problem and, secondly, the whole thorny matter of transport to, and within, the North area of Shetland. For the moment though — during the three decades of the reign of the *Earl of Zetland* and all associated with her — the folk in the North Isles in particular continued to appreciate a ship and her men. Like the old vessel she was still the vital cog in the wheel.

A COLOURFUL ROUTINE

The 1950s had seen diversity and diversification in abundance and the roller-coaster type progression of the second *Earl* continued towards the fourth quarter of the 20th century. In some ways she had been "living dangerously" because as early as 1953 — the *Shetland News* carried a headline: "Question of the *Earl of Zetland* being taken off" — her very existence was being debated in District and County Councils. The arguments revolved round the plus and the minus: "… the *Earl* would probably be taken off … it is very difficult for people getting off to the steamer (sic) in small boats in winter … soaked right through and having to remain like that until they get to Lerwick. If piers were provided the company might hold onto the *Earl*." And further: "… the idea of withdrawing the ship and putting everything overland is absurd. Anybody who knows anything about the Yell roads knows that it will be many years before they can carry the necessary traffic. In any case on the overland there are no public conveniences at the likes of Toft and Ulsta.

"There will always be a need for a boat to be based at Lerwick for carrying the heavy goods. The Council should do all they can to retain the *Earl,* keeping in mind the North Company is profit-making and cannot be expected to do the North Isles run at a loss. They cannot exist without a sea service. Is the Council prepared to subsidise freights to keep people in the North Isles?"

The major deliberations continued year by year, frustratingly, inconclusively. The *Earl* pursued her regular courses, appearing round headlands, skirting beaches and banks, dropping anchor at ports, boating off goods and passengers and animals as had always been, seemingly from time immemorial. The 1950s had come and gone and the *Earl of Zetland*, oblivious to all human indecision and infighting, continued her own imperturbable way like her predecessor.

Positive marketing of the additional excursions by the motor vessel expanded, the North Company being concerned on two counts, one to offer the public variety over and above regular voyaging and, two, keeping in mind the delicate balance of profit and loss. In fact, it was a tightrope to the extent that in 1961 the Secretary of State for Scotland agreed in principle to offer financial support to the North Company to keep the North Isles vessel in existence, while in a take-over background there was the prospect of a buy-out of the company by Coast Lines Limited.

There was no firm conclusion about this by Christmas 1961 but a "gift" to someone was in the offing; while the *Earl* ranged around. Her Christmas week took in intermediate ports to Uyeasound and back to Lerwick on 24th December; a break for Captain Johnston and crew; North Isles again, 28th December; and she called at Skerries on 22nd and 29th December.

The newspaper advert continued: "New Year week … Monday, 31st December, no sailing. Leave Lerwick, Wednesday, 2nd January, at 8am. Normal trip will call at Skerries, returning to Lerwick same night if conditions permit. Leave Lerwick, Friday, 4th January, normal sailing."

Then, adding to the timetable to Aberdeen fulfilled by the *St Clair* (III) and *St Ninian* (II) the *Earl* was billed to sail south: "*Earl of Zetland* to Aberdeen — Leaves Lerwick, Saturday, 5th January, at 5pm. Limited number of first-class passengers." There was no mention of passenger-carrying on her return, but sailing under new owners was imminent.

Interestingly, Coast Lines had absorbed a number of smaller firms in the relatively recent years, including Burns and Laird Lines Limited of Glasgow, and David MacBrayne Limited although this firm had been amalgamated as far back as 1928. In turn — in a developing age of take-overs — David MacBrayne was united into Caledonian MacBrayne in 1973. Then — and maybe finally? — there has been the fascinating change in that P&O Scottish Ferries who, in sequence, absorbed Coast Lines in the mid-1970s have themselves been ironically outbid for the Aberdeen, Orkney and Shetland services by a consortium of Caledonian MacBrayne and the Royal Bank of Scotland, with the not-inappropriate title "NorthLink". The change-over occurs in October 2002, coincidentally the 125th anniversary year of the coming of the first *Earl of Zetland*.

Below: At last another sturdy structure, with the ship securely tied up at Yell's most northerly port, Cullivoe, on a fine day of summer. Robert Spence, the local steamer's agent strides along the pier with a couple of gas cylinders. Sundry passengers find diverse things to look at. Above the foredeck is the top of the ridge of Valla Field on the west side of Unst.

Bruce Spence

The 21st century is now a far-cry from the late 50s and early 60s, although surveys and "feasibility studies" are so much part of life today, as then. Such a study was offered in 1958 by Mr W. MacGillivray, managing director of the Prince Line, who surveyed the islands transport questions at no cost to the County Council. He envisaged both steamer (sic) and overland services continuing, "at least for some time," but he believed it would be in the North Isles interests if the shipping company ran the overland service as well, or, at a minimum acquired a substantial interest in a joint company running it. He observed the need for a faster service and that it was the Council's intention to have various piers built, but the first, at Mid Yell, was not completed until 1953, and it could only be worked at certain states of the tide. Apart from that and an unusable erection at Skerries, no new piers at which the *Earl* could work had been established. "Losses to the company have been offset to some extent by the promotion of tourist traffic to the isles, but overall the service has been operated at a loss ..."

Then, as far as a balance between past and present is concerned Mr MacGillivray speculated correctly when he reported: "The question of introducing vehicle ferries need not be considered until the *Earl* is nearing the end of her useful life — on the assumption, of course, that the company are prepared to retain her till then ... it might be that the cost of replacing the *Earl* is so great that despite the attractions for tourists, the sea route would have to be abandoned in favour of vehicle ferries." In that context he was not far wrong but it was always unlikely that any shipping company per se would wish to have the onus of land and sea transport in the domestic Shetland scene. Admittedly P&O had developed extensive and valuable vehicle transport links with the South and into Shetland but were not offering a timetabled route as far north as Unst. That service has always been maintained by local operators, and rightly so, especially since the advent of vehicle ferries in the 1970s.

In the post-war reconstruction Lerwick Harbour Trust had looked to their own priorities — North Isles piers were outwith their jurisdiction — and the Victoria Pier was scheduled for improvement. While there was procrastination elsewhere, by 1953 work had begun; in fact the contractors, Wimpey, had equipment destroyed in the January hurricane.

During the summers of 1956 and 1957 work was forging ahead and the *Earl*, along with other North Company ships, was berthed at Alexandra Wharf as seen in the photograph on page 102. The pity is that North Isles piers could not have been scheduled in parallel with the Lerwick project!

That the *Earl* still had a very vital role in Shetland life was evident enough at the end of December 1958 when "in response to traders and others", a previously cancelled sailing to the North Isles on the last day of the year was reinstated. That trip did happen, but January brought the almost inevitable gales. The third week of the month was horrific; at exposed Saxavord on Unst a gust of 112 mph was recorded; for two or three days everything was affected — no movement — as blizzards prevailed; the *St Clair* could not berth at Lerwick and rode out the storm in the harbour; the *Earl* was stormbound with extra warps out. Up at Gutcher in Yell the old Bluemull Sound ferry-boat, *Viking,* sank at her moorings.

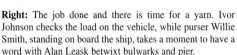

Left: Unloading at Mid Yell seems to be well on the way to completion. Ivor Johnson rests from his labours on one or two loaded lorries with goods destined mainly for the shops. Boxes and bags abound, while on the trolley below, the box on the extreme right carries the legend, "THIS WAY UP ... HANDLE WITH CARE". It is upside down!

John Nicolson, with cap, has his back to the camera and a group of men in the foreground appear to be engrossed – in something! As ever, passengers are interested spectators.

Right: The job done and there is time for a yarn. Ivor Johnson checks the load on the vehicle, while purser Willie Smith, standing on board the ship, takes a moment to have a word with Alan Leask betwixt bulwarks and pier.

Behind them a car with registration FNM 761E has an L-plate, suggesting that with the gradual arrival of more and more vehicles people are interested in learning to drive in the early 1960s. Willie Nisbet, wearing the light cap, is perhaps eyeing the sillocks in the water below the pier.

There were storms too in other areas, or at least disagreement, as a committee appointed to consider transport in the North Isles had ideas opposed to William MacGillivray's findings; their view was that those operating the overland service could take over the *Earl;* his was still that the shipping company could take over the ferry service! He pointed out that the motor vessel belonged to a company which had technical expertise and a shore staff equipped to deal with repairs and surveys, while a replacement ship could be easily found during refits. Being one of a fleet the *Earl* could be manned more economically, while so long as they owned her the North Company would be striving to foster tourism with all the promotional abilities and financial strength at their disposal, and in association with their other ships.

Despite complex deliberations the outcome was inconclusive, although the *Earl* continued to be a strong presence for all. In the May of 1959 she carried an official party from Lerwick to Fair Isle for — the opening of a new pier! The cruise ship *Meteor* was already at anchor near the entrance to the North Haven, her white hull and upperworks sparkling in the sunshine, and she was joined by the *Earl* looking small by comparison but very trim … In a toast to the new pier Sir Basil Neven Spence, Lord Lieutenant of Shetland, remarked, somewhat implausibly; "Piers in Shetland are like ashtrays in a house — you can never have too many of them …" Having lived most of his life on Uyea Isle off Uyeasound he knew about piers and their significance to a community … Only a month

Above: A yarn is interrupted for a photographer and the *Earl* is at full speed between ports. Bosun Lowrie Gifford, with his familiar pipe between his teeth, shares a moment in talking to donkey-man Bertie Pearson.

Behind them is the sealed off ventilator which had become redundant and on top of it a ubiquitous tyre, handy as a fender with a flit-boat at the well-deck. 1956.

Above: Relief Chief Engineer Alastair McRobb on board the *Earl* in 1956 at Lerwick. Born in 1930, with a Shetland mother, he was educated in Aberdeen and served his time in Hall, Russell's shipyard. Boyhood trips to the islands originated a lifelong enthusiasm for the "North Boats". After initial training and experiences he became Chief Engineer on the second *St Ninian* in 1962, thus he was well placed to further his great capacity for research and historical enquiry. The author of this book has cause to be very grateful for the in-depth ready assistance during research for the book *The Saga of a Ship – The Earl of Zetland* published in 1982.

Sadly, Alastair McRobb had a sudden and untimely death in 1998 before the text of his book *The North Boats* was completed, but friend Ian Somerville ensured the final section was rounded off. Maureen McRobb, his wife, donated the superb memorabilia collection to Aberdeen Maritime Museum.

Above: Three crew members in 1954. Left to right are Jimmy Winchester, then galley-boy, George Irvine, cook, and Alastair McRobb, relief chief engineer. He had a compulsive interest in all matters about the North Boats and maintained this throughout his lifetime. He was a frequent contributor to shipping magazines on the theme.

The three ladies names are unknown but they are passengers on the excursion round-trip to the North Isles from Lerwick in an era when the North Company was working hard at promoting such visits.

later in June the folk in Uyeasound were unanimous in not wishing a pier proposed for neighbouring Belmont. The pier wrangles were continuing!

Then Captain Johnston had arranged for the *Earl's* bunting to be looked out for the Queen's visit … six hundred and ninety six years since a reigning sovereign had visited Shetland … but at short notice there was cancellation, this due to information about a forthcoming addition to the Royal family. There was full approval for the good news; some disapproval at short notice given but very encouraging that the non-appearance was a postponement — probably until 1960 — and not a cancellation.

Seasonal gales arrived in the October. Once again the *Clair* was isolated offshore, a galling experience for some passengers sitting in mid-harbour within sight of their homes in Lerwick; members of a concert party expecting to play in the Garrison theatre that Tuesday evening were stranded on board; they amply entertained fellow passengers! The *Clair* had been on passage for 48 hours!

In Lerwick several of the new television aerials came down. Also the *Earl* stayed up in Unst waters overnight until wind and sea eased.

In February 1960 there was the heaviest one-night snowfall for a very long time; some old-timers reckoned the early years of the century competed for depth; some thought 1917 had seen the deepest. Winds

gusted to 80 mph which forced the *Earl* to abandon her Wednesday trip north: snow clearing (and snowballing!) occupied her crew …

Meanwhile, the silting at Linkshouse pier, Mid Yell, may or may not have been accounted for by gales … the east side was proving to be unusable for much of the time … on the west side the depth only allowed for berthing at half-tide, with rising water. Removal of the sand by Council under-water jetting equipment would be slow and expensive, thus an outcome which had been debated for years was hardly proving fully satisfactory …

This was in contrast to 10th August, 1960, when the *Earl* could display her bunting. As promised, Her Majesty the Queen, opened the harbour works, which had been ongoing since February 1955, by declaring about those responsible: "Their work will live on after them and will, I am sure, make an important contribution to the prosperity and well-being of these islands." Since 74 years had passed it was unlikely that anyone present in 1960 would be able to say, "I was there" when the old *Earl* was the first vessel to come in at the inaugural Victoria Pier in 1886; but she had gone on to make her own contribution as was happening with the new *Earl* in another era.

Yet the early 1960s were tending to be a period of concern, because depopulation was an insidious negative. In 1960 the Shetland figure of 18,000 was an all-time low, nevertheless a year later there was a further fall to 17,812; and a 13.8% decrease in landward areas. If there might have

Left: Jimmy Leask of Lerwick, galley-boy on the MV *Earl of Zetland* circa 1961. The setting provides a rather dramatic perspective of the ladder and the upper-deck abaft the funnel.

Below: Late sunlight glints on hull and superstructure, and the Bressay houses, as an evening cruise begins. The *Earl*'s unduly large lifeboats, from a proportion point of view, affect her appearance.

The group of four semi-detached houses were characteristic of what went up throughout the islands in the post-war period and they continue to serve today. In the foreground a youthful-looking figure in a peerie rowing boat tries his hand at the fishing. 1955.

Jimmy Winchester

Jimmy Winchester

been an influence on transport thinking for the country, this was modified when the hitherto long-term trend was reversed and the population began to increase again in the later years of the decade. Thus a long spell of transition was proving to be like the wind, changeable.

The *Earl of Zetland* was being subjected to the wind; the wind of change. Time and time again the name cropped up in official thinking, although the folk still regarded her as the essential lifeline while there were those — and not a few — who had been captivated by the romance of the Shetland lore witnessed through the ship.

Gordon Donaldson, to whom this book is dedicated, was one of them and in his delightful book "Isles of Home — Seventy Years of Shetland", published after his death, he expressed due sentiments which had also been told to me in the 1970s: "In the spring of 1966 I arranged a trip … Thursday night I was in the Queens Hotel in Lerwick before joining the *Earl* on the Friday morning … I looked out of my bedroom window over the harbour to see a singularly wintry landscape in Bressay, clad in white and with a lowering sky. My heart sank as I walked from the hotel to board the snow-covered *Earl,* but the showers soon gave way to sunshine. By the time we reached Mid Yell the snow had cleared on land but the ship's foredeck still carried a covering and the crew could snowball the men on the Linkshouse pier without fear of retaliation … it was well on in the day before we reached Baltasound, and a group of passengers hired a mini-bus to go to Norwick and then up to the top of Saxavord … a new and striking view of Flugga lying below as well as to the south and south-west over Unst, Yell and Northmavine — all seen in the waning light of an April day when there were many snow showers around and looking like the splendour of an old oil painting …

"This whetted my appetite and in September the same year I for the first time booked for one of the Company's inclusive tours … to pass Saturday night on the south boat at Lerwick and transfer to the *Earl* to spend Sunday night on board before making the round of the North Isles on Monday –Tuesday. That was another trip with an unexpected episode. It was the lamb-shipping season, so on the Monday we pushed on up to Baltasound, where we arrived — incredibly — about 2pm, were allowed four hours 'for a run ashore' as the skipper put it, and then left for Brough Lodge to ship lambs. We arrived off Fetlar to find the island brilliantly lit by the evening sunshine. I was briefly ashore to visit friends and then got back to see the *Earl* silhouetted against the setting sun, to rejoin her to cross to Uyeasound where we lay overnight. On the way south on Monday there was another special treat, for Captain Sinclair took the *Earl* close into the waters round the Horse of Burravoe which I used to know so well in a small boat.

"By this time completely converted to 'the steamer' and increasingly aware that her days were numbered, I made up my mind to miss no opportunity of a trip on her. I never went north overland again until I could go with my own car once a vehicle ferry to Yell appeared … I also became an addict of the Mini Cruises which offered a trip on the *Earl* as long as she operated … by this time I was remarking that my idea of paradise was a season ticket on the North Isles steamer …"

Gordon Donaldson was not alone in his enthusiasm. There were different categories: those who lived in Shetland, travelled on occasion, and regarded the *Earl* as essential and something of a much-loved tradition, those exiles or very interested parties who remembered both ships with affection and had enjoyed them; and those of a more specialist grouping whose pursuit was a broad one, embracing shipping in general.

Brian Patton comes into the latter category and in a book about Scottish coastal steamers including Shetland ships — specialist in its own right — he has mentioned how such vessels exercised a fascination for those who have known them, far greater than the interest aroused by similar ships elsewhere in the world.

Now two were becoming a part of folk memory — one gone from the scene and the other on her way to posterity in the Shetland sense — yet the second *Earl,* the ongoing subject of lively political concern in the affairs of local authorities, was still posing questions.

Sport was an unlikely element in the sheer diversity of the *Earl of Zetland's* cause and effect, although she had provided transport on occasion for the annual Orkney v Shetland sports meeting. But in March 1962 the North Company presented a trophy for annual competition between schools football teams in Whalsay, to be known as "The Earl of Zetland Cup". It was a much-appreciated gesture gratefully accepted by islanders of a big and very successful fishing community.

By the middle of August 1962 the Shetland County Council had decided to send a delegation to Norway to look at their ferry system, following a study and report by Mr H. K. Oppegaard, a Norwegian ferry expert, who was county engineer for More and Romsdal which had about 40 vehicle ferries working. He had covered the *Earl's* routes and distances overland, including all short sea links to Unst, Yell, Fetlar, Skerries and Whalsay.

Councillor A. I. Tulloch had pointed out that the *Earl's* life span was now limited (she was 23 years old). To replace her would cost £300,000, which would almost double her running costs. Meanwhile the government subsidy could only be a temporary measure.

Above: On the bridge Captain Case, Marine Superintendent of Coast Lines enjoys a draw on his pipe in the company of the skipper. He liked to make informal visits, sailing up to Lerwick via Orkney on the *Ninian,* making a round trip of the North Isles with the *Earl* and returning direct to Aberdeen on the *Clair.* Of course it had been confirmed that the North Company had been taken over by Coast Lines in 1961/62.

Above: Jimmy Johnston entertains a formally dressed gentleman on the bridge.

Mr C. G. Spence then "hit the nail on the head" when he commented: "We can go ahead with our outdated transport system for a year or two longer," he said. "It will eventually cost the council quite a sum for repair of existing piers and so on, but eventually we'll have to have a through service."

Rev H. A. S. Brydone had no objection to sending a delegation to Norway if they were going to achieve something. He recalled they had had the MacGillivray report and they did not like it. Two private companies were serving the islands at no cost and no trouble to the council. As long as one or both were prepared to continue he did not see why they should consider spending £300,000, especially on a problematical ferry service.

The Shetland Times editorial "The Old Rock" chipped in on 24th August, 1962, and commented; "No more complex problem has confronted Shetland County Council than that of transport to the North Isles. A political decision must soon be made ... now the views of two experts, Mr MacGillivray and Mr Oppegaard ... in fairness to the former the circumstances have altered; the life of the *Earl* is further expended and the need for ferry piers more clamant, while the delay in pier works through lack of long term policy is more distressing ...

"It is wise to send a deputation to Norway to see ferries operating in open water in winter conditions ..."

The editorial was reflected in County Council discussion about Uyeasound pier, also in 1962: "The convener explained that the future of the whole North Isles transport system depended on whether a vessel like the *Earl of Zetland* was going to be maintained or not. On that would depend the decision about a new pier ... a fair bet that things would remain as they are for perhaps another ten years — or the reasonable working life of the *Earl of Zetland*."

Jimmy Winchester

Above: An unorthodox glimpse of Brough Lodge, Fetlar, seen through a cabin port-hole in 1955. The silhouette of the unusual architecture is of particular interest, while a car stands at the lower end of the much-used slip.

Elma Groat

Left: The *Earl* is berthed along Alexandra Wharf, during the summer of 1956 or 1957, while work at Victoria Pier was in progress. There is ongoing work in the well-deck and on the quay, below the Brentham Place building at the back on the right. The familiar Fisherman's Mission was opened in the spring of 1962 on what had become waste ground on the other side of Harbour Street.

THE BEGINNING OF ANOTHER END

The speaker had it about right, for within the decade the phasing out of the *Earl* had begun, although her existence in the interim was not short of interest as evinced by Gordon Donaldson and Brian Patton. However, what became apparent was the gradual reduction in press advertising of excursion sailings compared to the 1950s when three notices could appear at a time in the *Shetland News* and *Shetland Times*. In 1963 and 1964 they were noticeable by their absence, replaced in the main by information about livestock movements, (although in June 1963 an advert featured senior and junior football teams from Whalsay playing in Lerwick).

"MV *Earl of Zetland*. To connect with calf sale at Lerwick above vessel will sail from Uyeasound at 6am on Tuesday, 15th October, 1963. Calves from Cullivoe, Feltar and Baltasound will be uplifted on Monday pm, 14th October.

"MV *Earl of Zetland*. Livestock. In connection with calf sale on Tuesday, 13th October, above vessel will sail from Lerwick at 7am on Monday, 12th October, calling at Whalsay, Skerries, Houbie, Mid Yell, Uyeasound, Baltasound; return to Uyeasound. On Tuesday vessel will leave Uyeasound at 6am, calling at Cullivoe, Mid Yell, Whalsay and Lerwick.

It was true that the *Earl* was providing an attractive dimension for holiday visitors in general but it is likely that, overall, excursions had not proved to be cost effective in the long term. The Mini-Cruises continued as long as she operated, while there were occasional outings. A cruise to Baltasound and round Flugga was planned at the time of a Historical Congress in 1969, but adverse weather put paid to that. The Shetland Antiquarian Society was more fortunate and made special cruises to Fair Isle and Fetlar.

In December 1964 there was an ominous press headline; "*Earl* runs up

big deficit." The government subsidy had been in place since October 1960, but four years later the operating deficit had risen above the £10,000 a year limit. A report stated: "The annual grant will be calculated so as to cover the (North) company's losses. There is also an incentive provision, so that in a good year the company will share equally with the Government the first £1000 of profit and in a bad year they will have to bear half the first £1000 of loss. The Government will retain control over the service provided and the rates and fares charged …"

Meanwhile, already approved in principle by North Isles councillors was the £300,000 vehicular ferry system to replace the "steamer" and existing overland services. At the other end of the scale of authority, in December 1964, Mr William Ross, Secretary of State for Scotland made his first speech on Scottish affairs in the Commons on the 55th day of the new Wilson Government. On his agenda was a draft undertaking to meet the shipping company's deficit for this year of over £10,000 and, if necessary, to deal with the matter over future years.

"One of the serious reasons for the increase in the grant is depopulation and the fact that the service is not being used because the people are just not there to use it," he said. The statement seems today unduly pessimistic because the actual depopulation figure between 1960 and 1961 had been under 200, albeit with a larger percentage from the country districts.

However, he went on to describe the importance of any agreement, "because we are dealing with people to whom communications mean life". One reason for the loss had been the transfer of passenger traffic to what was known in the islands as the overland service, in which boats about 25 feet long operated between islands. "If we develop this service it could well be that in the end we would have something much cheaper," he said. "It may be more efficient in the long run, but the prospect of that is years ahead …"

Jo Grimond the able and kenspeckle MP for Orkney and Shetland

Shetland Museum

Above: Loading or unloading? It is not easy to tell. The scene is typical in the handling of animals by steamer and the practicalities of dealing with cattle in islands with almost non-existent pier facilities. No doubt someone will know which port this is.

Brian Patton

Above: Firmly alongside at Mid Yell in 1972. The bow rope is as taut as it could be! By contrast a swathe of seaweed, probably from anchoring at Uyeasound, hangs down from the starboard anchor. There is plenty of onshore activity, although hardly of a bustling nature!

In the bottom left-hand corner is a glimpse of Bobby Tulloch's dinghy at the stern of his motor boat.

Michael Gray

Above: On the old *Earl* all mystery was removed from navigation as the skipper stood amid the passengers in conning his ship, but on the second *Earl* the bridge was of course modernised and essentially a place apart from passengers. As experienced and noted by that inveterate voyager Gordon Donaldson, "… a sense of all being in it together …" prevailed and became almost a tradition over the decades in the era of "Da auld *Earl*".

In some respects this continued on the new ship. Certainly the Captain could hardly be completely aloof due to so much direct involvement with the community and here we see a group of youngsters joining Willie Sinclair on the bridge as the *Earl* leaves what could be Baltasound. The deck space behind the actual bridge is another vantage point and a passenger makes his way up there.

added his voice: "These (*Earl's*) services are essential to the North Isles of Shetland even though Yell and Unst can be reached by a system of buses and ferries. The isles of Fetlar, the Skerries and Whalsay are almost entirely dependent on the *Earl of Zetland*, and in addition all heavy freight has to be carried by sea …" He added: "I do not want to delay the house in this draft undertaking which my constituents welcome … the servicing of this area … that transport should be considered not by itself but as part of a development policy …

"This is a matter which may affect a small number of people, but it affects them very deeply … they are people who are deeply devoted to their islands and their homes. They want to make a living there …" The House of Commons gave approval to the draft undertaking. The Secretary of State for Scotland and the Liberal MP for Orkney and Shetland had made their successful points. The *Earl* was granted her continuity — if only temporarily — and sailed on.

There was relief in the North Isles as the familiar vessel traversed her rounds, although in August 1965 another craft made a brief appearance. She was the Norwegian vehicle ferry *Rovdehorn* put through her paces at Gremista, Lerwick, and her visit was the result of SCC representation to Norwegian authorities. She revealed the capability of coping with nine varied vehicles. After a demonstration cruise round the harbour the cars and trucks were unloaded at a temporary ramp in just a couple of minutes.

Changes in shipping; changes in personnel. On Sunday, 10th October, 1965, an informal dinner party at Aberdeen, in the Station Hotel, honoured the retiral of Tom Gifford, Commodore of the North Company's fleet since 1959. The general manager Mr Norman Edmond and Mrs Edmond, accompanied by the assistant manager Mr H. W. Scott and Mrs Scott were

Below: An unusually telling focus on the *Earl's* working gear from the catwalk. Her well-used cargo winch is operated by Willie Sinclair at a North Isles port, accompanied by one interested passenger looking down at the unseen flit-boat, and a young couple with thoughts elsewhere.

Below the fall of the well-deck is the stock of the spare anchor and a notice: "Any persons embarking or disembarking otherwise than by the gangway do so at their own risk." It is a reminder that a day of poor weather in winter – or even summer! – could bring its hazards with a flit-boat rising and falling at the open doors of the well-deck. The North Company play safe with their notice!

Douglas Sinclair

hosts to Captain and Mrs Gifford and the new skipper, Captain Johnston and Mrs Johnston. Mrs Edmond presented Captain Gifford with a gold watch. Prior to the *St Clair's* departure from Lerwick, Maggie Sinclair, a stewardess and the youngest member of the crew presented her skipper with a portable typewriter, while Mrs Gifford received a bouquet.

With Jimmy Johnston moving on to take command of the *St Clair* his mate of some 14 years, Willie Sinclair, took command of the motor vessel with which he was so familiar, having skippered her too, from time to time. Of course his appointment marked a long family connection with the North Isles links — he was a grand-nephew of Captain William Nicolson, first-ever captain of the ship which initiated the famous name, *Earl of Zetland.*

David Carmichael (Michael) Gray became mate to Willie Sinclair, having had considerable experience on the North boats. Originally he had gone to sea in 1953 with a Shell scholarship from Gordonstoun School in Moray followed by a three year apprenticeship with Shell and a two-year contract with the firm, during which he sailed world-wide in tankers. He sat for his mate's ticket during that spell. By 1961, having wished to sail nearer home, he had "drifted" into the North Company at the time of the Coast Lines take-over and was second mate on the motor vessel the third *St Rognvald* for some weeks, then served on the third *St Clair* in the early summer of 1965 before being linked with the *Earl of Zetland* formally on 16th June, 1965. In the spring of 1964 he had sailed as second mate on the *St Clair,* captained by Tom Gifford and again with him, briefly, in 1966 on the second *St Ola* as mentioned below, in January 1966. Otherwise Michael Gray became another familiar figure associated with the *Earl* and had the distinction — although sad — of being her last working skipper on the North Isles scene in its fuller sense.

Meanwhile the "team" of Sinclair and Gray took the now venerable motor vessel into the New Year of 1966 when their first sailing then was Tuesday, 4th January, " … from Lerwick at 9.30am. Terminus Baltasound. Returning to Lerwick Wednesday, usual calls including Skerries".

Although the ship was due in Aberdeen immediately afterwards for refit, a bad south-easter forced a return when she was only an hour out from Lerwick. Her familiar replacement, the *St Ola,* skippered by Tom Gifford, temporarily out of retirement, with Michael Gray as mate, had already come up from Orkney and was on her way to the North Isles when she developed windlass problems and turned back … the *Earl,* coincidentally still at the Victoria Pier, immediately sailed for the North Isles then on to Aberdeen again … shades of the 1960 incident, although this time the North Isles did not lose out!

A different kind of crisis — and a serious one — emerged in May 1966 when the National Union of Seamen called a strike over wages and conditions. It was immediately problematical for all Scottish islands … the NUS initially rejected a telegram request from the SCC for a skeleton service to Shetland, cut off except for air services and there was consternation in all areas. The *Earl* made a beat-the-strike run to Unst, Yell, Fetlar and Whalsay, with 30 tons of fuel and foodstuffs but could not cope with last-minute demands, thus islanders began to sense frustration. The *St Magnus* had left Lerwick two hours before the strike deadline at midnight on 15th May, having brought "many hundreds of extra gallons of beer and over 70 tons — twice the normal amount — of flour and groceries".

An Army tank-landing vessel had arrived in Aberdeen to handle essential supplies to Orkney and Shetland; she was not expected to load until into the next week. Worst hit of all, economically, was the tourist industry, losing 300 visitors a week. The MP Jo Grimond flew to Shetland for an on-the-spot investigation into the situation.

Through council and other bodies appeals, and his good offices, the NUS agreed to basic supplies for Shetland through the *St Rognvald,* while Shetlanders believed the Army LCT made available was "grossly unsuitable". The NUS executive only grudgingly were permitting the *St Rognvald* to load at Aberdeen and the Shetland Council for Social Service, joined in the pleas for concessions: "No community has a harder economic struggle in time of peace than ours … no other community knows so well the conditions under which the merchant navy work or have as much sympathy for their present claims. It would be a sad irony if the first and most direct effects of the strike were to fall on the Shetland people."

By the beginning of June the seamen were informed after a Court of Enquiry that their strike was unjustifiable, but the action continued and the County Council, having heard on 21st June that there would be no more relief boats sanctioned by the strikers, decided to appeal directly to the Prime Minister. Meanwhile the *LCT Abbeville* loaded at Aberdeen … 24

hours later she was only about 40 miles into her 180 miles voyage, wallowing in heavy seas and confirming what had been said about her locally … and she had left behind about 70 tons of goods. In the House of Commons Jo Grimmond strongly expressed his disappointment at the inadequate vessel.

Perhaps there had been an element of conscience when the NUS allowed the *St Rognvald* to bring basic essentials to Lerwick … "we have no desire to cause hardship and suffering to ordinary citizens … in

Michael Gray

Above: A low slant of winter sunshine highlights the engine-room telegraph and bridge-house in December 1973 as Michael Gray pauses for a portrait. The *Earl* is heading up the east side of Unst towards Baltasound for her ultimate call there. The inevitable take-over by the much less intimate vehicle ferries is imminent. The skipper sports his Up-Helly-A' beard.

Dennis Coutts

Above: Loading at Victoria Pier. A general scene in the late sixties – a mixture of bustle and leisurely activity, with a strong hint that the *Earl* is being loaded. Striding purposefully along, the man on the right, Ian Mustard, wearing the formality of a tie seems to have deposited his barrow-load. A couple walk past showing little interest in all the ongoings.

Apart from the two oil drums on the left the boxes on the lorry are adorned by a variety of labels ranging through glucose, cream crackers and Ferguzade to, somewhat unexpectedly, what appears to be "Produce of Uganda". The vehicle registrations of PS 3669 and APS 702F are a giveaway about the period. The method of using wooden planks down which to slide boxes is apparent behind the third docker on the left. The mast of the yacht moored abaft the *Earl* is an unusual feature and a harbinger of the ever expanding use of the port of Lerwick by visiting yachts into the 21st century.

particular residents in a community such as yours …" They had previously rejected a telegram appeal.

A *Shetland Times* editorial suggested that, " … some North Company men must seriously be searching their consciences to see where their loyalties lie … sympathy for genuine deep-sea problems; misdirected support for militant elements; responsibilities to own communities. The editorial, commented: "But unless the union accepts that the bare minimum to 'keep us ticking over' (an apt phrase by one of our negotiators) is a weekly sailing without restriction … and in addition a weekly sailing of the *Earl of Zetland* to the North Isles, the call for alternative sea transport will be vociferous." The availability of the *Earl* to participate was not a question because she was being checked daily, her engines turned over, by the officers and could have been under way from Lerwick if allowed.

News of a temporary settlement of the seamen's strike came on 29th June — six weeks after its inception — and the *Earl,* having been sensibly kept "on the alert", was ready to go — to Aberdeen. Relief spilled over into celebration as the Shetland members of the steamer crews gave vent to their release from frustration as she headed out of "da sooth mooth" on Friday, 1st July, calling in by Kirkwall on the way. By the Sunday, fully crewed, the *St Magnus* — formerly *St Clair* (II) — had slipped quietly into her Lerwick berth from Aberdeen to a welcoming but quiet crowd, many straight from Kirk services. Her appearance would seem an answer to their prayers of some six weeks! It was also just about a year before another odd coincidence, since the *St Magnus* (IV) was due to be sold in 1967 exactly a hundred years after the advent of the paddler *St Magnus*; and 1867 was still a decade before the first *Earl of Zetland!*

The folk in the North Isles had had their particular problems with deficiencies during the strike, thus the appearance of "da steamer" was more than welcome, although there came a hitch later in the summer. There had been unwelcome vibration in the *Earl's* engine room which set up an alarming noise, thus it was decided to ground the ship at the north end of the fish mart. During the ebb the Malakoff diver discovered that pieces of the faring plates had worked loose and fallen down inside; also bolts on the plates, which protected the main propeller nut, were missing, hence the throbbing. If there had not been the prompt attention problems would have

escalated, thus a missed Monday sailing could have been the least of it.

Just as well the fault had been sorted out before bad weather set in, for a white Christmas proved to be a nightmare. Storms compounded by blizzards played havoc — electricity breakdowns; no power for 18 hours; air services cancelled; mail was seized up; a shed containing 120 animals on a mink farm was overturned; and unbelievably a dan buoy must have been whipped up from sea level to become impaled on the television mast on Bressay!

The *Earl* was under pressure from the raging storm, and a backlog of seasonal mail built up as she remained quay-bound, but the lull came and she was able to sail north before New Year, then by the end of January she had departed for Aberdeen and annual overhaul.

Perennial pressure from the winter Atlantic lows has been part of life in Shetland, probably from the beginning of time, and on not a few occasions has there been the headline: "Worst in Living Memory". The year 1967 was no exception. The first blast had come during the 1966 Festive Season, then that following February it was reported that not for many years had the North Company experienced such a disruption of its steamer services, including the sailings of the *Earl*. Probably she was fortunate to have "escaped" for that overhaul in Aberdeen!

But year by year "escape" was becoming a feature because there was the ever-increasing uncertainty of a service which was still vital and yet far from secure financially — in fact a liability. Freight costs were continuing to rise and becoming the greatest barrier to island development. Yet the *Earl* had had a £2000 subsidy to begin with and it had rocketed up to £18,000 by 1967, thus she was the subject of an enigma; indispensable as yet, but could she be afforded? To compound the ever-growing complexity the Prices and Incomes Board proposed that the North of Scotland Shipping Company (Coast Lines) should be subsidised through the rates! The Board were reporting on the company's application for a ten per cent increase in the fares and freights structure. Island reaction was strong in opposition … the Western Isles government subsidy was instanced … The MP Jo Grimond was also firmly opposed to the PIB. A. J. Cluness of the Shetland Council of Social Service added to the opposition in a letter to the press. By August 1968 an appeal was made by Shetland Civic leaders direct to the Prime Minister to prevent the ten per cent increase in fares and

Above: An interlude from the dancing during the ship's Christmas dinner dance in 1968. Members of the crew and guests are definitely in festive mood in the Grand Hotel, Lerwick. Included in the second row from the front are key men in the *Earl's* complement and their ladies. On the left is Bertie Pearson, then David Wilson, chief engineer, Willie Sinclair and his wife Marion, and Michael Gray and his wife Doreen. Of the three to the right in the front row, chief steward Bobby Scott is central to the group and to his left are seated Sandy Smith, cook, and Robert Burgoyne, steward.

freight on the *Earl of Zetland*. The Shetland telegram to the Prime Minister was to the point: "Insist you investigate immediately the annihilation of our economy as perpetrated by your Scottish Secretary in inflicting yet another substantial increase on our already penal shipping charges."

Whatever political or financial or economic manoeuvrings were ongoing Willie Sinclair and his intrepid crew continued to serve the folk, although there was a query about cabin accommodation: "More difficult is the provision of cabins on the *Earl* for local residents, a subject of strong complaint by one or two of my North Isles friends. Travelling with an infant is uncomfortable and embarrassing if no privacy is offered … with the very limited accommodation of the *Earl* I do not know the answer to this one." Criticism is always relative, thinking back to conditions on the old *Earl* or, as an extreme, the situation for the Jewish immigrants in 1947, twenty years before.

Livestock shipments figured in the autumn of 1967, then the New Year came in with "the most ferocious blizzard … some people go as far back as to say within living memory". And yet the same had been said the previous year …

So bad was the weather state that the *Earl's* radar could not function on a North Isles visit which took in Skerries, a remarkable achievement considering the wind and sea driving from the north-east. Adam Tait had described the challenge of getting out of the narrow mouth at the harbour there. Ten days after the 1968 storm Willie Sinclair took the ship away for the maintenance programme at Aberdeen, when an extensive refit was done, hinting that the company anticipated a few years yet before their ship was phased out.

That she still had a standing on the tourism circuit was confirmed when a correspondent wrote: "… I spent six annual holidays in Shetland and greatly enjoyed the hospitality of the inhabitants of several islands and not forgetting the *Earl* — without a trip on which no Shetland holiday would be complete." How many visitors would be around in April 1968 no one would ever know but the *Earl* was stormbound for some days in Lerwick. Even an excursion planned for Tuesday, 7th May, was cancelled "owing to bad weather", confirming the often fickle nature of the Shetland climate.

Below: Surging along at speed in the entrance to the voe at Mid Yell. At least one waving passenger, amid a fair complement on the foredeck, seems to be aware of the photographer. Another, probably female, traveller makes her way along the catwalk, while below her the roof of a solitary car can be seen, such an incredible contrast to the great volume of vehicular traffic using the ro-ro ferries on Yell Sound and Bluemull Sound in this 21st century.

Douglas Sinclair

Above: Formality and informality. The mate caught in action at the engine room telegraph which is lined up for "Full Astern" under his gloved hand on what is a breezy day of white caps on the sea.

The three rings of authority are tempered by the check cap worn backwards! Just where this is in the North Isles is open to question. The photograph may have been taken in the late 1940s when Tom Gifford was skipper or very early 1950s when Jimmy Johnston took over; certainly before the perspex screens were fitted to the bridge teak top.

Michael Gray

Shetland Museum

Above: An excursion to Fair Isle with the *Earl* lying at anchor and a small boat alongside. This is a magnificent setting with the banks of Mopul Head providing a fine backdrop. Below it are the delightfully named Wirvie Baas and Kubbi Skerry. The North Haven is in the foreground with the old tripod and derrick at the pier just visible. In this 21st century a very effective breakwater from the shore to the outlying skerry, originally the Stack of the North Haven, has helped to form a sheltered harbour.

Jimmy Winchester

Above: The heavily-laden Houbie flit-boat, an old sixareen which had fished out of Whalsay, on her way ashore during the mid-1950s; a peaceful scene with a calm sea. The two oarsmen are very far forward, while the boat is well endowed by people; one or two of them appear to be concentrating on something in or on the water at the stern. Perhaps an animal? Maybe the Board of Agriculture stallion?

In the background is Leagarth House, home of Sir Watson Cheyne, the great surgeon.

Fetlar Museum & Interpretive Centre

Above: A typical scene at Houbie. The ship lies quietly in waters only just ruffled by a breeze, with the Fetlar flit-boat at the well-deck on the *Earl*'s port side, as was standard. The derrick is swung out in the act of unloading.

In the far background left is the shoreline of the north end of the cliffs at the South Garth. To the right is an offshore rock, Scarf Skerry, which lies to the east side of the Wick of Houbie.

Since this is such a familiar scene it is appropriate to record the letter which appeared in *The Shetland Times* of 13th December, 1974: "With the termination of a splendid service to our island over the years by the familiar *Earl*, we, the members of the Hubie (sic) Flit-boat Committee, and on behalf of our fellow islanders, wish to state publicly that we have many regrets at the close of the service. We sincerely thank all those in the shipping company for a splendid co-operation." The letter was from, Charles Brown, Secretary, Fetlar Flit-boat Committee.

MILESTONES OF FATE

The Shetland Archaeological and Natural History Society had organised the day outing to Fair Isle on Sunday, 16th July, 1968, which emphasised how "when it is good it is very, very good and when it's bad it's horrid". Some 136 people disembarked from the *Earl* at the North Haven and had it very, very good. There was hardly a "lift" on the sea's surface in either direction, thus a hugely successful outing could be enjoyed to the full. Ashore, the Bird Observatory was a focal point, with an archaeology site at the Pund arousing much enthusiasm, then Captain Sinclair sailed through Mousa Sound giving well-satisfied passengers a close look at the broch. "At 7.45 the excursionists reached Lerwick, sunburned and delighted ..." It will never be known how many, if any, appreciated the fact that eighty-two years previously another, the first, *Earl of Zetland* had inaugurated "steamer" trips to Fair Isle; nor is it likely a thought would be spared for the hundredth anniversary of the formation of the Shetland Islands Steam Navigation Company in 1868; but maybe some were aware of how before war had broken out in 1939, almost 30 years before, there was abundant praise for the old *Earl* born of nostalgia yet had turned to indignation when she had to come back to release the new *Earl* for the Pentland Firth.

Meanwhile the subsidy factor rumbled on. The Government offered the carrot of a 75 per cent grant of £75,000 per annum, provided Shetland was willing to contribute from the rates. Orkney joined Shetland in the fray in the spring of 1969 and a joint submission was made to the Secretary of State. Shetland followed up with a claim for the North Isles (Shetland) service, stressing the crippling costs for the people there. There was then a snub from Willie Ross, Scottish Secretary, with a blunt refusal to both councils, let alone the North Isles problem ... effective way ... more modern ships and harbour facilities ... not the time to introduce a new short-term direct subsidy of the kind the councils advocate. Further representations proved to be futile and, in fact, by 1970 the emphasis had shifted to proposed vehicle ferries within Shetland in four years time.

A change of Government in 1970 gave some hope and Gordon Campbell, the new Scottish Secretary, agreed to visit Shetland following the ten per cent freight increase duly imposed earlier and although £55,000 was headlined as a subsidy to keep the *Earl* going in the short term, at the end of 1971 the Secretary stated: "As you know the Government are to pay 75 per cent of the capital losses on the new service. Meanwhile a subsidy of £55,000 will be needed this year towards the cost of the existing shipping service ..." The SCC were still not happy but the die had been cast ...

If frustration was the "in" word for the council, hindrance might have been appropriate for the subject of so much of the debate — the *Earl of Zetland*. Remarkably, she was delayed by snow when the relieving mate, Drew Georgeson, was caught in drifts on the winding road from Walls early in February 1969. The blizzards were described as "the worst in years". All the North boats were affected.

Mother Nature followed up with a blast in March which pinned down the *Earl* at Victoria Pier from the Friday until the Wednesday. Even a funeral in Yell had to be postponed because the Yell Sound motor boat was stuck at Toft. A Norwegian shrimp trawler *Straalau II* was struck by a lump of sea south-east of Bressay which smashed windows and the wheelhouse door; she limped into Lerwick with the lifeboat in attendance.

But then there had to be the balmy days of summer, and, indeed, Nature glowed for the Archaeological and Natural History second summer cruise. Fetlar, the Garden of Shetland, welcomed a party of 136 who had come north on the *Earl* by south-about Bressay and Noss and taking a close look at Skerries. The men of the flit-boat at Houbie equalled the warmth of Willie Sinclair and the *Earl*'s crew as they ferried the visitors ashore for a six-hour tour. Fetlar offered "open-house"; ladies provided tea at Leagarth Hall, after diverse scrutiny of places of archaeological and geological interest. Ornithologist and naturalist Bobby Tulloch had a party of 80 to observe the famous nesting Snowy Owls. As a thoughtful gesture by the society five Fetlar children at school in Lerwick enjoyed an unexpected day with the visitors, and their ain folk. The day was another clear success.

Whatever the future of the now 30-year-old motor vessel her closing years in Shetland were proving to be full and varied and even the routine runs provided scope for the visitor and a leisure run to Whalsay from Lerwick. Early overcast skies belied a fine, crisp day in September 1969; at Symbister a signpost just opposite the gangway indicated: "Bus tours

around the island as steamer (sic) discharges. Please hurry." Somehow the notice encapsulates the relaxed busyness; it will be a while before the steamer unloads and there is time for a bus tour but we'll need not to waste time … there will be folk today who remember the heavy run of goods at a port; load the flit-boat at the steamer, unload ashore, back to the steamer, load again …

That September at least there was by then a pier at Symbister, yet the vexed question prevailed elsewhere — still no pier. The passing of the flit-boat (two oars favoured) at Whalsay would have been a nostalgic moment for such as Henry Simpson and Andrew Bruce, just as today the flit-boat crews are remembered with warm sentiment.

But Whalsay was expanding and developing fast in 1969. The big impressive purse-netters of this 21st century were not yet in the offing but a new fishing boat the *Dewy Rose* symbolised ambition and expansion. A County Council dredger was hard at work in the inner harbour. There was a new shelter and toilets on the pier in contrast to the old wooden deckhouse, the "Toopic" where successive generations of Whalsay folk took shelter when awaiting the *Earl*. New domestic buildings abounded and more council houses were planned. The location of the airstrip was being discussed.

A day outing had revealed a spirit of optimism for the future and when

Above: Work begins at last. The presence of the "inter-island steamer" gives a scale to the proceedings as a digger loads a lorry at the start of preparations for the harbour works at Symbister in the 1960s.

Dennis Coutts

Shetland Museum

Above: A similar view to that on page 25. The *Earl* passes the lighthouse on Symbister Ness to make a routine call to Whalsay.

the *Earl* appeared again "fae da nort" she was joined by a big party of folk bound for a Lerwick/Whalsay wedding on the Friday, which encouraged a carnival hour of yarning between Symbister and Victoria Pier. It had been a good day.

Of course over the decades Whalsay would be the most visited of all ports by both *Earls*. The 1939 version would be there on the north and south runs at Christmas 1965 and New year of 1970. A newspaper notice warned shopkeepers: "North Isles merchants are again requested to have seasonal stocks on hand as early as possible to avoid disappointment due to unforeseen circumstances which may affect sailings or working of cargo." No doubt the advert was motivated by the frequency of winter gales … there was another the second week of December in 1969!

Then "stormy weather" prevailed over subsidies. A Lochgilphead, Argyll correspondent did not mince his words: "Dr J. Dickson Mabon's wasted one day holiday in Shetland ended, as was to be expected by everyone, in complete failure by emphasising his unwillingness to see any opinion other than his own. Mr Ross's previous official visit (of unhappy memory) required him to send his dogsbody on this occasion.

"Why should Orkney and Shetland be asked to raise £25,000 from the local rates as a condition of receiving £75,000 from the state to subsidise the Orkney and Shetland Shipping Company (sic), which I understand is paying 10 per cent to its shareholders. Have the mainland counties been asked to contribute to their sea transport?

Dennis Coutts

Above: An underwater extension of Whalsay harbour in progress and this picture shows a diver at work there. County Council staff are infilling the space between the seabed and the wavescreen of the breakwater to reduce motion in the harbour

" … I have lived for many years in Shetland and have found the people to be industrious, independent and well disposed. Their industry is being throttled by high freight charges …"

As a corollary, at an HIDB seminar on Shetland in April 1970 Board member Prophet Smith believed that there should not be talk of holding Shetland's population at 17,000 but increasing it to 20,000 or more. He was not to know then that a beneficiary to oil discoveries off Shetland would be population; and prosperity.

Managing Director of the General Shipping Division of Coast Lines jumped in: "… the increase in the Shetland freights has been made necessary on account of increased costs which have been unavoidable. The North Company is currently investigating ways and means to stabilise costs in the face of current inflationary tendencies, which I am sure will be recognised by your readers … the North Company is doing all in its power to satisfy the needs of the Shetlands (sic) within the context of operating a commercial concern."

But a panacea of fate was in the offing. *The Shetland Times* featured a headline on 10th July, 1970: "Car ferry plan approved." What had already been offered by the Secretary of State was confirmed. " … grant aid to be given on the capital costs at the rate of 75 per cent … four ferry boats and the creation of ten terminal points and the necessary roadworks — all at a cost of £1,000,000 … The islands to be included in the system are Unst, Yell, Fetlar, Whalsay and Bressay."

Just to add to the variety a dockers strike which involved Aberdeen affected the isles, although goods from the *St Ninian* were being transferred to the *Earl* on Thursday, 16th July, 1970. For a fortnight Shetland was living from "hand to mouth", however the *Earl* was able to carry supplies looked upon as essential. By the end of the month the crisis had passed. In expressing their appreciation Council Convener, Edward Thomason and Provost Eric Gray wrote: "… Without one exception each section placed the good of the whole community before their own immediate interests …"

In a September announcement about plans for the routes the North Company omitted all reference to the *Earl* other than, "… existing conventional ships being withdrawn as they become redundant", then, suddenly a week later *The Shetland Times* proclaimed in bold print: "P&O bid for Coast Lines." Next: "On the eve of local authority meetings to discuss the future of shipping services to Shetland comes the news that the North of Scotland Shipping Company may be added to the long list of companies in the P&O Group. Coast Lines Ltd of which the North Company is a subsidiary is said to be considering a take-over bid from P&O".

Lines from Andy Irvine's famous poem seem fitting for October weather with, "Da simmer and da hairst is past an' winter comes in surly blast." Home for the mid-term autumn holiday, school children were stranded on the islands when the *Earl* was unable to call at Fetlar, Skerries, and Whalsay on the trip to and from Unst. No doubt they would not be displeased. In fact, child experiences on the *Earl* would form a colourful tale … Colva Tait, whose father was John Spence, shepherd to John Smith of Berry on Uyea Isle, recalled how there were times due to wind direction

the Uyeasound flit-boat could not put off but the isle was relatively sheltered. John would row out in a fourareen or take a motor boat and the steamer would come in as close as she dared and almost stop, to enable Colva, on her way from school in Lerwick, to drop into her father's boat at an opened well-deck door.

By the beginning of 1971 all the portents of oil exploration and

Above: A tousle-headed grey-haired lady sits in what was a fine vantage point for passengers, while a man stands in line-ahead with Willie Sinclair as an approach is made to the bay at Symbister, Whalsay; an overcast day in 1972.

Above: The cargo winch and derrick in action at Whalsay as five crates of fresh milk from Freefield Dairy are swung ashore. The winch operator is Harry Johnson. Below the foredeck is a selection of light cargo for the North Isles, ranging from gas canisters to boxes and packages, while in the right foreground is a large tarpaulin-covered object, probably destined for the RAF Station at Saxa Vord, Unst; perhaps too big for the hold, or is it full?

Above: A family touch as a young man carries a child's buggy or pram down the gangway at Whalsay, following a lady carefully negotiating the wooden rungs. Suitcases are strewn around amid a variety of bystanders and vehicles. Fishing vessels and their gear provide an informal background.

experimental drilling were there. Shipping of a different nature appeared, geared for specialist work, thus the *Earl* had very varied company in Lerwick harbour during her closing years, while it could not then be known that she was due to have her own career, if extremely brief, in oil related matters. In the other development context P&O decided to absorb Coast Lines and Mr J. Stansby, personal assistant to Lord Geddes, vice-chairman of P&O came on a fact-finding tour of the islands.

Shetland was rapidly becoming a focal point in the world of oil and therefore in the financial world, both factors which were going to transform the previous depopulation and all the antipathy in finances. By the beginning of May *Staflo,* the giant oil-drilling rig was ready to drill off the coast. By the beginning of June it was announced that four inter-island ferries for Shetland would be built in Faroe. Ian Clark the county council's general manager, who was negotiating what was going to be a splendidly favourable oil deal for Shetland, was also to the fore in a scheme estimated at more than £1 million. The whole financial structure was altering almost overnight and presently the *Earl's* much discussed subsidy was put into a different perspective!

£0.60 return (Boating where necessary additional). This bracketed condition seemed an ironic reflection on the decades of procrastination about island piers at the expense of so many frustrated communities. No doubt when Charles Brown, boatman in charge of the Houbie flit-boat for almost twenty years retired in April 1972 he would have his thoughts.

Captain William Nicolson Sinclair would have his reflections too when he had the experience of travelling "overland" for the first time in his life in June 1972. He was going to RAF Saxavord and the Reading Room at Baltasound for retiral presentations. His company and crew had already honoured him on board the *Earl* on Saturday, 17th June. Manager of the North Company Herbert Scott presented him with a wallet of notes, while, as seen in the photograph on page 112 a gift of the inscribed fishing rod was proffered by purser Willie Smith. "One would think," said Mr Smith, "that someone who has had such an active life would find it difficult to pass the time in retirement, but Captain Sinclair has many interests. He is a pillar of the 'Big Kirk' and a member of the Masonic Lodge and its recreational club." Mr Smith handed over the rod, reel, tackle box and harness to a delighted, yet reticent, Willie Sinclair.

Michael Gray

"Annual income Twenty pounds, annual expenditure Nineteen Nineteen Six, result happiness. Annual income Twenty pounds, annual expenditure Twenty Pounds Ought and Six, result misery." The Dickensian remark had a relevance in the Shetland context. Certainly the freight problem was there and relevant despite the massive scale of finance. In a local sense, and highlighted by a report from a committee chaired by Professor Gaskin, people in Shetland were worse off than their counterparts in Aberdeen, for example. Yet more correspondence between the SCC and the Secretary of State was inconclusive, although the Secretary reiterated the commitment to pay 75 per cent of the costs of the four ferries … meanwhile at the end of December the headline was there: "£55,000 subsidy to keep the *Earl* going." She had cost some £52,000 brand new.

The words of the old song, "stormy weather, there's no sun up in the sky" would have been fitting in the winter of 1971/72, both figuratively and literally. There were the protracted stormy exchanges between Government and council, while January and March gales pinned down the *Earl.* On the first occasion she was turned back by heavy seas outside the north mouth and on the second she was alongside over a long weekend. But on the basis of hope springing eternal there was a final flourish in excursion trips when she was advertised for a North Isles to Lerwick sailing on Tuesday, 2nd May, 1972; North Ports £1.20 return: Whalsay

He reckoned that he did not know how to go about thanking everyone. He had to admit he would have been happier taking the *Earl* into Skerries with a north-east wind and an ebb tide! He felt it seemed only last year since he came down to join a North Company ship, a "poor peerie boy". He had been greatly relieved to find another, even peerier boy. That other boy was Robbie Tulloch. Willie Sinclair was just as glad to see him there tonight as he had been on that first occasion.

He was very touched — he had been given loyalty and kindness by his officers and crew, especially when he most needed the support.

Herbert Scott welcomed Captain David Carmichael (Michael) Gray on succeeding Captain Sinclair as skipper of the *Earl* and congratulated him, extending the good wishes of the P&O Company for his captaincy. In the absence of County Convener Edward Thomason, Mr Scott then read a message to Willie Sinclair: "Good, well maintained communications are essential … constant skill and effort. For nigh on 30 years your name and that of the *Earl* have been synonymous …

"On behalf of the people of Shetland and particularly the residents of the North Isles I offer you all good wishes … On a personal note, it seems a very short time indeed since I watched you start as a crane boy on the old *Sunniva.*

"A new era lies before us — before another twelve months the first of the vehicle ferries will be in service. I would like to think you would pass

Dennis Coutts

Dennis Coutts

Above: Another milestone in the annals of shipping in the North Isles of Shetland. Captain William Sinclair's departure into another path of life is marked by a presentation. The date is Saturday, 17th July, 1972, the place, a corner of the dining saloon on board the *Earl of Zetland* and, according to the clock, the time is 8.30pm. Some of the ship's bunting decorates the background.

Willie Sinclair's predilection for fishing is well known. Here he is clearly delighted to be handed a rod by the *Earl*'s purser William Smith, on behalf of the crew, while Michael Gray looks on approvingly. Captain Gray is Captain Sinclair's successor. In response to the gift Willie Sinclair remarks that he does not quite know how to go about thanking everyone. He said, "I am very touched by the gift made to me. I am not sure that I deserve it – I have always been given loyalty by my officers and crew when I most needed it."

Left: Confirmation of prowess as a sea angler! An understandingly proud Willie Sinclair with his magnificent catch. The rod has a strong resemblance to that of Willie's retirement presentation.

The fish is a particularly fine halibut, caught off Lunning Ness under the auspices of the Viking Sea Angling Competition held annually.

on to your crew, past and present aboard the *Earl* tonight the acknowledgement of Zetland County Council for their many years of toil."

Due to the post-1945 escalation of the so-called "Cold War" there had been an ever-expanding services presence on Unst, thus inevitably the *Earl* had an ongoing and developing role in taking materials and general cargo to Baltasound. Activity was steady as evinced by the photograph on page 124 with many such crates, and liaison with RAF Saxavord was healthy. The goodwill found expression when on Willie Sinclair's retiral a staff car was sent to pick him up from Lerwick and he was taken overland to Toft to sample the vagaries of the *Shalder* on Yell Sound — with another vehicle in between — and the *Viking* on Bluemull Sound before another staff car took the venerable skipper up to the Officers' Mess at Saxavord where he was entertained to a cocktail party with speeches. The same evening in the Reading Room at Baltasound, where Willie Spence had been feted in 1937, then the first *Earl* honoured in 1939, Willie Sinclair received from the people of Unst an inscribed cigarette case: "Presented to Captain W. N. Sinclair by the people of Unst, 19.6.72."

Willie Sinclair responded in his own unassuming yet inimitable manner and asked for a recitation of Andy Irvine's famous poem: "Da simmer and da hairst is past, an' winter comes wi surly blast … An' folk could never

get aboot, if it wisna for da *Earl's* toot … An' when da *Earl* gangs awa', We miss her — yea, baith ane an' a' …" It would be the ultimate public occasion for a hearing of an immortal piece of creative writing, not consigned to the dustbin of history but retained for posterity in memory; thus, again, people from the North Isles went on their way in the June "simmer dim" in reflective mood, contemplating this revolutionary change from the tradition of the pure sea-route to the overland and "ferries"; from the blanket term of "da steamer", applied often to both *Earls* to simply "the overland". The ferries would become to all intents and purposes an extension of the road system, with eventually other revolutionary thoughts about the fixed link concept of the bridges or tunnels for islands like Bressay, Yell and Unst, as applied successfully to Faroe and Norway.

Yet such contemplation was remote in the early part of the 1970s. Michael Gray and his crew had the task of the moment of overseeing the now "old" *Earl* through her closing time in Shetland. It was Mortimer Manson, former editor of the erstwhile *Shetland News,* author, politician for thinking of good report, and musician, who mused: " … if and when the day comes that no *Earl* anchors off a North Isles port or moves in and out of Lerwick's harbour, something vital will have gone out of the life of Shetland."

This was no longer merely a prospect but an inevitability, yet the ship's work was there to be fulfilled. Still under North of Scotland Orkney and Shetland Shipping Company Limited, MV *Earl of Zetland,* North Isles traffic, was a notice: "Commencing Monday, 12th February, 1973, … North Isles merchants are specially requested to have orders in suppliers hands in sufficient time to enable preparation and despatch of goods …" Then a few weeks later a full page *Shetland Times* notice: "Ferry Route. Toft (Mainland) to Ulsta (Yell). MV *Fivla* — Interim Timetable." And there it was each day of the week, Thursday apart, at approximately hourly intervals — commencing Monday, 21st May, 1973. What had been threatening for forty years and more was now fact. The romance of the highway of the sea was being replaced by the realistic practicality of the Overland. Initially no Thursday sailings aroused criticism but within a matter of weeks the omission had been rectified and the beginning of an ongoing ever-improving service was firmly established.

By that time the *Earl's* calls, already curtailed, were to cut out Mid Yell from 1st August, since the North Company, very reasonably, did not wish to compete with the new (road) haulage to Yell. There had been a reassurance from haulage contractor Norman Tulloch in Aywick, Yell, that he could handle all the goods usually brought in by the *Earl* … with what was a council proviso that the motor vessel would be made available in the event of ferry failure. Therefore at long last there was a bowing to the inevitable — shades of competition during the halcyon days of "da auld *Earl*"; the *Islander;* the *Innovator;* the *Norseman;* Davie Gray's Tuesday/ Wednesday trip — and the final twist of fate, the obvious coup de grace.

Perhaps Mother Nature was making a sympathetic point when the second ferry, the *Giera,* built in Faroe, had a tough passage. They had had a net wound round the propeller and were forced to turn back, then lost a couple of life rafts on the way to Lerwick. Presently, the *Giera* was on the Bluemull Sound run and a kenspeckle figure in councillor and ferryman Davie Johnson with his *Viking* motor boat, called it a day. Almost immediately Unst Shetland Council member Mr A. B. Fraser, was critical of the ferry service; the Yell ferry was late; he missed the mainland ferry at Ulsta; he was very late for a council meeting in Lerwick. His rejoinder was: "It will be the blackest day for Unst when the *Earl of Zetland* leaves." Such sentiments were echoed in what was overheard by Gordon Donaldson at the time of the end of the *Earl* at Mid Yell on 20th July, 1973. He overheard two women in conversation reminiscing and recalling the high hopes with which the ship had been welcomed in 1939. One said to the other: "Weel we'll maybe be waar off". Perhaps it was the perfect epitaph for the ninety-eight years of service by the *Earls*.

By the end of November 1973 the North Company stated they wished to withdraw the *Earl of Zetland* from service in January 1974 and because of the serious situation which would face the islanders of Fetlar, Skerries and Whalsay the County Council was in touch with the Scottish Economic Department. From them had come the reassurance that the ship would continue to be subsidised until suitable ferry communications were complete.

Then as a contrast to so many previous years the *Earl's* Christmas and New Year holiday sailing notice was replaced by an even larger newspaper panel stating the timetable of the *Fivla* on Yell Sound and the *Geira* on Bluemull Sound. The year of further reckoning, 1974, was imminent.

The worries of one of the three islands "out on a limb" emerged in a lengthy letter to the *Times* from B. Thorn, Head Teacher and Missionary to the Skerries folk, with copies to the Secretary of State and general manager of the North Company: " … I was informed by the local manager of the shipping company that we have a 'very good service'. In fact this is a one north-bound call per week … a once weekly delivery of mail, and a once weekly uplift … intolerable situation … to get to Lerwick I have had to leave Skerries on the *Earl of Zetland* at 10.30am on a Monday morning, arriving pm on a Tuesday, being unable to return to Skerries until the following Monday — and this for a journey of a mere 24 miles … And what is to happen to this community with the eventual withdrawal of the *Earl?*"

Any transition in transport systems will have teething troubles but Mr Thorn's concerns were very real to Skerries people; Whalsay was not so badly placed with easier and shorter access to the mainland. Fetlar, however had no fishing boats to fall back on for transport, thus concerns mounted there too. Meanwhile it was being demonstrated that no inter-island ferry system would run in profit. That proffered Government subsidy was always going to be vital and, in fact, the operating deficit for the first ten months of the vehicle ferries was £25,000. Freight was still a subject of concern; charges were tending to be hidden in the retail price of the goods in the shops that were generally providing their own road transport service since the demise of the *Earl.*

In the sequence of events a lighter touch happened in June 1974 when former *Earl* skipper Jimmy Johnston, now commodore of the North Company, retired. There was a gathering on the *St Clair* at Lerwick and, as at a recent retiral occasion, a fishing rod and tackle figured as a gift given on behalf of the North company by Eric Turner, general operations manager, standing in for general manager, Herbert Scott.

If Skerries had figured in *The Shetland Times* through their teacher and missionary, then Fetlar emerged in a slightly different context when some members of the recently formulated Community Association felt the island population problems were not well enough known and arranged a visit to Fetlar. At least the *Earl* was still there to take a party from Lerwick to drop anchor at Houbie on a bright, windy afternoon in August 1974, by which time a ferry terminal was being built at Oddsta. Thus Fetlar became historic in that a formal party was using the *Earl* for an island visit for near-enough the last time. And if depopulation was a subject to discuss in Fetlar, at least the Shetland number in the population was up to 18,500 by the end of 1974. Then it was in the December when Charles Brown wrote his letter of appreciation about the *Earl's* service over the years.

Michael Gray piloted the 36-year-old motor vessel over those final years, but even in such a short tenure he built up what had become an ingrained affection for his ship, before he left in February 1974. He was relieving on the *St Clair* for six weeks and was then sent to the *St Rognvald* to gain experience of Orkney ports before returning to the *Clair* again as permanent skipper. He retired in 1995.

Captain Drew (Drewie) Georgeson followed Michael Gray on the *Earl* and was there until the June of 1974. He, in turn, was succeeded by Captain Ray Ferrie who took the now old vessel through her final months and to a last refit in Aberdeen. It was then Captain Jim Tait who saw out her closing weeks as noted in the illustrations.

There was a poignant moment for all of them when the *Earl of Zetland* moved astern at Victoria Pier on Friday, 21st February, 1975, for what was to be a fleeting visit to the most visited — Lerwick apart — Shetland port by both North Isles steamers — the word is used advisedly because the islanders had aye referred to "da steamer". As simply as that an era — a saga of shipping — came to an end. At Whalsay more people than usual appeared to witness the *Earl's* very last call, but there was no fuss, no ceremonial; certainly no mass of folk. Only about a dozen figures stood on Victoria Pier that Friday as the ship moved away from Lerwick at 10am. The final voyage amid the familiar shores had few passengers, although significantly Willie Sinclair and Hector Strachan, who had often substituted as chief engineer, made the run to Symbister; their presence lent a touch of worthy sentiment to the photograph at the ship's gangway on returning to Victoria Pier.

That evening the "crew" marked the occasion with a private dinner party on board, but the town recognised the occasion when Provost J. J. Taylor invited the ship's complement to a brief reception in the Town Hall on the Monday forenoon, 24th February. It was the nearest to any ceremonial, although numbers of interested parties appeared on the first Monday in March as the Lerwick Brass Band provided a musical send-off with "Abide with Me" and "Auld Lang Syne".

TAKING A FINAL SENTIMENTAL VOYAGE – LOOKING FORWARD FROM THE FIRST *EARL* A THIRD PICTORIAL ESSAY

Sentiment: An expression of response to deep feeling.

Shetland Museum

Above: An idyllic situation. A setting sun reveals a perfect silhouette of the steamer as she lies at the north end of Colgrave Sound, off Brough Lodge. The sea-state reflects the peace of a perfect end to the day; only smoke and steam about the funnel suggests life on board.

Below: A beautifully evocative early morning atmosphere at Lerwick as the steamer goes astern from Victoria Pier, and turning to port, at the start of another run up to Yell Sound and the North Isles. The reflections of the *Earl* in the foreground water are particularly attractive, as are those of the Aberdeen trawler A597, on the wet stones of the quay at Alexandra Wharf. The sun glints on the sea; the *Earl* emits smoke in common with the other ships; the dining saloon bogey stove is lit, its smoke catching a light air behind the *Earl*'s funnel.

Shetland Museum

Right: Probably the only photograph of the *Earl* with a flying boat ...! A strong north-east wind stirs the harbour waters as the ship approaches her Lerwick berth. The aircraft is a Supermarine Southampton S1231 of 201 Squadron, moored off the location where the Lerwick Boating Club pier is today. The time would be in the late 1930s.

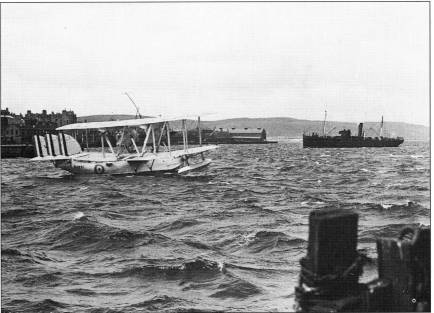

Shetland Museum

Fetlar Museum Trust

Left: A considerable proportion of the male population seems to be involved in organising this shipment of Shetland ponies from Fetlar. The end of the long slip at Houbie is in use, with the flit-boat only partially alongside in the ebb, and the water on the wet sand on the foreshore reflects the conglomeration of stones and seaweed, with wavelets breaking in a southerly breeze, a scene set in the 1920s.

To the left behind the pier is part of the Heog, a narrow point of land flanking the Wick of Houbie, and the Head of Lambhoga projects from the right, apparently at horizon level. The *Earl* lies awaiting the next turn of events.

Right: A moment captured on the after-deck in August 1933. The winch by the mainmast was seldom used, hence the canvas cover, although in the mid-1930s, as cars grew in numbers in the isles, the after derrick would hoist aboard the occasional vehicle – preferably small! On the mainmast the light fittings are evidence of the advent of electricity on board the *Earl* in 1921 and the lower part of the mast, by the cleats, is painted in simulated wood grain in an attempt at some refinement.

Willie Spence and Tom Gifford join passengers Ann Moar and brother "Sonny" Moar by the dining saloon companionway. They lived in Montgomery Street in Edinburgh where their parents' home was a "Mecca" for Shetlanders and many were the occasions of yarning and reminiscing. Ann Moar was an enthusiastic member of the always welcoming Shetland Association; also its educational counterpart, the Edinburgh Orkney and Zetland Association.

Kitty Moar

Left: A group of passengers seated by the after hatch on the way north during a fine, bright day in the late 1930s. Included among those identified are: top right Major H. W. L. Hunter of Unst, who spoke highly of the old ship, and top left Gordon Donaldson, one of Scotland's foremost 20th century historians. Although he lived in Prestonpans and latterly in Dysart, Fife, he admitted a life-long obsession with Shetland.

Gordon Donaldson

Right: The skipper takes a run ashore! Willie Spence sits back in the stern of the flit-boat at Brough Lodge on Fetlar as two of her crew go about their work, one apparently swinging a shovel – dealing with the aftermath of shipping animals perhaps? However, the heavy wood batten abeam the flit-boat is suggestive of vehicle carrying, which was not unknown by the 1920s.

The ship lies neatly anchored in quiet weather and part of the north end of the island of Hascosay is featured on the left.

Fetlar Museum Trust

Fetlar Museum Trust

Left: The steamer has come and gone, the flit-boat is almost emptied and the concrete slip at Houbie is a busy place. What was probably the first Massey-Ferguson tractor on Fetlar, driven by Bobby Coutts, takes off with a trailer-load, including two passengers. Standing behind the trailer is the figure of Charles Brown, skipper of the flit-boat.

Right: A forest of funnels, masts and rigging, in which the *Earl* joins … an early 1930s very busy day with mainly Scottish herring drifters in serried ranks plus people, goods and vehicles in abundance. The Diana Fountain is prominent in the foreground and the *Earl*'s stem is as far in as possible to the angle between the Victoria Pier and Albert Wharf.

Shetland Museum

Shetland Museum

Left: Judging by the display of flags this is likely to be a Victoria Day excursion round Bressay in the 1930s. Additional seating benches seem to have been provided. Various craft are on the horizon.

Right: A composition of contrasts! The slatted wooden ramp in the foreground, apparently at sea-level, is probably an ad hoc arrangement. The slip at Brough Lodge did not appear until the 1930s. The dog, so perfectly reflected in the wet surface, seems to be supervising the departure of the flit-boat which has two animals in tow! Reputedly the flit-boat was the last sixareen built by Hay and Company about 1900. She never was used for fishing and, tragically, to this day she is disintegrating on the Brough shore.

A stylishly clad lady looks back at the photographer, while upright in the bow is the figure of Sir Arthur Thomas Bennet Robert Nicolson, 9th Baronet (1842-1917), who is likely to be seeing off visitors to Brough Lodge.

But there is doubt about the ship awaiting them. At first sight she looks like the *Earl* yet her starboard lifeboat is too far aft and there would seem to be a deckhouse behind the bridge and mainmast … strange …

Fetlar Museum Trust

Left: Another view of that milestone of a day in the pathway of the two ships of the same name. Steward Robbie Gray keeps an eye on berthing, assisted by Lang Jeemie Jamieson, by the after-winch and derrick. The bridge and bunting of the new motor ship appear in the background to the right, with the stern of the *St Magnus* still out in the harbour to the left.

Shetland Museum

Right: Another informal moment. Mootie Jamieson and Captain Jimmy Wood stand by the wheel and are seen from the cat-walk. The wooden spar above was probably intended for an awning but was never put to any use until it was removed when an unsightly wheelhouse was built in the 1940s, too late to be of lasting value.

Shetland Museum

The Author

Left: Sheep have been a traditional feature of Zetland life and is confirmed by this photograph taken in the 1930s. The old *Earl* is lying at More's Station on Bressay with the Lerwick skyline behind. The masses of fine looking sheep in the front, hemmed in neatly by herring barrels, await shipment on one of the steamer's September runs to a Scottish Mainland port like Fraserburgh or Peterhead.

Right: A fascinating perspective shows the bridge-wing shelters and wheelhouse as effectively as could be wished. Why they were not fitted years previously will never be known. Could it be assumed there was a theory that the fresh sea air kept skipper and helmsman alert; or to prevent them falling asleep?

The old ship is in a transitional phase. It is 1946 and she is being "decommissioned" from wartime status. Her derrick is in the stowed position, while mate at the time, Willie Sinclair, rests his forearms on the canvas dodger – and above is the ship's identification board *Earl of Zetland II*. Armaments are still prominent aft. High on the mainmast a crewman makes adjustments.

Shetland Museum

Bruce Spence

Left: A day of quiet weather at Cullivoe around 1971/72. The new *Earl* glides gently astern with her cargo for the community stacked on Magnie Henderson's lorry. On the far side of the pier, largely hidden, is Robert Anderson's fishing boat *Winsome* while standing off is Alister Thomason's first *Madalia*. Apart from three figures at the head of the pier and another bending over by the *Winsome*'s foremast it is a tranquil scene. Bluemull Sound shows little evidence of its daily tide-race.

The pier itself is stark evidence of yesteryear and now engulfed by the highy enterprising and magnificent Cullivoe Harbour development opened on 21st May, 2001, by John P. Nicolson, vice-convener of Shetland Islands Council and councillor for Yell.

Right: The old, the new and the newer. The ancient wooden Cullivoe Pier, seen on the far right, has played a final role in aiding the construction of the modern concrete version. The main support of the sheerlegs rests on the old structure. Meanwhile the "new" *Earl* prepares to bring her well-deck alongside the face of the "newer" pier. She is still some yards away as dockers await a bow line. The month is September; the year 1971.

It is the *Earl*'s first call at the innovative pier following its opening, yet it is a futile exercise in terms of the North Isles vessel's service, since her days are already numbered. The pier development was the outcome of years of representations at local government level and its appearance was a triumph of perseverence. It was opened by Davy Johnston, councillor for Yell.

Michael Gray

Andrew Anderson

Left: Cullivoe was, of course, the most northerly of the ports of call in Yell and, given the right kind of calm sea and state of the tide, it was just possible to touch on the pier to land passengers and work cargo. Even at the other communities like Ulsta, West Sandwick, Burravoe, Sellafirth and Gutcher there was nothing suitable. Mid Yell was always a possibility, assuming near high-water. Other than the two ports, the flit-boats were essential even in the days of the first *Earl*. Baltasound in Unst remained the solitary place in the North Isles where berthing was feasible at any time.

This is an unusual grouping at the Cullivoe pier with the second *Earl* and five fishing boats tied up during the 1960s. It is near high water, the tide probably still flowing. The boats are: *Winsome* (LK704), *Snowdrop* (LK242), *Swiftwing* (LK192), *Ros Don* (LK703) and *Halcyon* (LK467). The *Winsome* and *Ros Don* are the two Cullivoe vessels.

The flimsy structure of the pier is obvious enough on the left side of the photograph; the whole body of it could shudder even with a relatively gentle nudge by a ship like the *Earl*.

Right: A very eventful day at Victoria Pier. Although the old *Earl* does not appear on this sunny afternoon in the late 1930s, the three-island *St Clement*, relieving for her, is in the customary berth. She had been built for the North Company in 1928 and was something of a utility steamer and served until April 1941 when, unfortunately, she was sunk in an air attack 20 miles south-east of Peterhead. It could well have been a fate suffered by the *Earl* too.

In this colourful scene the *St Sunniva* lies on the north side of the pier with the trim-looking *St Clair* across from her. The scene is enlivened further by the pipe band playing to a big crowd, with all the evidence of family gatherings.

Shetland Museum

John Manson

Left: The *Earl* being warped in up by the Alexandra Quay. The *Earl* normally lay port side to, overhanging the north end, and the south boat berthed starboard side to as close to the *Earl*'s stern as possible, to leave space at the south end for fishing boats to berth. Ship and shore men attend to the ropes, while a docker apparently uses a fender amidships. The derrick is in the stowed position and a fair number of passengers can be seen, especially below the funnel. This was during Jimmy Johnston's time. Is that him on the bridge?

Ashore, it seems an ambiguous situation. Are the sheep due to be loaded? The big corner fencing posts are certainly plentiful, whatever their destination.

LHT stores close to the berths used by the company were tight for space, hence the jumble of cargo and livestock visible in the photo.

Right: A glimpse of an annual overhaul in drydock at Peterhead in the late 1960s. The Mini Morris car beyond the foremast is probably an indication of the period, while a Land Rover is parked in the foreground. A mobile crane takes the weight of a piece of equipment and is being contemplated by two workers. Meanwhile the *Earl* is unusually devoid of life. In the distance, a 60s-style trawler is alongside the breakwater in the ebb.

The perspective shows the beamy nature of the ship with her very full underside amidships, perhaps an influence in her tendency to roll in heavy weather. In the right background a pier suggests a very tricky right-angled turn into the dock, a problem mentioned by skipper Michael Gray.

It is noted that both anchors, and possibly also the anchor cables, will have been lowered into the drydock for inspection and survey. The forward end of the port bilge keel is just visible close to the oil drum beside the Land Rover.

Michael Gray

Aberdeen City Archives

Left: A telling angle again on the six cylinder heads of the Polar Diesel engine M 46 M 840 BHP at 220 revs as specified in the order book. It was manufactured by British Auxiliaries Limited, Glasgow. The ten securing bolts on each cylinder head are of particular note.

Top right is the control wheel at the head of the extended spindle for shutting the watertight doors of the shaft tunnel. Also, above the upper handrail is the case for an oil fuelled lamp for emergency or when the generator was shut-down in port.

Shetland Museum

Right: It is New Year during the late 1940s and with holiday time the hatch is fully covered and inactive for the moment. Three young men watch the Lerwick Brass Band playing a selection in the well-deck.

Douglas Sinclair

Left: An effective perspective of the bridge interior so totally different from the completely exposed simplicity of the teak boarding and canvas dodger of the old *Earl*. "Chalk and cheese" would seem an appropriate analogy!

Here, the relative comfort is only too apparent. This scene, in the late 1940s or early 1950s (Tom Gifford or Jimmy Johnston as Captain) shows Mate Willie Sinclair at the wheel with an unknown passenger. Above the steering mechanism is the signal flags locker and above that a duffel coat for the inevitable wild day of weather. But no problem in a warm wheelhouse insulated from the elements.

Right: Right to the forefront! A photograph taken during an evening cruise round Bressay and Noss in 1955. The forestay and flagpole feature as "supports" for three happy-looking passengers, flanked by George Irvine, cook, left, and Bobby Burns, saloon steward, wearing his best "bib and tucker".

Central in the group is Muriel Murray, of Lerwick, with fashionable headsquare and handbag. Someone has a hand for the forestay.

Jimmy Winchester

Right: The skipper is "tripping the light fantastic" with Joy Goodlad at the ship's Christmas dinner dance in 1968, while on the extreme left Hunter Thomson, a guest from Hay and Company, dances with his wife Marjorie. About to make contact as they dance is Peter Black, local hairdresser, and his wife Betty, both guests of the *Earl*'s Christmas festivities.

Douglas Sinclair

Jimmy Winchester

Left: A moment of relaxation for Jimmy Winchester who served on the *Earl* from 1954 to 1964. He joined as a galley boy, was cabin steward and then cook from 1958. In the background are homes on the shore at Baltasound. On the deck above is one of the wooden life-rafts with grab-lines attached and which also served as seats on board. A box for life-jackets is on the deck behind Jimmy. Today James Winchester lives in Lerwick and, although retired, he is church officer at St Columba's Church, known as the "Big Kirk".

Right: A sense of togetherness on board! Bobby Scott, chief steward, Jeannie Smith, shore cleaner, and Sandy Smith, cook, are apparently in good form. A bright day at Lerwick in 1967.

Jimmy Winchester

Above: Three skippers of fame and tremendous experience share a moment for the record on a champagne occasion. They are on board the fourth *St Clair* at Lerwick.

Jimmy Johnston, on the left, became the *Earl*'s captain in April 1951 and served with devoted loyalty for over 14 years, until September 1965. Willie Sinclair, barring one or two isolated occasions, was his mate over those years until he assumed command in September 1965, guiding the *Earl* through her last spell in Shetland waters and in charge until he retired and Michael Gray took over in 1972.

Leonard Mainland, on the right, was mate on the *Earl* to Tom Gifford in 1945 when on 10th December she returned to Shetland after the war. *The Shetland Times* had commented: "The *Earl of Zetland* arrived on Tuesday at 1pm after a smart run from Aberdeen … in fine condition despite the large numbers of passengers carried over the war years … a credit to Captain Gifford, his officers and crew." Then Leonard Mainland had the unusual experience of being mate to Captain William Ramsay when 10 days later, the old *Earl* sailed from Shetland apparently for good, although she had a short spell of assisting the *St Ola* in Orkney waters.

Above: A social occasion in the 1970s. Willie Sinclair enjoys a pint in the company of Mrs Jeannie Smith whose husband Arthur (Attie) was a foreman docker at Lerwick with the North Company and who was a great stalwart with the Norscot Angling Club. Her son, Alex, followed in his father's footsteps working for the North Company and is married to Willie's eldest daughter Penelope.

Above: A glimpse of old Shetland before the days of traffic bustle; and this is the unmade road shown as it was around 1925. The old *Earl* is still in her heyday … some goods of indeterminate nature are being transported by Shetland pony … are they from the *Earl*? The next generation of pony seems to be supervising! Its leggy appearance contrasts the round-bellied adult animals. A motor van at the gable of the old "Tin" house at the west entrance to Baltasound implies the shape of things to come. Two residents appear to be having a yarn at the door of the east semi-detached house, while telegraph poles indicate improving communications amid the North Isles. The old "Tin" house, as it was dubbed locally, eventually was burned out in a fire in 1990s.

One end was the home of "Gibsie" Thomson, HM Customs and Excise officer in Unst, and veteran of the Battle of Jutland.

Above: A conversation piece at Baltasound and an informal moment, with the well-deck and forepart of the ship as a backdrop. Willie Sinclair and "Gibsie" Thomson pause thoughtfully in the midst of a yarn on the pier. It is a warm day of summer. "Gibsie" would be making a standard call at the ship as Customs and Excise official and obviously he has cycled down to the *Earl* – just as much a social, as official, visit – from his abode in the "Tin" house.

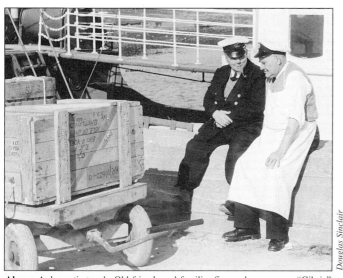

Douglas Sinclair

Above: A domestic touch. Old friends and familiar figures have a yarn. "Gibsie" Thomson in conversation with apron-clad cook Jimmy McLeod on the pier at Baltasound on a grand bright day. The year is 1959. Unloaded from the *Earl*, on the hand-cart is evidence of the RAF presence in Shetland, part of the UK early warning system during the then burgeoning cold war. "O/C RAF, Saxavord, Isle of Unst, Shetland" is lettered on the box crate.

Above: A group by the *Earl*'s berth at Victoria Pier, which hints at what the ship is all about; the breadth of family in Shetland. Captain Sinclair, in shoregoing gear, embraces next of kin and friends. His daughter, Dorothy (Mrs Watt), is on his left partially shadowed by the photographer. Muriel Coutts, wife of well-known photographer and naturalist Dennis, smiles broadly as befits a slant of afternoon sun in Lerwick, as does friend Rozanne Steadman on the extreme left. Her children join in. The transparent wind-break fittings stand out clearly on the bridge. It is noted that the ratlines now appear to have been removed from the mast rigging in this photo. Tammy Jamieson, head stevedore, is in the background.

Right: The ship eases alongside at Victoria Pier in 1947 after one of the first post-war Inter-county sporting events in Orkney. A north-westerly breeze sets the flags flying. Shetland had had success hinted at by the group standing on the monkey island with a cup being flourished and the obviously big crowd on the pier.

Willie Sinclair, then Mate, supervises the bow lines, while Captain Tom Gifford, behind the bridge canvas-dodger, keeps an eye on the fenders. Unusually the cargo-handling derrick is in the stowed position. At a later date the old-style dodger was replaced by angled perspex sheet.

Douglas Sinclair

Shetland Museum

Left: The Faroese passenger ship *Tjaldur* lies at the arm of the Victoria Pier as the *Earl* churns astern from her berth. To the rear, right, the *St Clair* (II) is in her customary place.

It is a scene typical of the late 50s or early 60s with an elegant styling of fishing boats, both Shetland and Norwegian, which is no longer a feature today.

Right: The master of the North Isles steamer, Willie Sinclair, eases his ship astern through sheltering fishing vessels in November 1968. About 70 boats sought shelter, more than half of them foreign, in one of the winter gales.

Left: A routine loading situation (or is it unloading?). The wire and hook of the derrick hang idle meanwhile, as dockers handle the goods by barrow. One cardboard box carries the lettering: "Burco C308 Model Enamel Finish, Electric Washboiler". Another, upside down, label states bluntly: "Don't crush". A photograph from the late sixties.

Behind the well-deck and framed by the catwalk is the wheelhouse of the well-known Cullivoe fishing boat *Winsome*, skipper Robert Anderson.

Right: The New Year scene at Victoria Pier with three North boats alongside. They heralded 1970 by sounding their sirens together.

Dennis Coutts

Shetland Museum

Above: A remarkably diverse scene, dated in a variety of ways. North boats are well represented with the third *St Clair* lying alongside the arm of Victoria Pier, her derricks in the raised working position, while there is a glimpse of the bridge and funnel of the fifth *St Magnus*, constructed as a "three island" ship.

The *St Clair* (III) was a motor vessel launched at Troon in early 1960, the last non roll on-roll off ship on the direct Shetland route, while the *St Magnus* (V) was a cargo-only ship built in 1955, designed to give refrigerated space and facilities for livestock. She had been ordered originally by Palgrave Murphy Limited then was bought by the North Company in 1967. She traded between Leith, Aberdeen, Kirkwall and Lerwick, but then Leith was withdrawn from the schedule and she was routed mainly between Aberdeen and Kirkwall with occasional appearances in Lerwick like this.

The *Earl* seems hemmed in by what would appear to be Scandinavian and Scottish fishing boats, a suggestion that there is inclement weather round Shetland's coastline. Also, judging by the three men standing below the well-deck cat walk, it is time for a break on the *Earl*. Certainly the seagull standing on the chimney-head in the foreground looks relaxed. But work awaits. The lorry-load of goods, plus trailer with sacks, and drums lying around, all imply that loading is not far away. Perhaps the car on Victoria Pier is due to be lifted aboard for the North Isles.

Also the range of vehicles on the Esplanade indicates the sixties with Triumph Herald, Baby Austin and Morris Minor Traveller, all evident.

Left: The year is 1953 and test borings are in progress under the auspices of Wimpey, the contractors, and pier extension is expected. In the background are the *Earl* and the modern motor-ship the *St Ninian*, like the *Earl of Zetland*, a compact, good-looking ship.

Right: Lord Geddes, vice-chairman of the P&O Group, who had bought over Coast Lines, and his party chatting with the master of the *Earl of Zetland* after the trip to the North Isles. Left to right: Mr H. W. Scott, general manager of the North Company; HRH The Princess of Hess; The Hon. D. C. Geddes; Lord and Lady Geddes; Captain Sinclair; The Hon. Mrs Geddes. It is August 1971.

Left: Tied up behind the *Earl of Zetland* is the first inter-island ferry *Fivla*, expected to start the Yell Sound service in about a fortnight's time. It is May 1973.

Right: Greenhead growth. The *Earl* follows her old routine on Monday, 22nd February, 1974, steaming in the north mouth while the emerging Norscot oil base spreads over an increasing area. Phase two of the Greenhead base is now underway, providing more storage and quay space.

Above: The *Earl* approaching Whalsay, still at full speed judging by the "bone in her teeth". Yet it is a poignant moment because in the foreground is the threat and reason for her demise, in the shape of a first generation inter-island vehicle ferry, *Grima*. Poised between her flying bridge and the onlooking crew members is a seagull – is this symbolic of the "Flight of the Spirit" of both *Earl*s? Certainly there is the symbolism of the end of a magnificent and highly evocative era of seafaring with both ships. Even the two narrow and lighter areas of water in the photograph seem to converge as if moulding the past into the present. Each *Earl* had given yeoman service to Shetland for nigh on 100 years between them, earning genuine affection from the folk, given expression in 1939 when the old *Earl* was "retired", and 1975 when the second *Earl* was withdrawn.

Top right: As reported in last week's *The Shetland Times* "the *Earl of Zetland* is no longer the North Isles steamer. She sailed south to Aberdeen on Monday, 3rd March, 1975".

Middle right: An informal, although neatly composed, group at the gangway in Lerwick, about the time of the ship's last voyage to Whalsay and back. Early afternoon sunshine highlights the situation. In the left foreground on the pier is Bruce Scott, formerly ship's bo'sun and immediately behind him is Captain Willie Anderson of the shipping office, also shore manager.

At the top of the gangway stands Hector Strachan, a senior engineer and on occasion relief chief. On his left is Eddie Knight, second engineer, and a familiar figure on the *Earl*. Wearing the peaked cap, Jim Tait, skippers the old, though still immaculate, ship as she traversed the "sooth mooth" for the final time on Monday, 3rd March, 1975. Bobby Scott, well known to passengers as chief steward flanks Jim Tait, while the bluff figure of Captain Sinclair, clad in shore-going gear and duffel coat, has a characteristic benevolent demeanour. Beside him is Hance Smith from Scalloway, who had sailed as mate with the company.

Bottom right: This is another significant occasion as the *Earl* heads north through the windswept waters of Bressay Sound on her last voyage to the isles. As mute witnesses, she has a cluster of Norwegian fishing craft, probably temporarily stormbound. Pools of water lie on the quayside after overnight rain and there is no visual evidence of people in the scene. Empty fish boxes abound. As the vehicle ferries linking the North Isles were introduced one by one, the *Earl* was withdrawn stage by stage, from Yell in August 1973, from Unst in November 1973, from Fetlar and Skerries after a final trip on 22nd November, 1974, and she finally ran only to Symbister. The very fine photograph shows the *Earl* en-route to Whalsay on Friday, 21st February, 1975, for a fleeting visit. As simply as that an era terminates. A period of 98 years when the northern island ports were served by an *Earl of Zetland*. No fuss, no formal farewell ceremony, but no small amount of sadness. It was Gordon Donaldson who, when the *Earl* made her last visit to Mid Yell in August 1973, under command of Captain Michael Gray, overheard two local women talking. "Weel," said one to the other, "we'll maybe be waar aff."

Right: A Captain and his ship. Michael Gray in pensive stance with the *Earl* at Mid Yell on a January day in 1970 or 1971. Perhaps he is reflecting on the time in the not too distant future when the ship would be consigned to Shetland's maritime history and a proud past.

Michael Gray

Dennis Coutts

Left: Seen on the bridge are Captain Jim Tait with, to his left, the local assistant manager of the North Company Captain W. Anderson, and Mr J. Turner, the new owner. March 1975.

Right: There was the very long reign of "Da auld *Earl*"; there was the long tenure of "Da new *Earl*". But now "new" becomes "old", for an epoch is ending. No doubt there are numerous still familiar faces here, seeing off the *Earl of Zetland* for her final sailing from Lerwick on Monday, 3rd March, 1975, but most significant is that of Willie Sinclair, third from the right – are his thoughts of the past? Inevitably so and, interestingly, his gaze is to the north …

The *Earl*, meanwhile, coasts gently away, her bunting marking a moving occasion. Her destination is Aberdeen … and at least she has avoided the breakers yard like her predecessor because she has been sold to a Mr J. Turner, of St Ives, Cornwall. Coincidentally, accompanying the *Earl* towards the harbour entrance there is a North Sea oil vessel, confirming the trend towards Lerwick becoming a focal point in the oil industry. Further, it has been said that the *Earl* is to become an oil-related survey ship.

Jim Tait is in command of the first motor vessel owned by the North Company, the others on board being the normal crew.

Included in the group are former purser Willie Smith, while in the immediate foreground stand Captain David Polson, harbourmaster with, on his right, Councillor Harry Gray.

Dennis Coutts

SOME COLOUR FOR A COLOURFUL SHIP

David Nisbet

Brian Patton

Above left: Sunshine and shadow in this panoramic vista of Mid Yell and parts of the North Isles. It reveals the sheltered nature of the voe itself, broadening out from the narrows between the point at the Glebe in the right foreground and the slopes of the Hill of Hevdagarth behind. The *Earl* has plenty of room to manoeuvre as she goes astern on a Friday afternoon in the late 1960s. She has deposited her cargo at the point of the pier, although there is no direct evidence of human activity and there is only one small boat moored. It is likely to be the motor boat *Consort* owned by the late Bobby Tulloch of Aywick after 1964, when he became RSPB Warden in Shetland. He was an outstanding ornithologist, naturalist, author and photographer, who loved to take his boat out of the voe beyond Kay Holm, seen on the right, to the shores of Hascosay, the island seen here in the middle distance, or Fetlar or Out Skerries to observe bird or sea life.

Of course each *Earl* had her quota of wildlife enthusiasts throughout the years and made trips with them ranging from the occasional call to Fair Isle to glimpsing Muckle Flugga, North of Unst, about 100 miles further north. In this photograph the islets of Sound Gruney and Urie Lingey are just visible on the right in the haze, with Uyea Isle and Unst beyond.

Above right: An overcast day at Baltasound in 1972. A forest of fishing boat masts implies some rough weather on the east side of Shetland. Certainly judging by the breaking water in the foreground there is at least a strong south-east wind.

Right: Taken in May 1972, this very remarkable photograph conveys a moment of truth! The *Earl* eases away from the substantial new pier at Cullivoe, leaving behind a formidable amount of cargo, and islanders pausing for a moment in stacking bags and boxes on the lorry. It is a "you name it, we have it" situation. Robert Spence, drawing on a cigarette, looks towards the departing ship, while others stand by, partially hidden. John Moar lingers in front of the vehicle, then heads identified are: Angus Henry, Magnus Henderson and Jamie Henry (from Sellafirth), with white cap. Wearing a light top is Georgie Henry.

The goods, mainly for the Cullivoe shops, are standard for a community and are wide-ranging. McEwans boxes of red cans are atop the pile! Other items are there in profusion: New Zealand produce (butter perhaps?), a box of Bisto, Zip firelighters, Tetley tea bags, Carnation milk, Golden Wonder crisps, Embassy Regal cigarettes, and no island consignment would be complete without bakeries from Malcolmsons in Lerwick.

Top left in the photograph, just visible, is the pleasing St Olaf's Cullivoe Kirk, built in 1830.

Brian Patton

The Author

Left: A boatload of autumn lambs at the open doors of the well-deck on an ideal September day. This is the big Cullivoe flit-boat, probably taken over to Uyeasound to catch the *Earl* on her south-bound run. The flit-boat named *John Tulloch* had come to Cullivoe in the mid-1950s.

There is plenty of fleece to get hold of on each animal, as the consignment will be manhandled up on board the *Earl*. Meanwhile the sheep are compacted into a mass of woollen jig-saw shapes. This would be typical of numerous North Isles ports in the late 1960s when lamb shipments marked the climax of the sheep breeding season, part of the vast culture of sheep-rearing in Shetland, which had developed incredibly fast to the extent that it eclipsed pure crofting. Arable land was swallowed up, sacrificed for grazing, and the sheer variety of the island landscape was not improved. The cultivated run-rigs were composed of standard crops like barley, oats, corn, potatoes, kale and turnips; each added its own colour and texture, often particularly noticeable from a ship and pleasing to the eye.

Here depicted in the immediate foreground is Bertie Tulloch of Brough and two of the three others are, left, Robert John Henderson of Mursetter and, centre, Robert Spence of Newhouse, steamer's agent. On board the *Earl* is Jack Goodlad from Burra Isle. He often relieved Willie Smith.

The Author

David Nisbet

Above left: Surrounded by small craft the *Earl* works cargo at the east side of the pier at Baltasound in August 1971 on an overcast day. A neat, brightly-painted fourareen in the foreground contrasts sea and sky.

In her heyday as the main transport to the North Isles, especially during the late forties, fifties and through the sixties, the *Earl* came to Baltasound on the Friday afternoon and sailed for Lerwick at the crack of dawn, normally 6am on the Saturday. She then could link with the south boat sailing from Lerwick that night. Frequently in the earlier years she would call at Uyeasound en-route to pick up mail, empties (barrels or drums) and/or passengers, depending on needs.

Of course in the uncertain days of the cold war, for near enough half a century post-1945 with RAF Saxa Vord manning the early warning installation, there was a great deal of movement of service personnel to and from Baltasound.

Above right: The seabirds on the foreshore in the ebb add a distinctive touch as the *Earl* lies across the end of the pier on a day of calm. Sunshine and shadow flit over the landscape at the sides of the voe at Mid Yell.

David Nisbet

Left: Loading livestock at Mid Yell. Postman Andrew Brown is in the foreground by the unloaded boxes. Willie Williamson, piermaster, manipulates the sling under the animal, while John Nicholson bends over in handling a rope and Willie Nisbet strides forward wearing a maroon jersey; Peter Thompson walks behind. Skipper Gray and various tourists note the ongoing activity.

David Nisbet

Right: The skipper traverses the catwalk. Behind, on the shore, is the new Shetland Norse fish-processing plant.

Above: Lying at anchor by the lighthouse buildings, Grunay, at Out Skerries. The buildings of the shore station are to left and right of the ship.

Maire Anderson

Bob Havlin

Michael Gray

Above: A striking aspect of the ship, enhancing the flare of her bow, as Michael Gray supervises departure in 1973 on a splendid day of weather. Passengers are grouped on the foredeck as the *Earl* pivots away from her mooring; others observe from the rail above the taught hawser amidships. Included in the Mid Yell pier staff are, left to right: Douglas Brown; a person unknown; Willie Nisbet; Alan Strachan and Jasper Mouat. The blue-painted machine is a rotavator.

Above: An Out Skerries fishing boat, the *Village Maid* LK3, acts as a flit-boat. Having loaded-up she is seen here pulling away from the well-deck. The canvas dodger of the *Earl*'s bridge suggests the mid-1950s.

David Nisbet

Above: A day of summer in Shetland can be captivating when all the elements are in harmony, in sky and sea and land; the year 1972. Robert Alan Jamieson, Shetland poet living in Edinburgh phrased it neatly … here are two lines: "… Cocooned in silken home, horizons familiar; In the greater womb of ocean, peat hills secured them."

Certainly Yell and peat are synonymous; those folk on the island who still cut and cure peat for fuel are never likely to find a shortage! The rolling, folding hills have their serried sections of peat banks near the roads and, although so many are abandoned, there is the evidence of annual casting to this day.

In the photograph there is the Glebe land of the Kirk Manse with its sunlit attractive variegated greens and behind is the lower slope of the hill of Lussetter, which had peat banks in former years for Mid Yell residents. On the horizon is Fetlar with the banks or cliffs, clearly etched on the south-west side, south of Brough Lodge.

The *Earl* lies at the Mid Yell pier, close in at near high water, small craft moored in front of her, each catching the sun in a sea picking up the blue of a cloudless sky. The pier itself is devoid of life although there are figures in the well-deck of the ship, while the grazing sheep in the foregournd epitomise the pastoral scene. The Mid Yell graveyard reminds us of the mortality of human kind.

David Nisbet

Above: Preparing to cast-of at Mid Yell on a brilliant day of high summer. A bank of cumulous cloud serves to silhouette Captain Michael Gray as he looks down towards the pier and the recently detached gangway. Alan Strachan and Jasper Mouat have just lifted it away, while Willie Nisbet, in the foreground, looks towards the camera.

The shadows on the immaculate white of the bridge indicate a late morning or early afternoon sun, then sea and land are, in the words of the hymn, in accord with, "Summer suns are glowing over land and sea …" and "Everything rejoices in the mellow air …"

Brian Patton

Above: Near enough midsummer, June 1972. Cloud-flecked overhead conditions and a stiff breeze from the south-east bring the sea to life with sparkle, light and shade. The surf breaks around the concrete marker on the reef named the Voder, then the Hoo Stack lies just to port of the ship as she gently rolls towards Lerwick to round off another North Isles trip. On the horizon is the north side of Bressay with the island of Noss to the left, the peak of the Noup of Noss rearing up beyond the Sneckan.

Below: A commemorative group at Mid Yell not long before the last of the voyages to the North Isles. The high sun dramatises the faces of the men. Central to the *Earl*'s crew on the well-deck are skipper Michael Gray and mate Ray Ferrie. The others (not as posed) are chief engineer Hector Strachan, second engineer Eddie Knight, purser Willie Smith, bo'sun Bruce Scott, able seamen Harry Johnson, Sammy Johnson, Robert Niven and Lowrie Smith, chief steward Bobby Scott, steward Brian Battles and cabin boy Lionel Smith. Donkeyman John Abernethy is on duty this day and not included.

On the pier are Yell men Willie Nisbet (agent) and Alan Strachan, both seated, and Douglas Brown and Jasper Mouat standing. Numerous passengers are interested onlookers through the windows.

David Nisbet

POSTSCRIPT

It is true that when the *Earl of Zetland* slipped quietly out of "da sooth mooth" on Monday, 3rd March, 1975, it was the end of her life and, therefore, her story amid the islands — which tale must always remain the fundamental reason for this saga. Yet as long as a ship exists her narrative endures and is relevant, therefore this supplement features a summary of the subsequent fate of the *Earl of Zetland* — the name continues — up to today.

Further, in the book about "da auld *Earl*" in the preface I remarked: "Undeniably, however, a ship and her voyages never end as long as we remember. And such memories can be vivid. These events live on in our minds, their significance in proportion to what we have seen and experienced, or heard. Thus the old *Earl* survives … those of us who remain, and who knew her atmosphere, live to tell of the epics and now record them for posterity."

If this comment was appropriate for one ship, then it is fitting for both. Certainly the *Earls* hold a fascination for those who have known them. It is probably as great as, if not more intense than, that of the enthusiasts who have been familiar with the famous steamers of the Clyde, especially in the late 19th and through the early part of the 20th centuries. Also those stylish vessels sailed in relatively sheltered waters and, in general, had piers at which to berth although the *Earls* had a parallel in the ubiquitous puffer beloved of the Western Isles whose exploits are legend; they had the

unusual, though time-consuming, advantage of being put ashore in the ebb to unload cargo at island beaches. Yet despite the limitations and inconvenience, unquestionably the flit-boats of Shetland added an extraordinary human dimension over the many years — all part of an island lifeline amid the seasonal peculiarities of the maritime climate in the North Atlantic.

Happily, the human aspect continues and thrives today. Essentially any ship is about people and if she can be of useful and progressive service, no matter what the stage in her life, then let her function. Arguably, continuing existence constitutes a tribute to her construction and atmosphere — the two ships named *Earl of Zetland* were not short of either! Therefore it is good the second *Earl* continues into the 21st century.

It would have been difficult, indeed impossible, to have speculated on the eventual existence (or destruction) of the old motor vessel as she headed for Aberdeen, skippered by Jim Tait, on a March day 27 years ago.

The late Gordon Donaldson, that inveterate North boats enthusiast, had noted her movements.

He caught sight of her at Flotta in Orkney after she had been sold, then, at a later stage, he mentioned that he had twice seen the *Earl* in London's dockland. The "twice" is confirmation of his strongly professed interest, for he had gone out of his way to see how she was faring, having had so much pleasure from the ship over the decades. Of course, for several years

Right: The style of the past … another glimpse of a bygone era with the *Earl of Zetland* seen off the pier at Mid Yell on a superb day of summer warmth. Here she was at her mature best in the island work during the late 60s and very early 70s, yet her time was running out. Piers like the one in the foreground at Linkshouse had, of course, come too late for the inter-island "steamer" – even the new *Earl* was given the title long after her namesake had gone to be broken up on the Shemen Beach at Haifa.

David Nisbet

The Author

Left: The style of the present … a shape of the past in the contemporary scene showing the *Earl* put into a perspective by the craft lying at an arm of the jetties at the Royal Quays Marina, North Shields. She is a symbol of success because she is a going concern, lying in surroundings where she is strategically placed to serve the folk who come. Her "custom-built" pier is there as long as she needs it, although a very different connotation compared to the "*Earl*'s berth" in the days of yore from the Lerwick past. Unlike the first *Earl* she has survived and looks likely to do so for a long time to come.

he had never missed an opportunity to make a trip on the *Earl*. There was little he enjoyed more and he always maintained that his concept of paradise would be a season ticket on the North Isles ship — or "steamer" as had been his wont.

After a brief lay-up in Aberdeen harbour the *Earl* was taken over from the North Company (P&O) by Mr J. Turner, St. Ives, Cornwall, on behalf of Middlesborough Ocean Surveys and renamed *Celtic Surveyor*. She appeared to remain "local" in that there was evidence of work in Orkney and Shetland waters. Shortly after her sale she had an unhappy re-appearance in the news when two divers working from her during the construction of the new oil terminal at Flotta were sucked into an underwater pipe and lost their lives. Also, she re-emerged in Shetland later in 1975 which caused interested comment, being unmistakable, even although she moored at the limb of the breakwater at the small boat harbour, a happening which was unprecedented. It was her first visit to Lerwick as *Celtic Surveyor*.

Further, she materialised unexpectedly when she was most inappropriately cast as a "doomed" vessel in a BBC soap opera about North Sea oil. By that time she had been altered in the first of a series of changes which would transform her appearance. A third mast was fitted immediately abaft the funnel and her lifeboats disappeared in favour of life-rafts.

Her work with Middlesborough Ocean Surveys was relatively short-lived since she was superceded by more specialist vessels as oil-related needs expanded and she was laid up before passing to an apparently ad hoc group with the name Cosag Marine Services, which in turn released the *Celtic Surveyor*.

Coincidentally Jack Lemon of Caister, by Great Yarmouth in Norfolk, had first seen the ship's potential when he had undertaken an electrical survey for the former owners, Cosag Marine Services. At that time, around 1981, she was laid up on the River Yare at Great Yarmouth with an uncertain future, but, Lemon and two partners envisaged the vessel as a focal point for a restaurant and entertainment centre and salvaged the former *Earl of Zetland* from virtual oblivion. She had begun to deteriorate, thus their involvement was timely. Another reprieve.

Having bought the ship, by mid-May 1983 a dream which had begun two years previously became a reality when the *Celtic Surveyor* had her official "launch", hailed as a tremendous asset for Great Yarmouth. Well over a quarter of a million pounds had been spent in a conversion lasting eighteen months and her presence offered many local job opportunities — a major investment. And the old *Earl* had been declared; "As sound as a bell and because of her age and beauty, and with her decor and all the brass, there's something about her."

At first there were thoughts about trips as far as Norway but the concept was found to be impractical, thus an anticipated permanent mooring at South Quay became the reality. However, with her Polar diesel engine still

Douglas Sinclair

Right: At a transitional stage in her ever-changing appearance. The ship is moored at a Great Yarmouth quay in the late 1970s. She has acquired an additional tall mast abaft the funnel which has a red triangle painted on it, a symbol of the survey company. The three masts have a hint of the style of the former Royal Yacht *Britannia* now at Leith! The *Earl*'s lifeboats have gone, presumably to be replaced by inflatable life-rafts.

Left: Another development of part of her career. Only two masts are in evidence in this view although there is as yet no evidence of the appendage aft which was to be part of a restaurant complex. Low, slanting sunlight catches the elegant curve of her port bow and the side of her foremast.

John Manson

intact and her wheelhouse restored to its former brass-polished glory, these were seen as prime attractions for the public. Promotional material heralded five bars, a dance-hall, and conference and reception facilities for 450 people, all a suitably ambitious projection. This was a far cry from the heady days of the original *Earl* when the music of George Stark, the blind fiddler and his band brought Shetlanders to their feet, or indeed, when students returning home at holiday time from the Anderson High School — or Anderson Institute as it was — would clear aside the basket chairs from the deck shelter (with its sloping floor!) for an impromptu dance on the new *Earl*.

There was even a deck to cater for children in the 1983 scheme, boldly described as "Great Yarmouth's Floating Entertainment" to be open all year. Many local firms participated in the imaginative initiative, providing everything from heavy duty engineering, through electrics and carpentry to catering and cleaning, thus the former *Earl* was the subject of a thorough refurbishment which would stand her in good stead. "It is a fairytale touch for Great Yarmouth," said Norfolk naturalist and broadcaster Ted Ellis as he opened the ship with borough mayor David Arnold, who added, "It is a tremendous asset not only for the holiday industry but for the people of the town …" Certainly, poised as she was at South Quay in a prime position outside the town hall, the ship was well placed to become the focal point her initiators visualised. Mid-May 1983 should have signalled the beginning of a long-standing relationship between the *Celtic Surveyor* and Great Yarmouth.

Up to a point the ship herself was succeeding. She was proving to be popular with townsfolk and visitors alike — including Shetlanders — but then financial uncertainties and difficulties arose with the parent group of companies and the asset of the *Celtic Surveyor* was not enough to offset the problems. The vision and enterprise of Jack Lemon and partners deserved

a better fate but their efforts were nullified by events outwith control. Berthed as she was by the town hall in a prime position, the distinctive former *Earl of Zetland* became a showpiece of entertainment success, and reverberated to lively parties with music late into the night, especially at week-ends.

However, the revelry and resultant noise was not to the taste of all and controversial concern was expressed, with the outcome that the *Celtic Surveyor* became a victim of her own success, the directors being obliged to adopt a modified stance which, exacerbated by the overall problems of the parent group of companies, led to receivership. Thus within a couple of years she was again available for any taker.

It may be that the veteran motor vessel had had a few detractors over her career yet they would be far outnumbered by admirers — hence her survival — and one of that majority came forward to again "save the day". She was towed south over the hundred or so miles to the River Thames in the late spring of 1986 after being purchased from the receivers by John Bevan, Submex Limited of London, and, as seen in the photograph on this page was moored beside the famous steam drifter *Lydia Eva* which had hitherto occupied what was the former *Earl*'s berth at Great Yarmouth.

Mr Bevan had commented: "A very recent underwater survey of the ship has shown that she is as strong as the day she was built and that past owners and operators have taken great care of her. I hope her 'retirement' will be even longer than her working life — I am certain she deserves it."

At that stage, amid a remarkably chequered few years, the plan was to have what was presented as "London Underwater Museum," an imaginative concept in conjunction with, and approval of, London Docklands Development Corporation. The West India Dock at the Isle of Dogs was chosen as a suitable location for what would be a home for historic diving equipment and under-water exploration to be run in

Above: Hemmed in with surroundings which could not contrast more, compared to any North Isles port, the ship, with the name *Celtic Surveyor*, is dwarfed by ongoing building construction at Isle of Dogs, London in 1987. Behind the *Earl* is the last surviving steam drifter, the green painted *Lydia Eva* YH89. She was built in 1930 and after fishing out of Yarmouth she became a target-towing vessel used by the RAF during the war. She was due for breaking up in 1969 but was rescued by the Maritime Trust, although subsequently her berth at South Quay, Yarmouth, was taken by the *Earl* when the future of the drifter was uncertain. What a pity there could not have been a Shetland equivalent of the steam drifter days of yore at the boom years of the herring fishing in the 1930s, that would have been something else saved for prosperity.

The *Lydia Eva* is here preserved as she was – a working ship – but her neighbour in the berth is already subject to radical change. With lifeboats removed, an awning has been fitted for the upper deck, a prelude to the subsequent access glazed stairway and encased "tent" structure as seen in later photographs. Inevitably the well-deck is no more, in the interests of useful space … it happened to the old *Earl* half a century before when she had become an immigrant ship.

conjunction with catering facilities for the visiting public. An additional aim was to have an on-board display of the ship's history and, in fact, John Bevan appealed to the Shetland Islands public for historical information and memorabilia from a productive and long life by any shipping standards — at the time, 1986, the *Celtic Surveyor* was almost half a century old.

As she lay in the London dockland her appearance had not yet been radically altered, although with the two lifeboats removed she had rails all the way round her upper deck abaft the bridge and the framework of an overall awning fitted. Immediately for'ard of the bridge-house was an access stair to the well-deck, while the cargo derrick was still in the working position, raised at an angle. She retained the three masts.

A snag materialised — ironically enough underwater — in that there was slight but persistent leakage at the propeller shaft to the extent that John Bevan arranged to have the screw removed, although at a much later date, along with the offending shaft, and the area plated in. But he retained the propeller, which decision was to be an asset to Shetland in due course. Again ironically, mute witness to the leak problem was part of the museum shore display in the form of a diving bell!

Although once more the subject of an ambitious and bold idea, after a year's operation the ship had not been well enough supported or patronised by visitors to pay her way, in many respects due to delays in the planned regeneration of the area where she lay, by the Dockland Development Corporation.

John Bevan then decided to lease her for entertainment purposes and she was taken over by City Fine Wines as a restaurant and wine bar at Marsh Wall in the dockland, under the managership of Mr Daniel Hart. With the ship now dubbed *Le Boat*, no doubt intended to be in keeping with the fine wines being purveyed, trade was steady over the first months from March 1988 at the beginning of what was thought would be a 20-year lease.

Yet, again the potential was not being fulfilled because after a first period of promising business, trade fell away. But an unexpected bonus came about when the staff of the *Daily Telegraph* newspaper moved en bloc from Fleet Street to a brand new building at the Isle of Dogs, an area subject to the redevelopment of docklands in the 1980s. This is well

illustrated in the photograph on the previous page where on the right is a completed structure with, beside it, the framework of a ten-storey block. These contrast the curved style of the past in shipping with the *Earl of Zetland* on the left and the famous Great Yarmouth steam drifter *Lydia Eva* astern of her.

At this time the old motor vessel still had her diminutive mainmast but it disappeared when circumstances decreed that the ship would need improved restaurant/bistro facilities to allow for not only the public but the staff of the *Daily Telegraph* as well. Under terms of the lease of the actual building the newspaper was not permitted catering facilities, thus the *Earl* was in the unusual position of being a canteen for the daily's staff and an eating and drinking place for the public. Another photograph taken from the offices of the *Daily Telegraph* — virtually an aerial view — on this page, gives a superb angle, showing the tent-like construction on the upper deck.   There is triple-access from the quay.

Being moored in a much more congenial area, and with "word of mouth" being a valuable publicity agent, the amenities of the floating restaurant were being well utilised and she proved to be a popular venue. The approach by the *Daily Telegraph* to John Bevan had been timely for both interested parties. Over a couple of years the arrangement, which was much too good an offer to refuse, proved to be a success, but then the *Daily Telegraph* staff of about 1000 were re-located to the brand-new Canary Wharf and the *Earl* was destined to move on yet again in the extraordinary sequence of events.

Happily the ship was at the "peak of her declining years" in 1989 when there was the milestone of her 50th anniversary, an occasion fortunately not forgotten or ignored — as it might have been — because, on board there was a traditional Shetland "reestit" mutton meal, initiated by the tenants City Fine Wines who were not insensitive to tradition and sentiment; and it was free to all employees of the *Daily Telegraph*! The choice of menu was beautifully appropriate because "reestit" mutton had been served when the then new *Earl of Zetland* came to Lerwick on 19th August, 1939.

On the re-location of the newspaper staff, and due to a great deal of competition with onshore restaurant and bar establishments abounding, it

The Daily Telegraph

Above: The *Earl*'s involvement with North Sea oil survey work had been short-lived. She was acquired for conversion into a floating catering establishment and here she is, still carrying the name *Celtic Surveyor* on her bow, but most inappropriately entitled "Le Boat Restaurant & Bar" on a banner at her rail, aft. As well as being a rather pricey wine bar and restaurant she serves as a canteen for the staff of *The Daily Telegraph*.

The view taken from the top of the newspaper building illustrates the trim proportions of the ship despite the varied alterations and inevitable "embellishments". Cars in the foreground are owned by staff of *The Daily Telegraph*. The former *Earl* is berthed at the old Millwall Dock at the Isle of Dogs by the River Thames, London, just over the river from Greenwich. The photograph is provided by E. Duncan.

was decided to seek pastures new, this time to Eastbourne where a new marina had been set up. John Bevan had developed a strong enthusiasm for the whole ethos of the *Earl of Zetland* — the reality of her working life; the romance of her reputation — and the new location at the south coast of England resort seemed to have ample scope for the ongoing saga of his ship.

The marina and council authorities at Eastbourne liked the idea of a floating restaurant resource and a two-year lease contract was drawn up, during which time the ship was dry-docked. It had been discovered that the *Earl's* propeller was an encumbrance which made the ship difficult to tow during the 1986 voyage from Great Yarmouth to the Thames in London and, since it was long past its functional life and with the water encroachment, the screw was removed and, like the diving bell at Isle of Dogs, became an exhibit on shore at Eastbourne's Sovereign Harbour, as the last decade of the twentieth century began to unfold.

In keeping with country-wide trends in the appearance of marinas, including Shetland, as the leisure sailing industry grew, the south-coast resorts with suitable surroundings were taking opportunities. Eastbourne was no exception and rapidly the number of berths occupied grew towards four hundred. This meant steady trade for the *Earl* in group visits and functions, and meetings, dinners, lunches, bar meals and calls for casual drinks. She was, in effect, highly successful. At last there was a fully supportive environment.

Above and below: Ample space for customer parking was a feature at Sovereign Harbour and once on board patrons had a very pleasant environment in which to dine. The lower view, looking aft in the dining area, constitutes the former boat-deck, a clever use of available space and an example of the *Earl's* post-Shetland versatility.

Above: Well established at Eastbourne amid a Mediterranean-like day and surroundings, beyond the bridge which sports the designated name "The Boat". In the foreground is the much-used anchor windlass from the *Earl's* long sojourn in the North Isles and the position shows how the well-deck had been covered over, with steps leading up to the resultant decking. Also, authentic-looking teak rails have been added.

Above: At least a name revived and retained! The *Earl of Zetland* at Eastbourne in April 1994, photographs taken by John Manson, formerly depute director of Design and Technical Services, Shetland Islands Council.

Of course the ship had been renamed *Celtic Surveyor* but when resold in the spring of 1983 the new owners apparently preferred the dignity of "The Earl". However, the additional title of "The Boat" seems hardly appropriate, while by no stretch of imagination even "reportedly" was the *Earl* associated with Dunkirk (1940) or to have had such a short career as implied by "… sailed between Lerwick and the Southern (sic) isles of Shetland 1975." But the lettering on the bridge is beautifully done – "Signwriting aboard by Paul Smith".

The two-year lease might well have been extended but the ship's very success was in some ways her undoing because it was decided to build onshore with ambitious catering facilities, thus it was "count-down" towards the *Earl*'s exit from the south coast. Three years had elapsed since her welcome to Eastbourne and, not surprisingly, there were those who were sorry to see her go. Meanwhile John Bevan was negotiating a transfer to another possible port, with Dover having potential. In the event it transpired that Newcastle was the likely destination due to a much more advantageous offer with brewery backing and the expected planning in a new marina as part of another major regeneration programme, at the River Tyne estuary, in North Shields.

While in Eastbourne the *Earl of Zetland* had been a worthy centre of attention with her fine charisma and amenities, busy by day, and at night brightly lit, attracting customers like moths round a flame. The contrast between that and her wartime days in Orkney could hardly have been more marked, highlighted — if that be the right word — by an isolated incident in 1940, and recalled in an evening of yarning so characteristic of the build-up to this book.

During those grim years of war, and considering the risk of German attack, the two ships of the same name *Earl of Zetland* might well have been subjected to more than one bombing attempt on each. It was ironic that there was a shot — literally a shot — fired in anger by "own side" at Scrabster, where the ship was moored, on Tuesday, 24th September, 1940. Outstanding Orcadian with a skipper's ticket, William Banks, was sailing as mate on the *Earl* and was duty officer on board that night. About 9.20pm a single rifle report disrupted the evening stillness. The bullet penetrated the steel side of the galley, wounding the mess-room boy R. Hutcheson on his right side and arm, also one of the ship's gunners on face and chest.

Acting spontaneously and irresponsibly a sergeant of the guard had allegedly spotted a light showing on the *Earl* and had taken it upon himself to fire.

Captain Tom Gifford had reacted strongly in a letter to Movement Control at Stromness: "... a serious incident and one which could have had grave results ... In view of the important and essential work you require the vessel to do I beg to suggest that very strong representation is made to the appropriate authority ... I would also point out that the same form of obscuring the lights has been in operation since the vessel was requisitioned (in January 1940) ... I have had no complaints."

William Banks had mentioned that the only lights burning that night in the top part of the ship were one screened light in the galley and one in the saloon. The galley window was covered by a fitted card-board, while all the curtains in the saloon were closely drawn.

No further evidence materialised while it was never reported what action, if any, was taken against the alleged sergeant of the guard culprit, but the polarised situations of bright lights and black-out could hardly have been better illustrated. The difference between peace and war.

THE *EARL*'S FINAL VOYAGE

The *Earl*'s bright lights of late 1996 burned until preparations were made for her departure for the north in February 1997. That the ship had had some impact locally was confirmed when the ITV teletext news of 30th January reported that the floating restaurant *Earl of Zetland* was due to be towed out of the Sovereign Harbour at Eastbourne to make room for a more conventional restaurant on land. Due to the time of year there was always going to be the chance of poor weather and, in fact, the tug *Towing Chieftain* had been delayed by bad visibility on her way south prior to the lengthy 400 mile haul from the south coast of England to the Tyne.

As had happened in Great Yarmouth and London Dockland in two locations, people of Orkney and Shetland connection found their way to the *Earl*, evidence of strong continuing interest, and visitors saw that the familiar funnel had acquired a coat of mid-blue paint which had a remarkable effect on her appearance.

In fact one visitor was Orcadian, Michael Clouston, who contributed an article to *Shetland Life* in March 1997. His father William (Dusty) Clouston had been bo'sun on the *St Ola* and when she went to Aberdeen for refit he transferred regularly to the Shetland ship. Michael Clouston had noted the colour change but instantly recognised the familiar funnel as he visited Eastbourne on the day of departure for the Tyne.

By early morning the *Earl* had been manoeuvred into the outer lock with the *Towing Chieftain* passing warps in readiness for the open sea and the several hundred miles to the north. There were two reasons for a stay of departure. The wind strength was Force 6 and ESE; insurance allowed towing in only up to Force 4, while, with a narrow exit-channel, the tide had to be at its peak. But by later afternoon on Saturday, 1st February, 1997, the *Earl of Zetland* began what would be her ultimate trip.

With the wind direction and its strength there was a sizeable swell in the English Channel approaches and as the two vessels rolled past Hastings and up to Folkstone and Dover, there were those of the ad hoc skeleton crew on the *Earl* who were aware of her reputation of being lively in a following sea. There had been others over the years who knew her vagaries well and who remembered, as crew or passengers, her skittish ways on passages between the likes of Uyeasound and Baltasound in a south-easter, or en route to Aberdeen for January refit.

It was that committed North boats man, the late Alastair McRobb, who recalled the extent of the *Earl*'s rolling. He served on the ship as engineer on numerous occasions in the 1950s, as seen in photographs. Voyages from Lerwick to Aberdeen varied from just over 16 to 23 hours. Masters involved were Tom Gifford (1954), Willie Sinclair — deputising — (1955) and Jimmy Johnston (1957 and 1958).

Although the 1954 trip was reasonably fast at near enough 17 hours, the ship was running before a northerly gale.

"Once we entered the Roost south of Sumburgh Head the well-deck disappeared with the hatch and bulwarks constantly submerged. It was a

Brian Patton

Left: The exposed east side of Unst can be subjected to heavy seas when strong winds prevail from the North Sea. South-east gales in particular can pose problems, as happened in the eras of Captains McMillan and Spence in the time of the old *Earl*. Off Unst is especially vulnerable for shipping today, as always.

Here is the scene looking aft with the ship north-bound as a confused sea sets up a pitching and rolling motion. It is a well known fact that the *Earl* could roll!

Contrast this with the same view looking aft, on page 142.

Peter Marfitt-Smith

Above: Manoeuvering with stern ropes to port and starboard to get alignment in the A. & P. Tyne Limited dock after the lengthy tow from the Sovereign harbour at Eastbourne in Sussex. She has been taken north by the tug *Towing Chieftain* and the two vessels had departed at 3.30pm on Saturday, 1st February, 1997. Would this indeed be the *Earl*'s final time at sea?

most eerie sight to stand in the wheelhouse and see a fo'c'sle ahead of us, apparently detached from the rest of the ship, and with solid water separating the two sections.

"The rolling was unbelievable. I remember sitting in the saloon for my supper and the windows were being totally submerged, on either side, with each roll. When standing on the bridge wing and looking aft, the boat deck could be seen touching the water each time she rolled. I don't think we made any attempt to measure the angle but it must have been considerable.

"The most amazing sight of all was to be in the engine room and see the bilge water swirling about the deck-head. We had the evidence of the tidemark on the white paintwork to prove to disbelievers once we berthed at Aberdeen. After that a trip to Skerries in an easterly gale was tame stuff indeed!"

Such gyrations would have been totally unacceptable during the lengthy tow up past Ramsgate, Margate, the Thames estuary, Lowestoft, the Wash, Grimsby, Scarborough, Whitby, Hartlepool and hence close by Sunderland and into the mouth of Tyne — a voyage which had taken her half-way back to Shetland and lasting three days. The *Towing Chieftain* had lived up to her name with an authoritative haul up the East Coast, and the *Earl of Zetland,* minus her screw, was delivered safely to be dry-docked at A. & P. Tyne Limited, Wallsend, for a thorough overhaul as evidenced in the photographs.

Meanwhile the Shetland Museum had become aware of the existence and availability of the *Earl of Zetland*'s propellor onshore at Eastbourne and an offer was made for its purchase through Tommy Watt, the Museum Curator in Lerwick. A 50% grant from the National Fund for Acquisitions clinched the deal and the propeller was uplifted in February 1997 by Shetland Transport and conveyed to Shetland, where it will become a feature at the fine new Shetland Museum and Archives destined to be established at Hay's Dock in Lerwick. It will be a fitting memorial to the halcyon days of two splendid ships which served the isles so comprehensively.

John Bevan was relieved at the safe arrival of the *Towing Chieftain* and her charge because there were always the inherent risks in towing, plus the insurance factors, especially in the winter month of February. However, in the circumstances all was well that ended well and, after a brief period moored at Wallsend, the *Earl* was coaxed into the capacious dry dock to be again checked, overhauled, particularly below the waterline, and have her upperworks further developed.

The new lease-holders, led by Newcastle business-man Peter Marfitt-Smith and in association with owner John Bevan, had ambitious ideas for a situation not unlike the marina at Eastbourne — a quality floating restaurant with a broad-based appeal to users of the brand-new marina at Royal Quays, North Shields, plus a discerning public looking for a different experience. Today, while these aims are being met, another dimension has been added in that the *Earl of Zetland* has been playing host

Peter Marfitt-Smith

Left: In great need of attention! In a curious way the coincidence of the channel for the ladder on the far wall of the dock suggests the line of the leading edge of the propeller but, alas, it is gone forever. Meanwhile, the rudder and the areas below the water line are badly affected by the sea growths and general pollution. A. & P. Tyne Limited are about to effect a transformation.

Peter Marfitt-Smith

Above: Dwarfed by the massive cranes and high dock wall and with the water pumped out the *Earl of Zetland* begins yet another lease of life in May 1997. Her predecessor had sailed from Aberdeen on 19th December, 1946, and coincidentally had been in the Tyne and London en-route to Marseilles for fitting-out. She was then "captured" by the Royal Navy in May 1947, 50 years earlier. The old *Earl* was in Gibralter on 1st February, 1947, and precisely 50 years later her successor was on her way for what may be a "swansong" in her long and worthy career in the service of people.

Below: Work well under way, with the *Earl* balanced on the central chocks of the dock bottom and showing her compact and shapely hull to advantage. The formidable wall on the right helps to frame the vessel, so agreeably lit by the sun.

Peter Marfitt-Smith

to crews of such renowned vessels as the aircraft carriers *Illustrious* and *Invincible*. The *Earl* thrives in all the diversity and with no apparent adverse circumstances!

Of course the expense of alterations has matched the ambition and in 2002 the ship is looking good in her context. The curved roof shape above the former well-deck, supported by the derrick now in the working position, has given a more balanced look to the much-altered super-structure — albeit a very different scenario from the *Earl*'s workmanlike appearance in Shetland waters; functional then, and stylish, but now needing a blend of the old and the new in the environment of catering for a fresh public.

That the new managers had faith in the project was confirmed when at the end of 1997 London-based John Bevan who in reality had "saved" the ship, elected to offer the *Earl* for sale. Peter Marfitt-Smith had decided that the enterprise was worth the investment, thus by January 1998 the *Earl of Zetland* had passed on to other hands once more, with a future of promise.

It was my privilege and pleasure to visit the ship in July 2000, June 2001 — with the Edinburgh Shetland Association — and again in October the same year. Financial outlays on the *Earl* have been considerable; well in excess of £2.5million. She had cost over £52,000, in the first place and her predecessor around £7000. The matter is academic but still reveals the

Above: Here is an update on the chequered history of the second *Earl of Zetland*. Currently she is the popular focal point of the 400-berth marina at the regenerated river area at North Shields on the River Tyne. This photograph could hardly be a greater contrast to the *Earl* in a seaway, with sunlight creating strong patterns of light and shade, again looking aft on the starboard side, with the eternally calm water of her berth beyond. It may be a travesty of her Shetland function … but she is still serving people at the time of this photograph, taken on 15th July, 2000. Blooming flowers (*Petunias*) in boxes add to the contrast!

Left top: A balancing act? Dry-docked at Wallsend, the *Earl of Zetland* exudes power and grace in this towering graphic and dramatic perspective, observed in 1997. The clear definition of her plates and riveting belies her 58 years. Remarkably, her underside at the bilge keels shows daylight at each side above the chocks while the supports for the hull to port and starboard appear to be somewhat flimsy for her bulk!

Left bottom: There is equal strength and delicacy in this stern view and again the bilge keels are obviously clear of the chocks. The fresh very dark anti-fouling paint enables the ridges on the plating to catch the sunlight below the waterline, yet there is a poignancy about the disappearance of the propellor which drove her and many a precious cargo of humans, animals and goods for hundreds of thousands of miles in Shetland and Orkney waters. The *Earl*'s port of registry is still well defined in the metal letters but her name, once removed, has been repainted directly on to the hull plating. Temporarily the hull is blue.

Peter Marfitt-Smith

In her heyday the *Earl* needed no "Welcome Aboard" sign for, like her predecessor, she had that by reputation. Over the decades each ship had her own particular and very distinctive warm hospitality on board, proferred by the succession of skippers and crews. Here she is being coaxed into her present resting place at North Shields in October 1997, by tugs fore and aft, now a powerless hulk, yet still retaining that essential character despite the cosmetic on-deck additions. Surely it is better that she survives as yet, serving folk and escaping the ignominy of the breakers yard. Within three years the rather barren background has been transformed into a well-designed industrial, commercial and residential complex with the superb marina as a focal point. It is acknowledged that the visits of the tall ships to the Tyne in 1985 and 1993 were a catalyst for the outstanding regeneration of a desolate area. The *Earl*'s hull and funnel are (temporarily) painted blue from the previous owner, while, as a sign of the times, oil rigs are moored out in the River Tyne as seen in the upper photograph.

Peter Marfitt-Smith

Left: No mistaking the finely-crafted flare of the bows with anchors highlighted, and evoking memories of time-honoured and innumerable calls at any island port with anchor down and a flit-boat easing alongside the port well-deck doors, the hinges of which can be seen.

It is good to see her derrick in the working position, supporting the roof structure of a ship's bar above the former well-deck. The roof shape almost echoes the curvature of the bows in inverted form. A Union Jack is stiff in the breeze and one of two covered access gangways shows on the starboard side.

Right: Looking down the starboard side showing the well-formed covered gangways fore and aft. Since the photograph was taken in July 2000 the porthole-shaped windows on the gangways have been replaced by larger rectangular panels similar to those edging the Bo'sun's Bar above. The shore-end of a mooring device to hold the ship in place can just be seen below the rear gangway; likewise shore to ship cabling.

To the right, there are boats in the marina backed by examples of the attractive housing at the site, while on the left, above the *Earl*'s stern is the unusual funnel of a big North Sea ferry. North Shields is a terminal for European ferries.

Left: A detail of the old and the new. The bridge structure and the deck shelter windows are basically the same as yesteryear. The distinctive red rectangle for the port sailing light is as it was and that compact funnel is unmistakable. Below it is the galley with its row of windows, strip-lighting showing within. Immediately behind the funnel is the mast fitted not long after the ship left Shetland.

It does not need much imagination to picture successive skippers on the bridge wing, peering down at a flit-boat alongside. What would men like Tom Gifford, Jimmy Johnston and Willie Sinclair have thought of the fate of the *Earl of Zetland*? Michael Gray, her last full-time captain, is an interested observer.

recent investments which make a tribute to the quality of a truly remarkable ship from the yard of Hall, Russell and Company Limited 63 years ago.

In the nature of things the Royal Quays Marina has to be her final berth, or resting place, because the wider entrance to the marina has been sealed off, leaving a lock-width capable of taking only smaller craft.

Once guided into the marina, having left the dry-dock with her underside carefully reconditioned — and with amazingly little wear in her plates — she was put close alongside the quay by two tugs for months of interior refurbishment and decorating, with much care lavished on her. By early 1999 the work was completed and the *Earl of Zetland* was opened for the public.

She was permanently moored some metres from the quay wall, held in place by two black painted cylindrical bars fitted approximately amidships and two covered access gangways, specially manufactured, one to the well-deck and the other to the after deck. In theory, four rigid structures should have held her immoveable yet as I enjoyed a bar lunch on 15th July, 2000, in the for'ard lounge above what had been the well-deck, and looking out through the windows on the port side over the marina, I had a "double-take". Was she or was she not rising and falling, if not rolling? And assuredly, if almost imperceptibly, there was movement. I lingered and looked and remembered … what a blessing, she survives!

The Author

Above: An unusually powerful blue of the sky complements the freshly-painted buff funnel, exactly as it was in the ship's heyday, although an interesting addition is the current logo which pays tribute to the name and the *Earl*'s "date of birth" in 1939. Previously the twin ventilators before the funnel were also buff with pale blue interiors, but the bridge house, the back of which can just be seen, has not been altered. Today it serves as a compact office.

The Author

Above: The distinctive logo of the *Earl*, promoting her as she is today. This insignia is repeated on approach roads leading to the Royal Quays Marina, thus visitors are well guided to the ship's abundant catering facilities.

Vaila Irvine

Above: The warm colour-scheme and welcoming atmosphere are evident enough in this interior as in June 2001 during the visit of the Edinburgh Shetland Association whose 75th anniversary happens to fall in 2002. This restaurant structure was raised on the boat deck during the mid-1980s and has proved to be an asset in the ability of the ship to handle good numbers in catering; thus the *Earl of Zetland* continues to serve people.

Vaila Irvine

Left: Yesterday and today. The past and the present. The bridge woodwork is the same; the windows are identical; the current owners are sensitive to the links with the past. A further common factor with each administration has been the retention of the Clearview Screen as seen here on a starboard side window. It has remained from the old days and worked on the principal of fast-moving rotating glass to throw off rain or sea water. On the former bridge this screen was set above the chart table, although it was not all that well placed in that mast and derrick tended to obscure the view. However, other older North Boats like the *St Magnus* and *St Clair* had a Clearview Screen fitted.

It is appropriate that it remains today in the *Earl* at North Shields amid the fittings for a neat office on board. The computer screen and keyboard are a far cry from the days of the *Earl* in Shetland.

Left: The setting of a new lease of life. Style and size would appear to be two of the ingredients serving to ensure the ship's survival and this glimpse of her shapely cruiser stern is a reminder of her quality. Immediately behind the flagstaff is the modern administrative and control centre of the Royal Quays Marina, while at the first of the pontoons an ever-expanding range of small boats appears alongside. Some are similar to those lying in Shetland marinas. At the far side extends the type of appealing housing surrounding the marina.

The Author

Right: Miniature flags silhouetted above the eye-level give a castellated effect, framing the view from the Bo'sun's Bar built over the former well-deck and with a roof suspended from the derrick. It was here that the author was aware of the movement of the *Earl* as discerned from a lower seated position, lining up the window ledges with the quayside beyond … somehow a vessel still alive.

The Author

The Author

Left: "It seems like yesterday". How frequently is the remark made, particularly by those of a less recent generation! "A trip down memory lane" often features too. Both comments may apply here as members of the Edinburgh Shetland Association and guests renew acquaintance with the *Earl*, her bulwarks emblazoned with the very familiar name.

The date is Sunday, 3rd June, 2001, and the visitors are about to board the coach for Edinburgh after a tour of the ship taken by Benjamin Hardaker, manager, and a fine dinner on board … shades of the past … "Aye, we hid mony a laff wi dem" (the crew); "… but could she roll …!" Memory lane indeed.

In a touch of appropriate sentiment Andrew Thomson of Unst, Association Council member, has presented the old – or is it "new"? – *Earl* with a photograph of her at Baltasound, taken by his mother. It seems so right that the ship can still exist … serving people.

The author kneels, bottom right in the photograph.

John Bevan

Above: The pre-planning for the Eastbourne marina is evident from this outstanding perspective. Undeniably the *Earl*'s fitness for purpose shows in these surroundings. She is neither too big nor too small for such a setting beside the motor boats and yachts moored at the berthing arms on her far side. It is not surprising that the ship offered scope for her owners at a similar North Shields enterprise, hence her purchase and transfer to the Tyne, although her amazing latter-day career would have astonished those marine architects of Hall, Russell away back in the late 1930s when the ship was being designed. They could hardly have been expected to anticipate that she would not only be the vessel which continued and enhanced a great and cherished tradition of sea communication in Shetland but which showed her versatility and adaptability in such style and in such diverse places. Like her forerunner "da auld *Earl*" she has been unorthodox – not for her the breakers hammer immediately on "retiral". Admittedly the first *Earl of Zetland*'s "stay of execution" lasted for little more than a year, yet prior to her demise she had made a big impact for such a tiny steamer, spoken about and commemorated even in modern day Israel as well as remembered with affection in her "home" waters. The "new" *Earl* has survived 27 years beyond her Shetland life expectancy and she looks set to surpass her predecessor's 70 years …

Below: The timelessness of an oil painting by marine artist W. A. Smith is a fitting tribute to an apparently ageless ship. This evocative work hangs on board the *Earl of Zetland* in a public place and was commissioned when she lay in London Docklands.

John Bevan

BIBLIOGRAPHY

The work of numerous authors is gratefully recognised; their expertise has been both extremely helpful and stimulating;

CAMERON, James: ....*The Making of Israel*
(Martin Secker and Warburg Limited, London 1976)

CLUNESS, Andrew T: ....*The Shetland Isles*
(Robert Hale Limited, London 1951)

DONALDSON, Gordon: ....*Northwards by Sea* (Second Edition)
(Paul Harris, Edinburgh, 1978)

DONALDSON, Gordon: ....*Isles of Home – Seventy Years of Shetland*
(Scottish Academic Press, Edinburgh, 1994)

GRANT, Roderick: ....*The Lone Voyage of Betty Mouat*
(Impulse Books, Aberdeen, 1973)

IRVINE, James W: ....*The Waves are Free*
(The Shetland Publishing Company, Lerwick, 1988)

KIRK, James: ....*Her Majestys Historiographer, Gordon Donaldson*
(Scottish Academic Press, 1996)

McROBB, Alastair: ....*The Second St Ola*
(Thuleprint Limited, Sandwick, Shetland 1977)

McROBB, Alastair: ....*The North Boats*
(Ferry Publications, Narberth, Pembrokeshire 1999)

NICOLSON, James R: ....*Shetland*
(David and Charles, Newton Abbot, 1972)

NICOLSON, James R: ....*Lerwick Harbour*
(Lerwick Harbour Trust. The Shetland Times, 1976)

NICOLSON, James R: ....*Hay and Company*
(Hay and Company. The Shetland Times, 1982)

PATTON, Brian: ....*Scottish Coastal Steamers*
The Lines that Limited the Lochs.
(Silver Link Publishing Ltd., Peterborough, 1996 and 1999)

SANDISON, Charles: ....*Unst My Island Home and its Story.*
(The Shetland Times, Lerwick 1968)

TAIT, Ian: ....*Rural Life in Shetland*
(Shetland Museum, 2000)

TAYLOR, Harry P: ....*A Shetland Parish Doctor*
(T & J Manson, Shetland News, Lerwick, 1948)

TULLOCH, Bobby: ....*A Guide to Shetland's Breeding Birds*
(The Shetland Times, 1992)